Making Sense of Microeconomics

Exercises may be downloaded at:
http://www.herzogsystems.com/resources

Making Sense of Microeconomics

Revised First Edition

John P. Herzog

University of Dayton

Bassim Hamadeh, CEO and Publisher
Jennifer Codner, Senior Field Acquisitions Editor
Carrie Baarns, Manager, Revisions and Author Care
Kaela Martin, Project Editor
Abbey Hastings, Production Editor
Jess Estrella, Senior Graphic Designer
Natalie Piccotti, Director of Marketing
Kassie Graves, Senior Vice President, Editorial
Jamie Giganti, Director of Academic Publishing

cognella® | ACADEMIC PUBLISHING

Contents

Chapter 5   Making Sure We All Have What We Need

Chapter 6   Elasticity

ACTIVE LEARNING

This book has interactive activities available to complement your reading.

Your instructor may have customized the selection of activities available for your unique course. Please check with your professor to verify whether your class will access this content through the Cognella Active Learning portal (http://active.cognella.com) or through your home learning management system.

CHAPTER ONE

Why Study Economics?

IN CHAPTER 1 you will begin to understand some of the underlying terms for and issues about microeconomics that will help you to better understand things in later chapters. It will define microeconomics and give you an overview of why it is important to understand.

If you are in business and if you are concerned about whether you are maximizing your profits, you will need to study microeconomics.

If you are a manager in any organization and want to maximize the use of your resources, you will need to make sense of microeconomics.

If you want to retire, and therefore if you have or will someday have saved money for your retirement, you will need to have some understanding about the stock market in order to know what is happening to your retirement fund. Therefore, once again, you will need to get a good understanding of microeconomics.

Everyone uses economics every day without using the word *economics*.

There are many reasons that it is necessary to understand the subject of microeconomics, but these are the three most common reasons and the three most important.

WHAT IS ECONOMICS?

If you are **economical**, that means you are using all the resources you have to the max. You are not wasting them. Using your resources to the max is needed for many reasons. Everyone has a different perspective on this. You can use them to make yourself financially wealthy. You can use them in the way of using your talent, whether it be in business, theatre work, or social work, or wherever you choose to maximize them. There are many who believe in God and that there is a life that follows this one; therefore, many choose to maximize the use of all of their resources to prepare for that permanent life rather than for temporary things in this life.

Our focus in this book is from the financial perspective. From that standpoint, the formal definition of **economics** is that it is a social science primarily concerned with the description and analysis of the production, distribution, and consumption of goods and services. It is the branch of knowledge that deals with the production, consumption, and transfer of wealth from one person to another, or from one organization to another. Economics is also a social science that studies the choices that individuals, organizations, and sometimes entire societies make as they deal with the scarcity of resources. It also studies the things that impact those choices. These choices can be on the part of buyers of goods and services, while other choices involve those who produce those goods and services. When we discuss the laws of supply and demand, for example, these choices will be seen in action.

Many times, people make the mistake of making predictions about what people's choices will be based upon pure math, but the study of our social tendencies shows that it is driven just as much by psychological behavior as it is by math.

For example, it is assumed that when government raises our tax rates, it will collect more in taxes from the people. That is the assumption made if we simply use math to predict the outcome of a tax increase. In some cases, however, higher tax rates can actually lower the tax revenue collected by government if the high rates discourage people from seeking extra work. If workers or producers feel that they will keep a lower amount of their wages or profits after taxes, then they often feel that there is no reason to put forth the effort to earn those wages or profits. Some even refuse to report all income when tax rates go up, and that, of course, is illegal and absolutely forbidden.

Higher taxes have also been known to cause workers to lose their jobs as employers move their operations to other countries where they have lower taxes. When people lose their jobs, the government has less income that they can tax, and thus they often collect less tax revenue.

If you are in business and if you waste resources (on a micro level), you raise your costs of doing business, and thus your organization can't compete.

On a national level, when government does not encourage people to manage their resources properly or economically, it causes shortages, which raises costs and retail prices. Higher costs and retail prices can ultimately cost jobs in our country as people seek products with lower prices abroad. Shortages, high prices, and a lack of jobs would create unrest in any country.

The study of **microeconomics** shows us how to make the best choices on a smaller level, in our individual businesses and markets, for best results.

Macroeconomics is the study of the performance of the national and global economy in an attempt to gain full employment in our societies with stable prices, acceptable wealth and income distribution, and a sufficient supply of what we need in the way of goods and services.

Proper application of economics will tell us *what* should be produced, *how* it is to be produced, and *for whom* it will be produced.

The study of microeconomics allows us to have a better understanding of how these things happen. By studying it, you can learn how to make decisions that will give your organization more financial health and allow your firm to work smarter and with better results. It studies things on a more localized, microscopic scale. It studies or analyzes the activity of individual organizations and markets. For example, if you are in the pizza business, and if these same three questions would need to be answered by you, you would need to decide if *what* you produce should in fact still be pizza, *how* you would best produce the pizza, and *for whom* you would likely be producing your pizza.

The next important thing you need to understand is the pool of **resources** from which everyone will choose. The resources we want to use economically are those used for production. They are called the **factors of production** and include the following:

1. Land
2. Labor
3. Capital
4. Entrepreneurship

Land is a factor of production for two reasons. First, it is the space we occupy in order to produce goods and services. Second, land is where many products can trace their origins. When you see a component part to a car, for example, the steel or rubber from that part came from resources that come from plants, trees, or the ground.

Obviously, none of those resources will ever be used if we don't take the time to have someone extract or harvest them from the land and turn them into something useful. The people and the time it takes to do these tasks is what we know as **labor**. Labor is also used to perform tasks such as medical or financial services, which do not include the use of tangible things.

The resource of **capital** primarily refers to the tools and equipment that anyone uses to make production happen. Anything such as a farmer's plow, a conveyor belt in a factory, or a computer on someone's desk is in this context considered capital. Many think of capital as being money. Others think of it as stocks and bonds. Both of these are correct, but in this context, capital refers to machinery for production. Money capital is needed to purchase the capital tools and equipment, which is commonly referred to as **capital equipment**; therefore, in this context capital will strictly be considered equipment.

Entrepreneurship is what makes the other three factors of production valuable. Nothing happens in an economy until someone steps up to the plate and becomes an entrepreneur (or business owner) who utilizes these resources to give us the goods we need and the jobs we seek.

The problem is that there is a limit to the available quantity of these resources; hence, they can become scarce, causing shortages of goods and services. As a result of scarcity, to say yes to producing one thing often means saying no to producing another. This is called **opportunity cost**.

Opportunity cost is not a bad thing. College students may say no to taking a job when they finish high school that pays them the minimum wage in order to go to college. Over a four-year period, their sacrifice could add up to over $60,000 of income thrown away. Is that bad? Not really. College students are very wise to turn down that $60,000 in the hopes of going to college first, betting that a college degree will help them earn far more than the minimum wage and thus make up for that loss of $60,000 in the long run.

It works the same way in production. If you choose to make cars with *all* of the resources you have, there would be nothing left with which you could produce any other product or service, such as refrigerators, perhaps.

Which one would you choose to produce? If you are in business to make a profit, it would most likely be the one that brings you the most profit.

The **production possibilities curve** shows you your production possibilities, and it will help you decide *what* you will produce. It is the combination of things you could likely produce at a given time with the resources you have. For example, looking at the chart in figure 1-1A, suppose you decide to produce only cars using all of your resources. That means you could produce no refrigerators because you would have used up all of your resources to produce the cars. Therefore, the coordinate representing production of both items would be at Point Y, right on the Y axis: only cars would be produced and no refrigerators.

However, if you decide you would like to produce at least a few refrigerators, then you would have to give up producing some of the cars. Your new coordinate could likely then be at Point B. Perhaps you choose to produce even more refrigerators. Once again, you would have to produce even fewer cars and your coordinate could likely then be at Point C. Maybe you choose to produce still even more refrigerators. Again, you would have to produce even fewer cars and your coordinate could likely then be at Point D. If you choose to produce no cars, and only refrigerators, your coordinate would then be at Point X, right on the X axis.

On the other hand, you may choose to produce fewer quantities of both the cars and the refrigerators. In other words, you may choose not to use all of your resources. You may then be producing at Point A, inside the production possibilities curve in figure 1-1A.

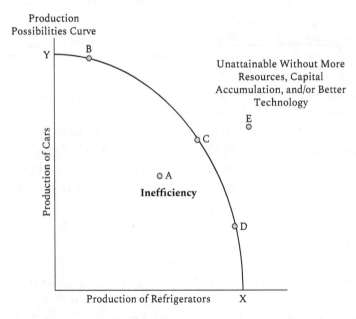

FIGURE 1-1A   Production Possibilities Curve

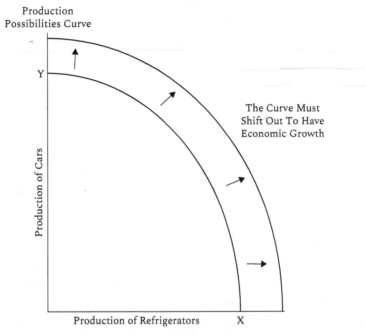

FIGURE 1-1B Production Possibilities Curve Shifted Out

Point A represents waste or inefficiency. If you don't use all your resources, many of them you can't get back in the long run. For example, if you do not use the labor of all of your employees today, tomorrow you can't hire someone to fill the time you wasted today. Why would anyone want to produce at Point A? It may be that they have no choice. If there is high unemployment in our economy, if business is bad for everyone, or if there is a lot less buying going on than usual, you may want to produce at Point A because you may not be able to sell all the items you produce while using all your resources. Later in this book we will discuss the many things that motivate producers to reduce production and to not use all their resources.

To produce outside of the production possibilities curve is not possible. Why? Because you would not have enough resources with your current situation to do so. Point E, for example, is a point of production that is unattainable with what you now have to work with. The only way that you could produce at the level of Point E would be to shift the entire production possibilities curve outward, or to the right. This can be done if you obtain more resources, make better use of the resources you have, or become more efficient, as shown in figure 1-1B.

So how does one do that? There are several options.

First, in addition to what has already been said about it, you can use technology to improve your output. **Technology** often, but not always, requires more capital equipment. Therefore, some refer to this as **capital accumulation**. Technology can also come in the form of ideas that yield a better way of accomplishing the same things. If I can produce something today in ten steps that used to take twenty steps, then technology is at work, even it doesn't involve equipment or if it's just figuring out a better, faster way to accomplish the same objective.

If you don't shift the production possibilities curve outward, or to the right, you are never going to have **economic growth**. In other words, your level of output, and likely your profits, would remain the same. On a national level, if all firms choose not to push their production possibilities curves outward, the economy will not grow and those who are without jobs will have no way of finding work.

THE ECONOMIC ENVIRONMENT

Another thing to consider is the environment in which you are doing business. It can either enhance or inhibit your ability to operate your organization. The **economic environment** is influenced in large part by how much the government gets involved with managing the economy and what kind of an economic system it is in which you operate.

There are those who believe that government should intervene and regulate our economy and our economic activities in many ways, while others believe that government should not get so involved. It is believed by many that when the government tries to regulate an economy, it always fails to achieve its goals while simultaneously making things worse. One of them was **Adam Smith (1726–1790),** who wrote the book entitled *The Wealth of Nations* in 1776, which discussed **the invisible hand theory**. He felt that the answers to the questions of what, how, and for whom things are to be produced should be answered by the free market and not by the government. He professed that government should practice a **laisse-faire** (hands-off) mentality and not regulate the economy. He also preached that producers don't produce things out of concern for society's needs but rather out of their greed for profit. He felt that no matter how much society needs a certain product or service, producers will not produce them unless there is adequate profit to be made.

The theory is now called the **market mechanism**. For example, if consumers demand fewer cars and more refrigerators, fewer cars and more refrigerators will be produced; thus, workers who produced cars will then shift to other jobs such as producing refrigerators, changing the mix of output. Government doesn't have to tell you to produce fewer cars if people have stopped buying them, nor does it need to tell you to produce more refrigerators if they are very popular. Producers are smart enough to cash in by producing the things people want to buy and are willing to pay dearly for. Producers are also smart enough to stop making the things that people are no longer willing to pay for. This natural shift from producing one thing and then to producing another is the invisible hand theory at work, managing the economy. It just happens to work itself out. In this scenario, therefore, the questions would be answered as follows:

- *What* will be produced? Refrigerators.
- *How*? With the use of those who are skilled at producing refrigerators and are willing to produce them for the prices consumers are willing to pay.
- *For whom*? For those willing to pay a price for it that generates adequate profits for the producers.

Notice, therefore, the essential element of the market mechanism is the **price signal**. People will not produce refrigerators for you unless you are willing and able to pay them the price that will give them the profits they want.

Adam Smith believed that these questions are best answered by those who are engaged in the free market rather than by having government decide.

There are many countries in the world besides America that are predominately free-market societies. Many of these same countries, however, have a very imbalanced economic status, with only 1 or 2 percent of the people possessing nearly all the wealth, and the remaining 98 percent of the people living in total poverty. So, if we are also a free market, why do *we* not have such problems? Many believe, for example, that our antitrust laws, which prohibit people from conspiring to monopolize a market, are what help us to have a better distribution of wealth and income than the other countries. Therefore, many believe that there is some level of need for regulations.

While many economists don't always agree, there is evidence that productivity and prosperity, along with acceptable wealth and income distribution, usually don't happen without involving some level of government regulation.

When you set up shop, therefore, it's important to know where you are and what the economic environment is where you are doing business. It may be that you can't operate your business profitably unless you are in an economic environment where the taxes are lower and the regulations are fewer. Whatever the case, you must deal with the circumstances of where you are.

These are the things that our government typically provides for business organizations:

1. Provision of the legal framework
2. Environmental protection
3. Consumers protection
4. Labor protection
5. Infrastructure protection (such as our power grids, highways, bridges, airports, and communication networks in order to facilitate sales and production)
6. Provision of services (such as emergency services, law enforcement, and military services)

WHAT KIND OF AN ECONOMY DO WE HAVE? CENTRAL (PLANNED, SOCIALIST, COMMAND), FREE MARKET (CAPITALIST), OR A COMBINATION OF BOTH?

Economics Myth #1: The United States operates in a pure free-market economy.

If you are doing business in this country, you are working in an economy that is predominately a free market, but the United States does not operate *completely* in a **pure free-market**

economy. That is an economy in which private businesses provide goods and services to satisfy all our needs with no goods or services provided by the government. The reason that we are not operating in a completely pure free-market economy is that there are many things that society needs that the free-market system cannot provide. This is known as **market failure**.

Every society has a different economic system. Some gravitate more toward having a *pure free market*, while others gravitate toward the other end of the spectrum where you would have *pure* **socialism,** where the government decides what, how, and for whom things will be produced (See Figure 1-2).

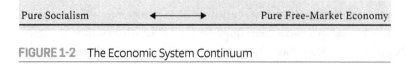

| Pure Socialism | ←——→ | Pure Free-Market Economy |

FIGURE 1-2 The Economic System Continuum

It is important to know what economic system it is in which you are working, whether you are doing business here or abroad. We are in a global economy, which means we can do business in any country we want to as long as their economic system will allow it. Even if they do allow it, their regulations and government involvement will likely differ from ours here in the United States.

While **communism** and socialism share many similarities, they are not the same. Many argue that communism is actually a form of socialism that is much more extreme.

Communism is an economic and political system, while socialism is only concerned with the economy. It is believed, therefore, that socialism can exist within more than one political system, including capitalism. Socialism maintains that personal ownership is allowed, while Communism does not. Socialism promotes the idea that people should be able to make choices in areas such as their careers, religion, or education, but communism does not.

Capitalism is another term for an economic system embraced by countries that would prefer to allow private individuals to control industries and trade at a profit rather than to have them controlled by the government. Therefore, let's focus more on socialism and how it works in relationship to the free market.

It is often referred to as a **planned economy**, a **central economy**, or a **command economy**, where a centralized entity, such as the government, decides what will be produced, how, and for whom. The only way it can succeed is if the government truly knows what people want and don't want to buy.

For example, some have referred to the term *socialized medicine*. Many people feel that it is a type of socialism, where, once again, the government answers those three economic questions by creating a national health care system.

Over many, many years, some countries have moved from one end of the continuum toward socialism, while others have moved to the other end of the continuum toward the free market. A country tends to move toward a free-market system when it appears that the government isn't producing enough of the necessary goods or services needed by the public. On the other hand, a country may move toward socialism if it appears that it is having market failure, where the free market fails to give society all that it needs. Examples of these needs in the United States that the free market usually can't provide at a profit are our military services, highways, and emergency services. No entrepreneurs are likely to be able to make these things available at a profit; therefore, the government needs to pass the hat (by charging taxes) to create them. This is why we say that the United States is in a **mixed economy** due to market failure, in that the free market cannot satisfy all of society's needs.

In some countries, economies have been known to drift back and forth, from socialist economies to free-market systems as societies and their leaders see fit.

The United Kingdom, for example, has **socialized medicine**. It took some time to achieve this and get it to the point that it is today. Some argue that it still isn't satisfying needs, while some disagree. Still others argue that other societies need to do what the United Kingdom has done. Regardless of where you are on this debate, it shows how countries move up and down the continuum.

The United States has far more goods provided by the private sector (or the free market) than it does by government, so our mixed economy would put us on the right of the center of the continuum between socialism and a free-market society.

Government failure exists too, however, as it sometimes fails to make the economy prosper or is unable to produce what we need that the free market can't produce in high enough quantities and at an affordable cost. Sometimes government tries to solve social problems but makes them worse instead.

HOW TO BENEFIT FROM THIS BOOK

When we use economic theories in this book, they are those primarily agreed upon by economists in our country and around the world. **Economic theory** exists when people, usually economists, prescribe what people need to do to reach economic objectives. The theories we discuss here will prescribe the cause and effect of different actions and strategies. I have often thought of these theories as **financial physics**. They are often used to make predictions that use the concept known as **ceteris paribus**, which means other things being equal. For example, economists say that if prices go up, purchases will decline, ceteris paribus. In other words, purchases will decline with higher prices if nothing else changes. The problem with such thinking is that seldom does one thing happen without many others simultaneously changing.

Another problem exists in that once theories are applied, either at the micro level, or the macro level, reality, through politics and imperfect knowledge and information, hints at the flaws in these theories. We can only apply these concepts when we have good information about our circumstances, either about our business or the economy as a whole. Unfortunately, information is often inaccurate and/or late. When government tries to regulate the economy, it may take months for politicians and government to determine the status of the economy, a few months more to determine how to fix any problems, more time to implement the policies aimed toward fixing those problems, and then even more time for those remedies to take effect. This is called **legislative lag**. Applying the right remedies to economic problems, just as a doctor prescribes medication and remedies to a patient, is also less effective if it is done so with bad information or when the status of our economy is not correctly reported.

Needless to say, as we study various economic theories and models, we must bear in mind that they have their limitations, and we must often make adjustments when necessary.

CHAPTER 1 REVIEW

QUESTIONS TO THINK ABOUT

1. Why study economics?
2. What is economics?
3. When managing the economy, what are the three questions that you must answer?
4. What is the focus of this book?
5. What do economists feel is the ideal economic environment?
6. What are the things that our government typically provides for our economy?
7. What kind of an economy do we have?
8. Explain the weakness of economic theory.
9. What myths are described in this chapter?

TERMS TO KNOW

Adam Smith
Capital
Capital accumulation
Capital equipment
Central economy
Ceteris paribus
Command economy
Communism
Economic growth
Economic theory
Economical
Economics
Entrepreneurship
Free-market economy
Government failure
Inflation
Invisible hand theory

Labor
Land
Legislative lag
Macroeconomics
Market failure
Market mechanism
Microeconomics
Mixed economy
Opportunity cost
Planned economy
Price signal
Production possibilities curve
Socialism
Socialized medicine
Technology
The Wealth of Nations

CHAPTER TWO

The What, How, and for Whom Goods are Produced

IN CHAPTER 2, we will now focus more on *what* is produced by producers and how we measure it. We also look at *how* we produce them. Are we using labor or are we using machines to produce our goods?

WHAT WE PRODUCE

The monetary value (not including subsidies, or **transfer payments**, discussed later) of the **final goods** of what a nation produces, and ultimately sells, over a given period of time (quarterly or annually) is known as **gross domestic product (GDP)**. The key word here is "final goods." If your firm buys a component part and adds value to it by putting it on a product and then reselling it, such goods would not be considered a final good, but rather an **intermediate good**. The reason that these types of goods are not counted in GDP is that doing so would be counting them twice: once at their purchase by the manufacturer and then a second time when the manufacturer sells the product to which that component part was added.

Intermediate Goods That Are NOT Counted in GDP Purchases	Final Goods that ARE Counted in GDP Purchases
Tires, Steering Wheels, or	Cars, Vans, or Trucks Sold to Car Consumers
Headlights Sold to Car Manufacturers	

FIGURE 2-1   Examples of What Are and Aren't GDP Purchases

Gross Domestic Product is found by adding up the purchases of goods and services in our country within four different categories:

1. (C) **Consumer Goods**: This includes anything purchased by a citizen for personal use.
2. (I) **Investment Goods**: These are things purchased by a business for business use only and not added to a product for resale to their customers. These investments are not to be confused with investments in things such as stocks or bonds. They are called investment goods because businesses hope to enhance their profits by purchasing them, and it is their hope that the money they spend for them will increase production, reduce costs, and increase profits, just as anyone would get returns with any investment.
3. (G) **Government**: This would be any and all spending by the federal government except for transfer payments. **Transfer payments** are those made to citizens for economic aid. They include things such as welfare, unemployment, and Social Security payments (or money transfers) to those in need or entitled to them. These are not counted in GDP.
4. (X_n) **Net Exports**: This would be the sale of consumer goods and investment goods, mentioned above, that are sold to anyone outside of our country minus any imports we Americans may have purchased from other countries. This number has been negative for many years, because the money value of what we have imported is far greater than the money value of the goods and services that we have produced and then exported.

Up until the early 1990s, the US government's focus was more toward the measure of **gross national product (GNP)**. It measures income of people in this country. For the most part, income of Americans as measured by GNP should be the same as GDP because every time you purchase something it becomes someone else's income. However, income may reflect more than that. For example, there are many who earn dividends and interest from investments they make in foreign firms. The profits from those firms are not derived from sales or production that create jobs here. Another way of defining GNP is by taking GDP and adding net income that Americans receive from outside our country.

The measure of GDP is very important, because it tells us the status of our economy. This is why GNP is no longer used, because it gave us a slightly inflated job creation figure when it included income of Americans from investments of businesses of other countries that did not create jobs here. There are three different statuses that can exist in any economy. A **recession** exists if there is a small decline in output by our country's producers, which causes an increase of unemployment by a few percentage points. A **deep recession** exists if there is a *huge* decline in output, causing unemployment to climb above 10 percent or so. A **depression** exists if there is an astronomical decline in output, causing unemployment to soar to nearly 20 percent or above.

When GDP falls for two consecutive quarters, it is then determined by economists that a recession exists or that our economy is in a state of recession. At that point, **unemployment** (an increase in the number of the Americans in the workforce who cannot find jobs), bankruptcies, and foreclosures will rise while company profits and prices will fall. An economy has not really recovered from a recession until it has returned to the level of GDP that existed before the recession. Another way of looking at it is that a recession is not completely over until your economy reaches **full employment**. Full employment is not necessarily zero unemployment; this is something that will be studied later. Figure 2-2 shows what the GDP has been in the United States since 1929.

U.S. Real GDP Since 1929

Date	Real GDP	Date	Real GDP	Date	Real GDP
2016	16.85 trillion	1987	8.29 trillion	1958	2.92 trillion
2015	16.55 trillion	1986	7.94 trillion	1957	2.85 trillion
2014	16.22 trillion	1985	7.71 trillion	1956	2.84 trillion
2013	15.79 trillion	1984	7.40 trillion	1955	2.78 trillion
2012	15.38 trillion	1983	7.00 trillion	1954	2.61 trillion
2011	15.19 trillion	1982	6.49 trillion	1953	2.54 trillion
2010	14.94 trillion	1981	6.59 trillion	1952	2.53 trillion
2009	14.54 trillion	1980	6.50 trillion	1951	2.40 trillion
2008	14.58 trillion	1979	6.50 trillion	1950	2.27 trillion
2007	14.99 trillion	1978	6.42 trillion	1949	2.00 trillion
2006	14.72 trillion	1977	6.02 trillion	1948	2.04 trillion
2005	14.37 trillion	1976	5.73 trillion	1947	1.96 trillion
2004	13.95 trillion	1975	5.49 trillion	1946	1.96 trillion
2003	13.53 trillion	1974	5.36 trillion	1945	2.22 trillion
2002	12.96 trillion	1973	5.46 trillion	1944	2.24 trillion
2001	12.71 trillion	1972	5.25 trillion	1943	2.07 trillion
2000	12.68 trillion	1971	4.91 trillion	1942	1.77 trillion
1999	12.32 trillion	1970	4.71 trillion	1941	1.49 trillion
1998	11.77 trillion	1969	4.72 trillion	1940	1.27 trillion
1997	11.21 trillion	1968	4.62 trillion	1939	1.16 trillion
1996	10.74 trillion	1967	4.40 trillion	1938	1.08 trillion
1995	10.28 trillion	1966	4.29 trillion	1937	1.11 trillion
1994	10.05 trillion	1965	4.10 trillion	1936	1.06 trillion
1993	9.65 trillion	1964	3.78 trillion	1935	0.94 trillion
1992	9.41 trillion	1963	3.60 trillion	1934	0.86 trillion
1991	9.02 trillion	1962	3.42 trillion	1933	0.78 trillion
1990	8.91 trillion	1961	3.28 trillion	1932	0.79 trillion
1989	8.85 trillion	1960	3.08 trillion	1931	0.90 trillion
1988	8.61 trillion	1959	3.06 trillion	1930	0.97 trillion
				1929	1.06 trillion

Source: U.S. Bureau of Economic Analysis

http://www.multpl.com/us-gdp-inflation-adjusted/table

FIGURE 2-2   GDP Trends

If GDP in your country is greater than that of another country, it doesn't always mean that your country's economy is doing better. It can often be because the population in your country is different than that of another.

In 2016, for example, China had a much higher GDP than that of the United States, but the population of China is much greater than that of the United States. It is misleading to look at only those figures and conclude that China had a stronger economy. Figure 2-3 shows figures from 2016, with China at the top.

Country	GDP (millions of $Int'l)
World	11,51,65,700
China	2,14,17,150
European Union	1,97,21,689
United States	1,85,69,100
India	87,02,900
Japan	52,66,444
Germany	40,28,362
Russia	33,97,368
Brazil	31,41,333
Indonesia	30,32,090
United Kingdom	27,96,732
France	27,73,932
Italy	23,12,559

FIGURE 2-3   (From the International Monetary Fund [IMF]) Country GDP

This is why economists prefer to measure **GDP per capita**. It is equal to GDP divided by the total number of men, women, and children in that country. During 2016, the United States had more than $57,000 in GDP per person or per capita, but China's was less than $9,000. Figure 2-4 shows that China was not even among the top-ranked countries when calculating GDP per capita.

Country	GDP
Qatar	1,27,660
Luxembourg	1,04,003
Singapore	90,151
Macau	87,855
Brunei	76,884
Kuwait	71,887
Norway	69,249
Ireland	69,231
United Arab Emirates	67,871
Switzerland	59,561
San Marino	59,058
Hong Kong	58,322
United States	57,436
Saudi Arabia	55,158

FIGURE 2-4   (From the International Monetary Fund [IMF]) Country GDP per Capita

Per capita GDP helps to make numbers practical to analyze a country's economic status, but it has its weaknesses.

First, it is not an indicator of the actual distribution of a country's wealth. For example, it appears at first that each person in the United States is earning over $57,000 annually. But that is only an average. There are many who earn far less than that, while others earn millions of dollars per year. As far as wealth is concerned, it is not necessarily measured by income. Many retirees have a great deal of wealth but very little income. A person's wealth can include savings accounts at various banks as well as stocks, bonds, cars, homes, and much more. Sometimes people gain this wealth as heirs to estates, from generations of money that has been passed down many times, while others accumulate wealth by saving for retirement and their children's college education fund over many decades.

HOW WE PRODUCE

After studying what we produce, we then study how we produce, by analyzing our productivity. **Productivity** is measured by taking output and dividing it by the number of inputs used to produce it, inputs such as output per labor hour or per element of capital equipment. For example, if you are producing ten products with the use of five labor hours, your labor productivity would be two hours of labor per product produced.

As a country, the United States and other developed nations (such as Canada, Japan, and member states of the European Community) have higher productivity with labor because they have organizations that are **capital intensive**. That means that through the use of capital equipment, we produce more goods for every hour of labor we employ. Manufacturers tend to have operations that are very capital intensive, as they use a great deal of equipment and automation, while industries in the service sector of our economy such as accountants, attorneys, and cleaning companies are more **labor intensive**, using more people skills than equipment for production.

Over the years, the United States has dominated the world in productivity. While many other countries have made huge improvements and strides in productivity and the use of capital equipment, the United States is still the leader.

Labor intensive industries, or countries that tend to be more labor intensive than capital intensive, utilize what is called **human capital.** This is the level of skills and knowledge your human workforce has. Cheaper help is not always better help. The United States has the advantage here too, with labor in our country being among the best educated and skilled for production.

Another thing that we have going for us in the United States is **factor mobility**, the ability for our workforce to shift from one firm to another when their existing employers have slower or negative growth or when layoffs ensue. Skills that workers use in one organization can often be plugged into that of another. This helps to keep productivity in our country higher and can help reduce unemployment.

THE IDEA OF MARGINAL CHOICES

In our study of economics there is a term that is used quite often: marginal.

In this context, the word *marginal* means a change or the amount of change. For example, is it worth studying one additional hour as you prepare for an exam? The added benefit from studying that extra hour would be the overall change in or the **marginal benefit** derived from that added studying. The added cost of an activity is the **marginal cost**. In this example, the change in effort and time (or the added effort and time) spent for studying would be that marginal cost. Time and effort costs you, whether you pay a monetary value for them or not. **Marginal analysis** is a concept, therefore, that helps us to decide if it is wise to take a certain action. If we are to act in a way that is economical, marginal analysis would tell us that we must not take an action where the marginal cost exceeds the marginal benefit.

Returning to the studying example, if you begin to study for an exam, each hour of time (cost) in studying will likely give you a greater marginal benefit (the increase in your knowledge and preparation for the exam per extra hour used for studying). Therefore, marginal analysis would suggest that you are wise to spend the added time studying and that it is justified by the benefit. However, suppose you have been studying for fifteen straight hours and you are weary and tired. The added time (or the marginal time) or effort in studying will not likely give you much more (or marginal) knowledge, as you will be too tired to grasp any more information. In that case, marginal analysis would recommend that you stop studying and that you rest for a while before resuming.

As we continue to reap benefits by what we buy or by what we do, the marginal benefit tends to diminish. In our studying example, more time studying made you weary, thus the marginal benefit declines. The same thing is true when we buy certain products or services. As we continue to buy them, we get tired and bored with them, thus the cost is no longer justified by the benefit. This is called the **principal of decreasing marginal benefit**. It simply says that marginal benefit goes down the more we do a specific activity or the more we consume of a product or service.

ANOTHER WAY OF LOOKING AT THE "WHAT" WE PRODUCE

Comparative advantage is the ability of a firm or an entire country to produce a specific good or service at a lower opportunity cost than its competitors or competing countries. You or the producers in your country should produce what makes you the most profitable. Oil producing countries, for example, would not be wise to begin to produce cars, because if they use up their resources to do so, they have fewer or no resources left to produce oil that is more profitable. Their profits from making cars would likely be much lower than what profits they would make if they just keep producing oil. It is always recommended that you or the people of your country do what you do best. **Absolute advantage**, on the other hand, is the ability of a firm (or country) to produce a specific good or service with fewer inputs or resources (including capital or labor) per unit of output than its competitors. In other words, the firm, or country, can do the production cheaper. However, when deciding what to produce, it is always best to produce products or services with which you have comparative advantage rather than that of absolute advantage. It doesn't matter if you can do it cheaper. It matters more if you can do it better and with more profit and with lower opportunity costs.

Many of the people in the oil-producing countries spend their time making profits in oil production, while buying the products that we in the United States do best, such as car production.

YOUR PROFITABILITY AND ITS COST TO SOCIETY

Sometimes organizations make decisions about what they produce and how they produce it that actually injure people in our society. For example, some cars have been produced over the years at lower costs but at the expense of the safety of those who drive them and their passengers.

While we do have a moral responsibility to maximize profits for shareholders, we must do so in a way that is legal and ethical. In the long run, firms that cut corners in costs while endangering their customers, polluting our environment, or hurting society are not likely to increase the firms' profits. In time, such practices are discovered and exposed by the public, and when they are, it causes far more economic damage and creates more cost to those firms than any profits or benefits they may have derived from those actions.

ECONOMIC COORDINATION AND COOPERATION

In order to produce economically, it is often best for people to specialize. People can be more productive when they focus their efforts on a limited number of products and services. When people try to serve all needs of all people, they often fail or are inadequate at doing so.

The problem is that to specialize, there must be some level of economic coordination and cooperation between at least two people or two institutions and the markets. For example, if you choose to focus your efforts toward production of software, it doesn't do you much good if your customers have no computer hardware or computer networks on which to run that software. There are often those, however, who can produce the computer hardware and networks to make software run. Software developers are at the mercy of such networks and hardware running smoothly to run their software. Therefore, a great deal of cooperation and coordination between software, hardware, and network providers and their institutions and markets must exist.

MARKETS

Markets are not necessarily a place. A century ago most markets were comprised of people doing business and making sales face-to-face in the center of cities and towns. Vendors would set up shop on a weekly basis, or they would have a store in a business district. The only way most business transactions took place was by people coming to those market places.

In this day and age, many markets have become more like networks. Many transactions are facilitated by making deals with the use of telephone equipment, fax machines, and computer links with many buyers and sellers around the world who may never meet in person.

With markets now being unlimited in their possibilities, the doors are open to many opportunities, but they are also open to the thieves who steal your ideas and make imitation copies of your products. Therefore, markets only work when property rights exist.

Property rights are what give you the sole right to the use and sale of your ideas, products, or services. They are social arrangements that govern ownership. The property types include **real property**, such as buildings, plants, equipment, and land. They are tangible. On the other hand, **financial property** includes things such as stocks, bonds, and savings accounts. They are not tangible, but they are very valuable. Finally, you have **intellectual property**. Intellectual property is also intangible. It includes creative work, such as books, music, computer programs, and inventions, all of which should be copyrighted and/or patented.

When property rights are enforced, you have the incentive to specialize and produce the goods in which you have comparative advantage to maximize the use of said property. When an environment exists where such property can be easily stolen, or where copyrights and patents can be infringed upon without consequences, much effort and many resources must then be used to protect said property. Such resources would then be wasted when they could have been used to produce more goods and services.

CHAPTER 2 REVIEW

QUESTIONS TO THINK ABOUT

1. What is gross domestic product, and how does it indicate our current economic condition?
2. How does the United States stand worldwide regarding GDP and productivity?

TERMS TO KNOW

Absolute advantage	Double-dip recession
Capital intensive	Factor mobility
Comparative advantage	Final goods
Consumer goods	Financial property
Depression	Full employment

GDP per capita
Government
Gross national product (GNP)
Human capital
Intellectual property
Intermediate good
Investment goods
Labor intensive
Marginal analysis
Marginal benefit

Marginal cost
Net exports
Nominal GDP
Principal of decreasing marginal benefit
Productivity
Real GDP
Real property
Recession
Unemployment

CHAPTER THREE

The Circular Flow

DOES ONE SALE generate another sale? Absolutely! Otherwise our economy would falter. Chapter 3 will show you how important it is for one sale to generate many more sales. We will also discuss how a loss of sales in one respect can be replaced by another.

When a sale is made, there is always a process that takes place.

1. If I am a consumer, I take my money and buy something from the **product market**.
2. That product market is either a business or it buys the goods or services we buy from another business.
3. Businesses buy their resources from people like you and me when they
   a. pay us for the land we own or by paying rent for the use of the land we own,
   b. pay us for our labor (paying a wage to one of us to produce the good or service for the product market),
   c. buy capital equipment from one of us,
   d. give us profits (if we are the entrepreneurs) when they buy from our businesses.

Once someone like you or me is paid, we can once again become consumers, and we can take our money and buy more things from the product market. At that point, the process starts all over again and steps *a* through *3d* are repeated.

This process is known as the **circular flow**. It must go around and around as long as possible and as strong as possible or our economy could likely fall on bad times. Please see figure 3-1.

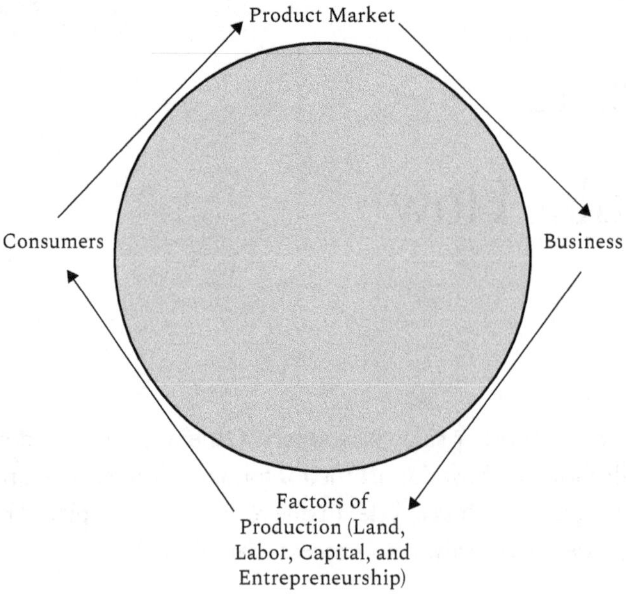

FIGURE 3-1   The Circular Flow

Sometimes, however, the circular flow can spring a leak. Just like the plumbing in your house, if the leak isn't fixed or if the water that leaked out isn't somehow reinjected into your plumbing, eventually your pipes will have no more water to circulate and they dry up. We never want to see our economy dry up. We must keep the circular flow moving and remove such **leakages**.

What kind of a leakage could occur?

The first is **taxes**. When you are paid, you are not able to spend all of your money because a large part of that income must be paid to the government, thus that money is leaked out of the flow. How is that money reinjected?

Taxes find their way back into the circular flow when the government takes your tax money and buys things from the product market just as a consumer would. They can also pay money directly to landlords for land, to workers for labor, to those selling capital equipment, or to those in business (entrepreneurs) who take care of some of the things government needs.

Another leak comes from **savings**. If people put money aside in their savings accounts after they have earned it, the money won't be spent, and that would create another leakage in the circular flow.

Savings find their way back into the circular flow, however, as long as the people who save money don't put it in a shoe box under their bed. They must put it into financial institutions such as banks, mutual funds, or investment firms that sell stocks and bonds. When that happens, those financial institutions turn right around and make that money available to those who need it to buy homes, cars, appliances, capital equipment for business, and much more.

The final major leakage from the circular flow comes from **imports**. If the American people are buying goods from other countries and not from here, that money once again escapes from the American circular flow. The reinjection of that money then comes from exports of our products that we sell to people abroad.

There is a problem here. As mentioned earlier, the exports our country sells abroad are far fewer than the imports we Americans purchase. For many years, the reinjection of exports to compensate for lost sales in imports has not been adequate, and as discussed before, our net exports have been a negative number.

So then, why doesn't the circular flow of our country dry up as a result of that?

One major reason is that the **reinjections** of government spending and loans from banks more than make up for the import/export leakages. The government spends much more than they receive in tax revenue. Also, when you put money in banks, much more money is created by those deposits than the deposits themselves. Does that sound impossible? When you study macroeconomics, you can see how money deposited into savings accounts actually multiplies.

CHAPTER 3 REVIEW

QUESTIONS TO THINK ABOUT
1. Describe the circular flow in your own words.
2. How can we better fix the leakages in the circular flow?

TERMS TO KNOW
Leakages
Reinjections

CHAPTER FOUR

The Laws of Supply and Demand

NOW THAT THE circular flow has been discussed, chapter 4 will show what drives the level of sales based upon how much people are willing to buy and produce under various circumstances. Remembering the circular flow will also make it easier to understand the concepts of supply and demand of goods and services.

So, what does it mean to demand something?

In order to **demand** something, you must

1. want it,
2. have the means to purchase it (meaning you have the money to buy it or you have enough credit to borrow to buy it), and
3. be willing and able to take the action to purchase it.

All three of these three things must happen if demand is going to take place.

Demand is defined as the ability and willingness of a given person to buy given quantities of a good or service at a given price, ceteris paribus. The **law of demand** basically states that as sellers continue to raise their prices, the quantity demanded of those goods and services will decline, ceteris paribus. The opposite is true. Lower prices will bring an increase in the demand of goods and services.

There are two reasons for this. The first is called the **income effect**. Everyone has a limit to what they can afford because we all have a limit to our income. Even the richest people in the world have limits to what they can purchase. Therefore, if prices go up, people cannot afford to buy as much; thus, demand will fall. The second reason that fewer goods and services are purchased from you as a producer when you raise your prices is the **substitution effect**. If you are a producer or seller and if you charge more and more for your goods and services, your customers will look for another way, a less expensive way, to satisfy their needs. They will find other goods or substitutes (**substitute goods**) to do so. Substitute goods could be one of your competitors' goods and services or something that is comparable to your product that will satisfy your customers' needs.

Back in the late 1970s, many people became overwhelmed by the increases in energy costs. Unfortunately, the utility companies had no competitors. Therefore, many, many consumers began to look for other ways to heat their homes. They used products such as kerosene stoves and fireplace inserts. As a result, the energy companies experienced a significant decline in sales, because those heating their homes found substitutes to satisfy that need.

Let's take a look at an example of how a typical firm's demand for their product or service might work.

As we did in a previous chapter, let's assume that you own a pizza restaurant. Suppose you have a potential customer who, if asked, would tell you that if you charged $5 for a slice of your pizza, they would only demand one slice per year. But as you lower your price, they may agree to buy more. The schedule shown in Figure 4-1 could be an example of how much pizza your customer might buy in a given year if you are selling pizza. This would be an **individual consumer's demand schedule**.

Price Per Slice	$5	$4	$3	$2	$1
Demand	1	2	3	4	5

FIGURE 4-1 Price per Slice (Individual Buyer)

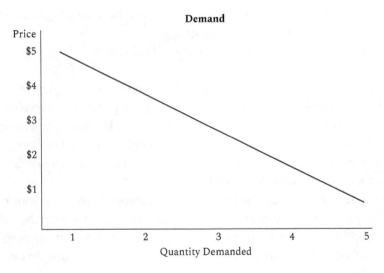

FIGURE 4-2 Demand Curve (Individual Buyer)

If you were to graph that demand schedule, it would look like what you see in figure 4-2. This is called the **demand curve,** which shows demand at many levels at various price levels.

Every potential customer has their own individual demand schedule and, ultimately, their own demand curve for your product or service.

Now assume that there are 10,000 of these potential consumers, like the person mentioned above, in a given market area that become potential buyers or demanders of your pizza. The schedule in figure 4-3 could then be an example of how much pizza your firm may have demanded from it during a given year. This would be called the **firm's demand**.

Price Per Slice	$5	$4	$3	$2	$1
Demand	10,000	20,000	30,000	40,000	50,000

FIGURE 4-3   Price per Slice (Firm's Demand)

Now assume that there are 10,000 pizza parlors in the country. The schedule in figure 4-4 would show how much pizza would be demanded in our country in a given year. This would be known as the **market demand** for the pizza industry.

Price Per Slice	$5	$4	$3	$2	$1
Demand	10,00,00,000	20,00,00,000	30,00,00,000	40,00,00,000	50,00,00,000

FIGURE 4-4   Price per Slice (Market Demand)

Now assume that there are 100,000 different industries with average prices such as these in the country. The schedule in figure 4-5 would show how much would be demanded in our country's entire economy in a given year. This would be known as the **aggregate demand** for our entire country. Aggregate demand, therefore, is the same as gross domestic product (GDP).

Price Per Unit of Sale	$5	$4	$3	$2	$1
Demand	10 Trillion	20 Trillion	30 Trillion	40 Trillion	50 Trillion

FIGURE 4-5   Price per Slice (Aggregate Demand)

If we were to graph the aggregate demand in the preceding schedule, you would be creating what is called the **aggregate demand curve** as seen in figure 4-6.

Therefore, the first major determinant of demand is the price that producers charge for their products or services.

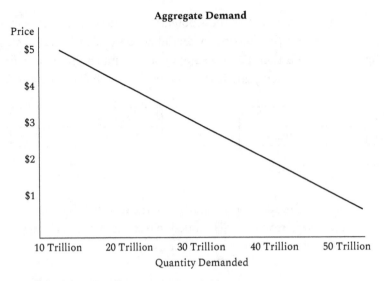

FIGURE 4-6   Aggregate Demand Curve

Let's now return to the idea of graphing only your pizza shop for a moment. Since this is microeconomics we're talking about, we need to focus on the individual pizza shop. Using the numbers mentioned earlier (seen again in figure 4-7), the demand curve for your pizza shop could look something like what is seen in figure 4-8.

Price Per Slice	$5	$4	$3	$2	$1
Demand	10,000	20,000	30,000	40,000	50,000

FIGURE 4-7   Price per Slice (Firm's Demand)

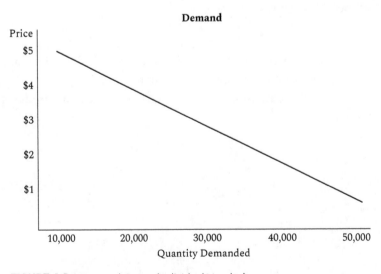

FIGURE 4-8   Demand Curve (Individual Vendor)

If the price that your pizza shop charges for each slice sold drops from $5 down to $4, your demand would increase to 20 thousand slices. As your prices continue to change, going either down or up, your demand would move up and down along your demand curve. Therefore, the only thing that causes demand to move along the demand curves of businesses in this country is a change in the prices they charge. There are other determinants of demand besides that of the prices charged by producers.

TASTE (LIKING OR DISLIKING OF YOUR FIRM'S PRODUCTS)

Let's return to your pizza shop. Suppose, for example, that people stop liking your pizza. It could be that your products are no longer liked by your customers as much as before. Many may begin to feel that they prefer a different taste, or maybe they perceive that the quality of your pizza has declined. Even if your prices remain the same, demand for your pizza would decline. If the price you charge is $4, demand could possibly decline to Point D or somewhere in that vicinity, as is illustrated in figure 4-9. If you charged approximately $3, then demand could possibly decline to Point E or somewhere in that vicinity. If you charged $2, then demand could possibly decline to Point F or somewhere in that vicinity.

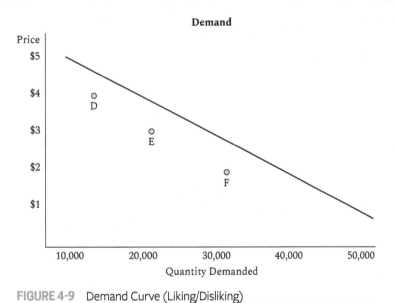

FIGURE 4-9 Demand Curve (Liking/Disliking)

If you connect those three coordinates—D, E, and F—you would have a new demand curve. In other words, if fewer people like your pizza, your demand would decline even if your prices are unchanged, and your demand curve would shift to the left (from Point A to Point C) as seen in figure 4-10. That is bad news for your business. It is important to note here that whenever a curve shifts, the old curve ceases to exist.

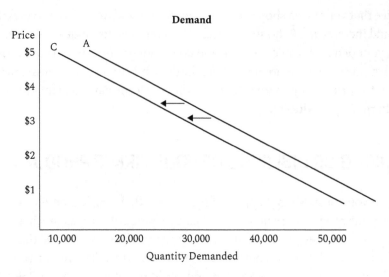

FIGURE 4-10 Demand Curve Shift Left (Liking/Disliking)

The opposite is also true. Suppose, for example, that people began liking your pizza *more*. Suppose they have developed a taste and craving for it. Even if your prices remain the same, demand for your pizza would increase. Your demand curve will then shift to the right from Point A to Point B, as seen in figure 4-11. That would increase your sales and perhaps your profits. This is good news for you!

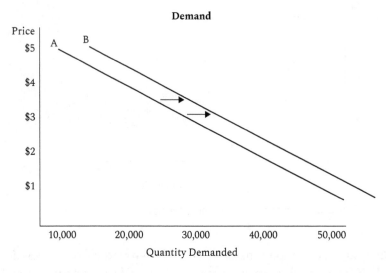

FIGURE 4-11 Demand Curve Shift Right (Liking/Dislike)

INCOME (AFTER TAXES)

Suppose now that the income of families in your market area began to decline. It can happen by higher unemployment, high-paying jobs leaving your area, or people in your market area taking pay cuts for various reasons. A tax increase could also reduce the amount of **disposable income** of the people in your market area. This is income people have left after they pay their taxes. If taxes go up, your potential customers would have less of their paychecks left over that they could spend. Even if your prices remain the same, demand for your pizza would decline. If the price of your pizza is approximately $4, then demand could possibly decline to Point D or somewhere in that vicinity as seen in figure 4-12. If you charge approximately $3, then demand could possibly decline to Point E or somewhere in that vicinity. If you charge $2, then demand could possibly decline to Point F or somewhere in that vicinity.

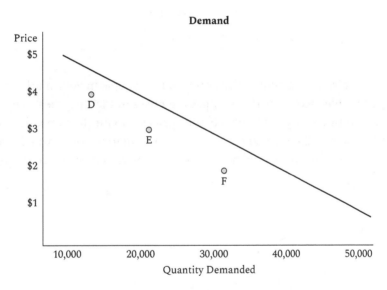

FIGURE 4-12   Demand Curve (Income)

Now, if you connect those three coordinates, you would have a new demand curve. In other words, if income after taxes of families or for people in your market area declines, your demand curve would shift to the left, from Point A to Point C as seen in figure 4-13. Again, this is bad news, because a drop in sales could lead to a drop in your profits.

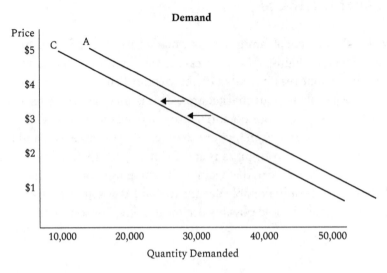

FIGURE 4-13 Demand Curve Shift Left (Income)

The opposite is also true. Suppose, for example, that people in your market area begin to earn higher disposable income, perhaps by getting raises in their paychecks, by lower taxes, or by a decrease in unemployment. Even if your prices remain the same, demand for your products would increase. Your demand curve will then shift to the right from Point A to Point B as shown in figure 4-14. That would increase sales for you, and again, this is good news!

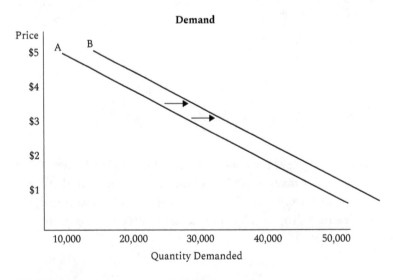

FIGURE 4-14 Demand Curve Shift Right (Income)

OTHER GOODS: SUBSTITUTE GOODS

We have spoken about the idea of the substitution effect. If people find other, better, or less expensive goods than yours to satisfy the same basic needs, those products would be referred to as **substitute goods.**

Now suppose, for example, that the price of those substitute goods declined while the quality of those goods was perceived as being relatively the same as yours. It could be that other pizza shops, or any shop that could produce a meal for people that satisfies them in the same way your pizza would, lowered their prices. Also assume that your prices remain unchanged. That would make those goods more attractive than yours to buyers, and demand for your products would decline. If the price of your pizza is approximately $4, then demand could possibly decline to Point D or somewhere in that vicinity as seen in figure 4-15. If the price of your pizza is about $3, then demand could possibly decline to Point E or somewhere in that vicinity. If the price of your pizza is approximately $2, then demand could possibly decline to Point F or somewhere in that vicinity.

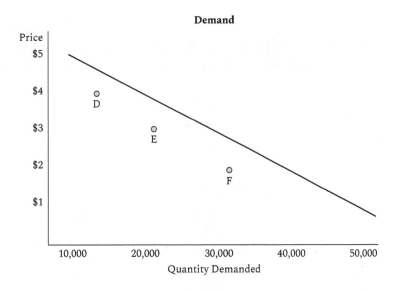

FIGURE 4-15   Demand Curve (Substitute Goods)

Once again, if you connect those three coordinates, you would have a new demand curve. In other words, if people can buy substitute products just as good as yours at a lower price, your demand curve would shift to the left from Point A to Point C as seen in figure 4-16. That is bad news, because this means that your demand will fall, and once again your profits—and, in a sense, your weekly paycheck—will also decline.

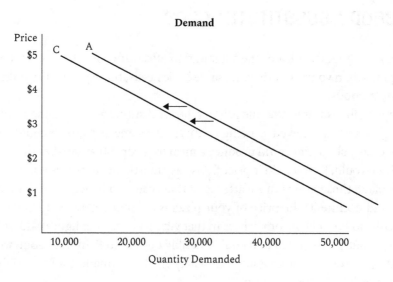

FIGURE 4-16   Demand Curve Shift Left (Substitute Goods)

The opposite is also true. Suppose, for example, that prices for substitute goods rise, while the prices of your goods remain the same. Demand for your products would increase. Your demand curve will then shift to the right from Point A to Point B as seen in figure 4-17. That would increase your sales, and profits. Good news again!

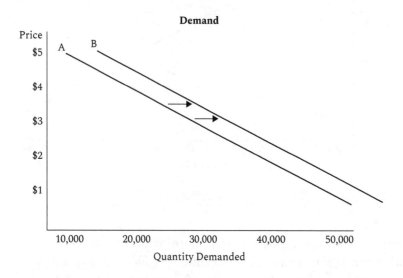

FIGURE 4-17   Demand Curve Shift Right (Substitute Goods)

COMPLEMENTARY GOODS

There are many goods out there that require the purchase of another good or service in order to own and operate them.

For example, you are not likely to own a telephone if there is no telephone service or network available. At the same time, you would not need to have access to a telephone network if you do not have a telephone. Another example would be cars, lawnmowers, or any gasoline-driven products. You can't operate them without gasoline, and you would not have much use for gasoline without those products. These are called **complementary goods.** If the price of a complementary good rises, therefore, it becomes more expensive to own the product that requires it. For example, if the price of gasoline goes sky-high, the sales for cars would decline because it would be more expensive to own and operate cars. The same would be true for telephone service. Few telephones would be purchased or leased if people could not afford to pay for access to a telephone network.

A pizza shop might consider soft drinks a complementary good, because you likely can't eat anything without having to wash it down. This example may not be as good as that of the relationship between cars and gasoline, but let's run with it to help you to understand this concept. Now, suppose, for example, the price of soft drinks increases significantly. If that happens, you could see a decline in sales. Even if your pizza prices remain the same, demand for your pizza would decline. If the price of your pizza slices are approximately $4, then demand could possibly decline to Point D or somewhere in that vicinity as seen in figure 4-18. If the price of your pizza slices is approximately $3, then demand could possibly decline to Point E or somewhere in that vicinity. If the price of your pizza slices is approximately $2, then demand could possibly decline to Point F or somewhere in that vicinity.

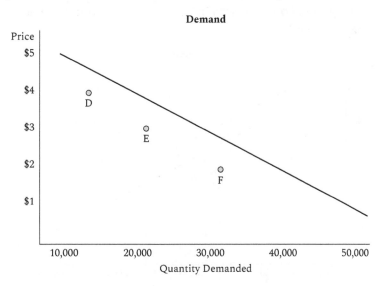

FIGURE 4-18   Demand Curve (Complementary Goods)

If you connect those three coordinates, you would have a new demand curve. In other words, if the price of goods that are complementary to your pizza goes up, your demand curve would shift to the left from Point A to Point C as seen in figure 4-19. Again, this is bad news, because a drop in your sales hurts your pizza shop's profits.

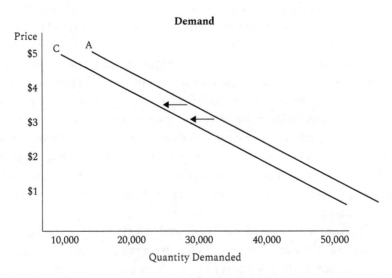

FIGURE 4-19 Demand Curve Shift Left (Complementary Goods)

The opposite is also true. Suppose, for example, that prices for soft drinks decrease while your prices do not. Demand for your pizza would increase. Your demand curve will then shift to the right from Point A to Point B as seen in figure 4-20. This would increase your sales and profits. Happy, happy, happy!

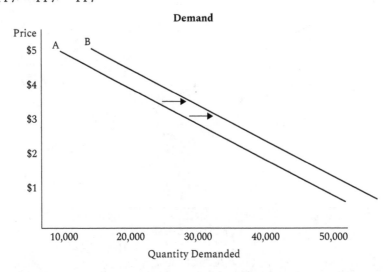

FIGURE 4-20 Demand Curve Shift Right (Complementary Goods)

EXPECTATIONS (Future)

If your customers expect that the foreseeable future for our economy is bleak, and therefore if they feel that there is a chance that they can lose their jobs, they will likely not buy things unless they absolutely need them. For example, the purchases of homes, cars, and appliances will often decline when the future of our economy is perceived to be bleak.

It has often been said that when the economy gets a cold, Detroit gets pneumonia. That's because the automotive industry is a major provider of jobs there. When people expect a bad economy and they stop buying cars, Detroit, as well as other towns that depend on car manufacturing jobs, appliance manufacturing jobs, or construction jobs, will see much higher unemployment than other parts of the country that do not rely on such jobs. Businesses would also likely buy less in the way of capital equipment. They are not going to expand their output capacities if they feel that business is about to take a bad turn. An expected drop in consumer spending (C) would cause a drop in business investment (I), both of which are major components of GDP.

Let's revisit the pizza shop scenario. Bleak economic outlooks don't usually hurt food service industries as much as they do to manufacturing jobs. Still, there will likely be some decline in your pizza business as people start to watch their spending more closely. They may choose to eat at home more often to save money. If this is the case, you would see a decline in sales in your pizza shop.

If your price for a slice of pizza is still $4, then demand could possibly decline to Point D or somewhere in that vicinity as illustrated in figure 4-21. If the price of your pizza is approximately $3, then demand could possibly decline to Point E or somewhere in that vicinity. If the price of your pizza is approximately $2, then demand could possibly decline to Point F or somewhere in that vicinity.

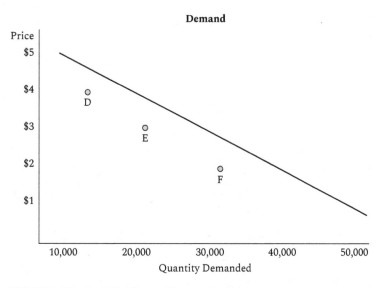

FIGURE 4-21 Demand Curve (Expectations)

If you connect those three coordinates, you would have a new demand curve. In other words, if expectations for the foreseeable future of our economy are pessimistic, your demand curve would shift to the left from Point A to Point C as shown in figure 4-22. As always, a shift to the left of your demand curve means fewer sales for you and lower profits.

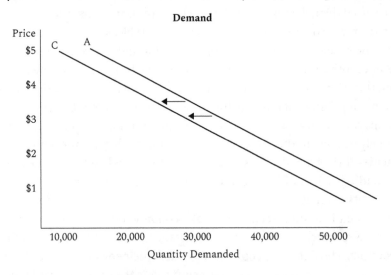

FIGURE 4-22   Demand Curve Shift Left (Expectations)

The opposite is also true. Suppose, for example, the outlook of the economy looks very good. More people will then buy your pizza. Your demand curve will then shift to the right from Point A to Point B as shown in figure 4-23. That would increase your sales, and, you guessed it, hopefully it will bring you a prosperous time. More good news!

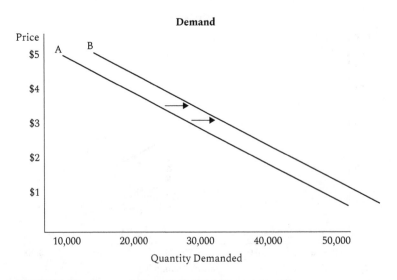

FIGURE 4-23   Demand Curve Shift Right (Expectations)

NUMBER OF BUYERS

Many believe that a higher population can hurt society, but when population declines, so too does the number of potential buyers of our goods and services, bringing demand down. If the population in your pizza market area declines, you lose customers.

If the price of your pizza is approximately $4, then demand could possibly decline to Point D or somewhere in that vicinity seen in figure 4-24. If the price of your pizza is approximately $3, then demand could possibly decline to Point E or somewhere in that vicinity. Do you feel like you've heard this before? If the price of your pizza is approximately $2, then demand could possibly decline to Point F or somewhere in that vicinity.

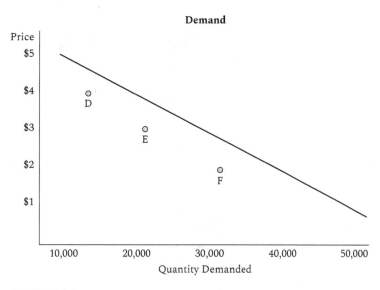

FIGURE 4-24   Demand Curve (Number of Buyers)

If you connect those three coordinates, you once again would have a new demand curve. In other words, if population decreases, your demand curve would shift to the left from Point A to Point C as shown in figure 4-25. Once again, this means that sales and profits for you will decline.

The opposite is also true. Suppose, for example, that you see a major increase in population in your market area. Even if your prices remain the same, demand for your pizza would increase. Your demand curve will then shift to the right from Point A to Point B. This would increase your sales, and prosperity would be yours again, as seen in figure 4-26.

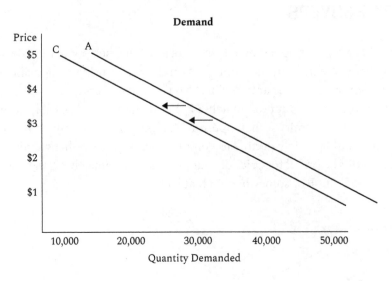

FIGURE 4-25 Demand Curve Shift Left (Number of Buyers)

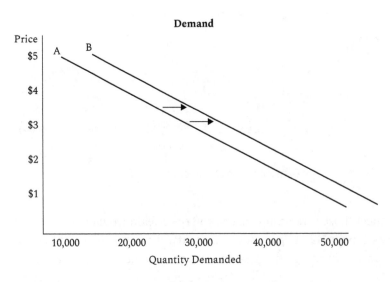

FIGURE 4-26 Demand Curve Shift Right (Number of Buyers)

TIMING

Demand for some goods and services depend very highly on timing. A pizza parlor is going to have lower demand on weeknights, but in the evening on a weekend, demand for pizza will surge. There are special times that demand will change, perhaps on nights such as New Year's Eve, or during the World Series or the Super Bowl.

A lot of retailers will see lower demand after the Christmas rush is over but will see much greater demand in the weeks before Christmas. Every industry has their busy and slow times, and demand will shift right and left accordingly.

SUMMARY OF DETERMINANTS OF DEMAND

- Prices of producers move demand along the aggregate demand curve.
- The remaining determinants of overall demand will shift the curve. Those determinants are mainly as follows:
  - Tastes
  - Income (after taxes)
  - Other goods (substitute and complementary)
  - Expectations
  - Number of buyers
  - Timing

SHORTAGES CAUSE HIGHER PRICES

If you want to sell the only gallon of milk that exists in the entire state you're in, I guarantee you that there would be many people willing to pay you far more for that milk than the current prices charged at the supermarket. Shortages, therefore, cause higher prices. This is something that applies to many elements of our lives, and therefore we will discuss it again later in this book.

WHEN DEMAND IS THE INDEPENDENT VARIABLE

Up until now, we have been discussing what will happen to demand if prices and other determinants of demand would change.

What happens to prices, however, when demand is the independent variable? In other words, what happens to prices when demand changes?

If demand rises, it will also typically drive prices up as well. One of the reasons for this is that higher demand can possibly create a shortage if producers can't keep up with that demand. As mentioned earlier, shortages cause higher prices and/or inflation. Another reason is that when a product is popular, many want to get their fair share of it. People don't want to be left out. If everyone is buying a product, it's only wise in the minds of many that they want to be like everyone else during such a fad. Such rushes to buy hot products drive up prices, because people are willing to pay just about any price that would keep them from having to do without the products or services they want or need.

For example, there have been times when stock prices rose, not so much because they were good investments but because the other available investments, such as bonds, were very unpopular. Therefore, many people chose to buy or demand stocks as the lesser evil, driving up the prices, and erroneously making people think that those stocks were making great returns.

The opposite is also true. When demand for things falls, there is often a surplus of goods in warehouses and stores. It is costly to store things, especially if they are not selling. Stores start having sales to get those unpopular goods out of their stores to make room for more.

Because so many people were out of work during the recession of 2008, many businesses had to lower their prices to entice buyers to come back to them. Housing during that time also saw prices plummet. People knew that demand for them was very low; therefore, people chose not to buy homes until they believed that the prices had bottomed out. If consumers know that demand, and therefore prices of given products, is declining, they are less inclined to buy them today, knowing that if they wait, they can get those products at a much lower price.

High Demand Causes High Prices	Low Demand Causes Low Prices

FIGURE 4-27   High vs. Low Demand

Now we move our discussion toward the concept of supply.

If a person is to **supply** something, this means that they are willing and able to supply it, produce it, or make it available for someone else (most likely for purchase).

In order to supply something, you must

1. be willing to supply/produce it,
2. be able to supply/produce it, and
3. be prepared to take the action to supply/produce it.

All three of these things must happen if supply is going to take place.

Supply is defined as the ability and willingness to sell or produce given quantities of a good or service at a given price, ceteris paribus.

The **law of supply** says that if the price that people are willing to pay a producer goes up, the producer is likely to supply more, ceteris paribus. It's the price signal. Higher prices paid to you for what you do motivates you to produce more. Not only are you motivated to do so by higher profits, but the higher price paid to you makes it more practical for you to produce your products or services at a profit.

The opposite is also true. If people are no longer willing to pay you a high price for what you produce, you are not motivated to do so. In fact, you may not even be able to afford to do so without losing money.

Let's return to the example of your pizza shop.

If you feel that you would be willing to supply, perhaps, 50 thousand slices of pizza during any given year if people are willing to pay you $5 for each them, then the grid in figure 4-28 may be a schedule that would describe how much you would be willing to supply as the market price for your pizza slices changes. This would be the **firm's supply**.

Price Per Slice	$5	$4	$3	$2	$1
Supply	50,000	40,000	30,000	20,000	10,000

FIGURE 4-28   Price per Slice (Firm's Supply)

Now assume again that there are 10 thousand pizza parlors in the country. The schedule in figure 4-29 shows how much pizza would be supplied in our country. This would be known as the **market supply** for the pizza industry.

Price Per Slice	$5	$4	$3	$2	$1
Supply	50,00,00,000	40,00,00,000	30,00,00,000	20,00,00,000	10,00,00,000

FIGURE 4-29   Price per Slice (Market Supply)

Now assume that there are 100 thousand different industries with average prices such as these in the country. The schedule in figure 4-30 shows how much would be supplied in our country's entire economy. This would be known as the **aggregate supply** for our entire country. Aggregate supply, therefore, is the same as gross domestic product (GDP) as long as everything that is supplied is also demanded.

Price Per Unit of Sale	$5	$4	$3	$2	$1
Supply	50 Trillion	40 Trillion	30 Trillion	20 Trillion	10 Trillion

FIGURE 4-30   Price per Slice (Aggregate Supply)

If we were to graph the aggregate supply from the preceding schedule, it would create what we call the **aggregate supply curve**, which would look something like the curve shown in figure 4-31.

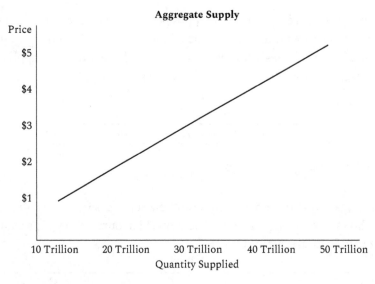

FIGURE 4-31 Aggregate Supply Curve

Once again, we need to keep in mind that our focus here is at the micro level. Let's recall the supply schedule for your pizza firm. If the public is willing to pay you the prices below, you could likely be willing and able to supply pizza at the levels listed in figure 4-32.

Price Per Slice	$5	$4	$3	$2	$1
Supply	50,000	40,000	30,000	20,000	10,000

FIGURE 4-32 Price per Slice (Firm's Supply)

Therefore, the first major determinant of supply is the price that consumers are willing to pay you for what you produce. If the price paid to you drops from $5 each down to $4 each, your supply would decrease to 40 thousand. As the prices in your pizza business would continue to change, going either down or up, your supply would move up and down along the supply curve. Therefore, the only thing that causes supply to move along the supply curve is a change in the price paid to producers. To graph this relationship, we would create the **supply curve,** and it would appear something like what you see in figure 4-33.

There are other determinants of supply besides that of the prices paid to producers, as we will now discuss.

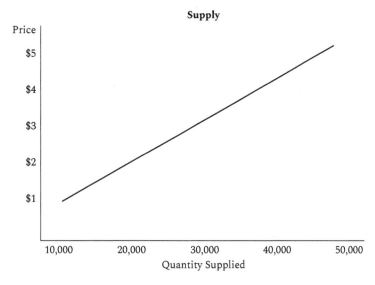

FIGURE 4-33 Supply Curve (Vendor)

TECHNOLOGY

Suppose, for example, that you begin to find more efficient ways to increase your output by the use of technology. Even if the market prices paid to you remain the same, supply for your products would increase. If the price paid for your pizza is approximately $4, then your supply could possibly increase to Point G or somewhere in that vicinity as seen in figure 4-34. If the price paid to you for your pizzas is approximately $3, then your supply could possibly increase to Point H or somewhere in that vicinity. If the price paid for your pizza is approximately $2, then your supply could possibly increase to Point I or somewhere in that vicinity.

If you connect those three coordinates, you would have a new supply curve. The supply curve has thus been shifted outward, or to the right, which is what you see in figure 4-35. In other words, if more and/or better technology is used in your firm, your supply (or output) will increase. Your supply curve will likely shift from Point X to Point Y. This is good news for your customers, and your workers. Your customers are less likely to face shortages of your pizza; thus, there is a good chance that prices will remain stable. It also is good news for workers, because more production helps their job stability.

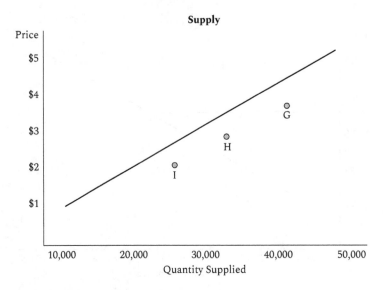

FIGURE 4-34   Supply Curve (Technology)

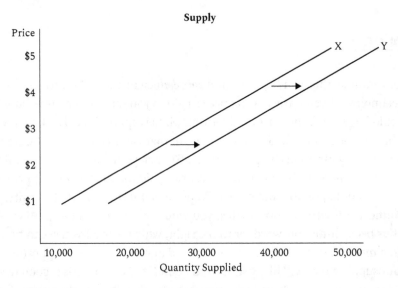

FIGURE 4-35   Supply Curve Shift Right (Technology)

Some may ask what would make your supply curve shift to the left as a result of a change in technology. The only time that technology would drive the supply curve to the left, or reduce supply, would be if existing technology is abandoned, neglected, or removed from your business, but this is not likely to happen.

FACTOR COSTS

If your cost of doing business declines, this is an indication that the **factor costs** (costs of the factors of production such as land, labor, and capital), which are the costs of your resources, may be falling as well. These costs could include your rent, your labor, your pizza dough and sauces, your pepperoni, or anything you use in the production of your pizza. That's good news for you because your profits per unit of output can rise even if your prices don't. You are then motivated to produce and supply more pizza to cash in on the added profits. If the price paid to you for your pizza is approximately $4, then your supply could possibly increase to Point G or somewhere in that vicinity as shown in figure 4-36. If the price paid for your pizza is approximately $3, then your supply could possibly increase to Point H or somewhere in that vicinity. If the price paid to you for your pizza by your customers is approximately $2, then your supply could possibly increase to Point I or somewhere in that vicinity.

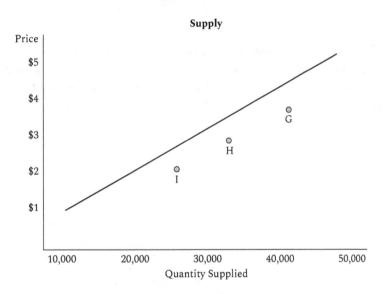

FIGURE 4-36   Supply Curve (Factor Costs)

If you connect those three coordinates, you would have a new supply curve. In other words, if factor costs for production of your pizzas decline, your supply (or output) of your pizza would likely increase, thus shifting your supply curve to the right from Point X to Point Y as shown in figure 4-37. This is good news for your customers and workers, for reasons mentioned earlier.

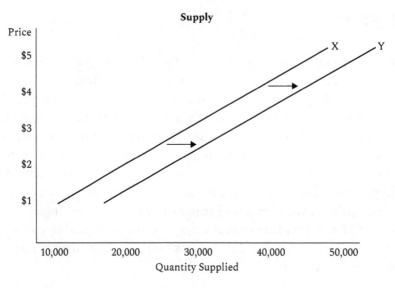

FIGURE 4-37   Supply Curve Shift Right (Factor Costs)

The opposite is true. If your cost of doing business goes up, this is an indication that the costs of factors of production are likely rising as well. If you aren't being paid higher prices, your profits for each pizza you produce is going to fall. You are then less motivated to produce pizza, thus your supply curve would be shifted to the left from Point X to Point Z as seen in figure 4-38.

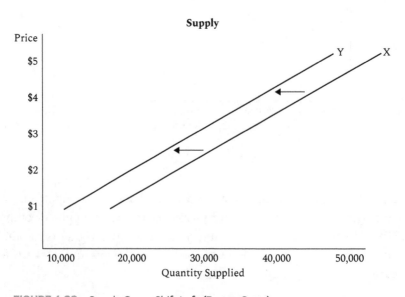

FIGURE 4-38   Supply Curve Shift Left (Factor Costs)

TAXES

Economics Myth #2: Lowering taxes for businesses is wrong and immoral as it gives big corporate fat cats more money while not giving any benefit to the middle class.

Many people oppose the lowering of taxes for business. They fear that businesses would not be paying their fair share of taxes. There are a few things that must be considered here. First, 80 percent of the businesses in existence in this country are **small businesses**. They are not "big corporate fat cats" who crush the middle class. Second, if the country is experiencing high unemployment, the lowering of taxes can put many unemployed people back to work, because it can increase disposable income and increase demand.

Lower taxes are also good motivators for producers to increase output. Even if the price that businesses collect per unit of sale stays the same, they get to keep more of the profits they earn. Politicians of both political parties have proposed, voted for, and implemented legislation granting tax cuts for businesses over many years, especially during times of high unemployment. Many contend that when the government gives a tax cut, the tax revenue lost by the government is not something they can ever recoup. However, it has been proven mathematically that tax cuts bring in far more revenue for government than is lost. When tax cuts occur, that money is usually spent. When it is spent, it becomes someone else's income. That person will then likely spend it as well. This process is repeated over and over again, creating more taxable income and thus more tax revenue for the government. This is something that you will see when you study macroeconomics.

If the price paid for your pizza is approximately $4, then your supply could possibly increase to Point G or somewhere in that vicinity as shown in figure 4-39. If the price paid to you for your pizza is approximately $3, then your supply could possibly increase to point H or somewhere in that vicinity. If the price your customers are willing to pay you for your pizza is approximately $2, then your supply could possibly increase to the point of Point I or somewhere in that vicinity.

If you connect those three new coordinates, you would have a new supply curve, shifting your supply curve to the right from Point X to Point Y as shown in figure 4-40. In other words, if taxes are lowered by the government, your supply (or output) would likely increase. More output leads to more available goods, lower prices, and more jobs. The added jobs created by increases in production are another reason that tax reductions can help the economy and thus help create job security.

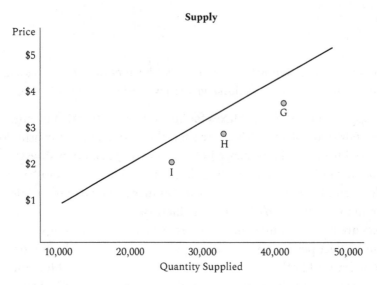

FIGURE 4-39 Supply Curve (Taxes)

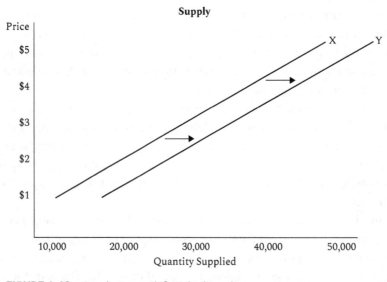

FIGURE 4-40 Supply Curve Shift Right (Taxes)

The opposite is true. When the government raises taxes, producers are less motivated to supply goods and services because they don't get to keep as much of their profits. Some say, "Why bother working so hard and producing so much if the government is going to take such a huge portion of my profits away?" Some businesses actually move to different countries to avoid high taxes, which certainly reduces supply on an aggregate scale in our country. That would shift the supply curve to the left from Point X to Point Z as seen in figure 4-41. As a result, in your firm, as in many firms, higher taxes lead to reductions in supply, and thus they lead to cuts in production.

This is bad news for your customers and your workers. With a cut in production (or supply), fewer goods are available and shortages can begin, and thus higher prices may ensue. Cuts in production also cause layoffs and unemployment.

Higher taxes also have an impact on workers' attitudes toward their supplying of labor hours. With higher taxes, people are often less inclined to work that extra job at night or on the weekends. The middle class can then be hurt too when fewer people are willing to supply their labor hours to businesses, as it causes a decline in supply, thus shortages and higher prices could occur as well.

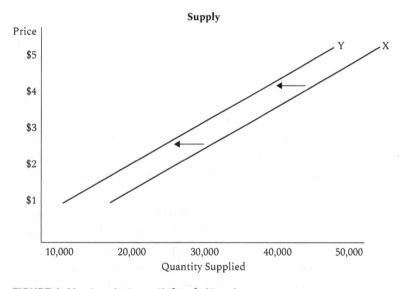

FIGURE 4-41   Supply Curve Shift Left (Taxes)

While we are still on the topic of taxes, it must be noted here that corporate profits after taxes are what drive the value and income of those who have retirement plans or the investments made by parents who are saving money to put their children and/or grandchildren through college. Increasing taxes on "the rich" or corporations actually hurts those looking for jobs as well as those saving for retirement or for their children's future. The value of those investments made by the middle class is driven by net profit after taxes of all corporations, which creates dividends. Higher taxes reduce those dividends, thus reducing the value of their investments, and creating a strain on retirees and on families with children wishing to attend college.

REGULATIONS

Economics Myth #3: Deregulation only makes society less safe.

Deregulation is an attempt to remove any and all of the unreasonable regulations that are imposed by governments that are not effective. Deregulation is not always a bad thing, as long as the regulations that have been cut back or removed have been proven to be ineffective toward making society better. Many regulations were removed by the government over the years and it actually helped rather than hurt society.

Economics Myth #4: Deregulation has only been done by one political party.

Actually, both political parties have fostered a great deal of deregulation over the years. Jimmy Carter was the president who began a wave of deregulation in many industries in the late 1970s and early 1980s, and that wave has continued through many presidential administrations of both political parties since then.

When the government chooses to ease regulations, you are often inclined to increase output. Even if the price you collect per unit of sale stays the same, fewer regulations make it more likely that you can afford to produce more pizza and/or that it will be easier to produce. Regulations are often expensive, and it is often difficult to comply with them. Suppose the government was requiring you to take measures for cleaning your pizza shop that truly didn't make your shop any cleaner. Suppose also that it was very costly and difficult to comply with those regulations. Now suppose that the government no longer required you to take those measures. Your motivation to stay in business, or perhaps to make more pizza, would increase. If the price paid for your pizza is approximately $4, then your supply could possibly increase to Point G or somewhere in that vicinity, as you can see in figure 4-42. If the price paid to you for your pizza is approximately $3, then your supply could possibly increase to Point H or somewhere in that vicinity. If the price paid to you for your pizza is approximately $2, then your supply could possibly increase to Point I or somewhere in that vicinity.

If you connect those three new coordinates, you would have a new supply curve, thus shifting your supply curve to the right from Point X to Point Y as seen in figure 4-43. In other words, deregulation in your industry can help your supply (or output) to increase.

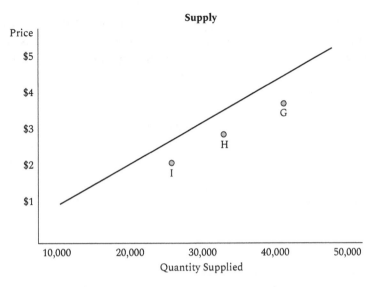

FIGURE 4-42   Supply Curve (Regulations)

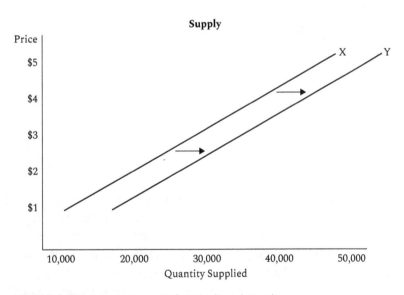

FIGURE 4-43   Supply Curve Shift Right (Regulations)

The opposite is true. When the government imposes more regulations on you and the producers in your industry, you are less motivated to supply those pizzas, and there is a very strong chance that you would be motivated to cut production. The regulations could also make it too expensive for you to produce, thus causing losses in business, to say nothing of the burden and stress that those regulations could cause you. You will likely begin to feel that <u>producing your pizza</u> <u>simply isn't worth the trouble anymore</u>, and you may then decide to <u>end production</u> altogether. Assuming that you would stay in business but simply cut production, your supply curve would shift to the left from Point X to Point Z as seen in figure 4-44.

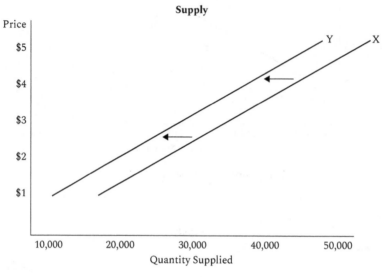

FIGURE 4-44 Supply Curve Shift Left (Regulations)

SUBSIDIES

There are some industries that cannot produce the output needed by society because they are so competitive. An example of this would be the farming industry. If the market price of corn is too low, many farmers will not produce the corn because they will lose money, or they may not be able to make enough profit to make an adequate living. When this happens, the government will often ask, "What price do you need per bushel of corn in order to make a profit?" Suppose the going price is $4 per bushel, but the farmers would need $5 per bushel to make a profit. The government will not stand for shortages in food. That would cause major social uproars. Therefore, the government may be inclined to pay the farmers the extra dollar they need in order to produce the corn at the profit they desire. Such an act by the government is called a **subsidy**.

When the government offers subsidies to producers, the supply of those goods and services will increase.

It is very unlikely that the government will pay a subsidy to pizza producers, but what could happen if they paid you a dollar above what you are now being paid by your customers? If the price paid for your pizza is approximately $4, then your supply of pizza could possibly increase to Point G or somewhere in that vicinity as seen in figure 4-45. If the price paid for your pizza is approximately $3, then your supply could possibly increase to Point H or somewhere in that vicinity. If the price paid for your pizza is approximately $2, then your supply could possibly increase to Point I or somewhere in that vicinity.

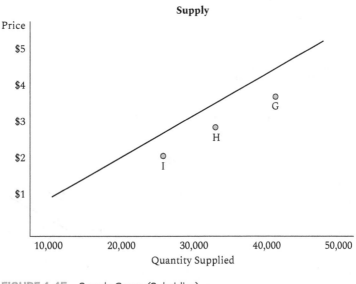

FIGURE 4-45   Supply Curve (Subsidies)

If you connect those three new coordinates, you would have a new supply curve. In other words, if more subsidies are made available by our government, your supply (or output) would likely increase and your supply curve would shift out from Point X to Point Y as seen in figure 4-46. Once again, this is good news for your customers and workers.

The opposite is true. When the government chooses to reduce subsidies in their fiscal budget and if you are a recipient of one of those subsidies, you will likely be inclined to reduce your output or supply. Your supply curve could shift from Point X to Point Z (see figure 4-47).

This is bad news again. Your customers may see shortages of your pizza, and many of your workers will likely be let go.

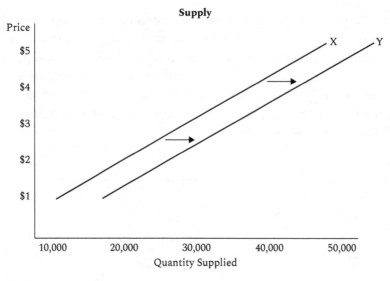

FIGURE 4-46   Supply Curve Shift Right (Subsidies)

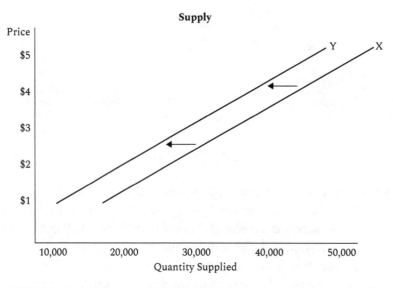

FIGURE 4-47   Supply Curve Shift Left (Subsidies)

EXPECTATIONS

If you are a producer and if you expect the economy to boom in the foreseeable future, you may be inclined to increase your output/supply in order to cash in on the good times ahead. Such expectations will likely compel you to supply more pizza and to increase your output capabilities.

If the price paid for your pizza is approximately $4, then your supply could possibly increase to Point G or somewhere in that vicinity as portrayed in figure 4-48. If the price paid to you for your pizza is approximately $3, then your supply could possibly increase to Point H or somewhere in that vicinity. If the price paid for your pizza is approximately $2, then your supply could possibly increase to Point I or somewhere in that vicinity.

If you connect those three new coordinates, you would have a new supply curve, thus your supply curve will shift out from Point X to Point Y (see figure 4-49). In other words, if you have better expectations of the economy or if your optimism increases, your supply (or output) would likely increase. You guessed it. This is good news for your customers and workers.

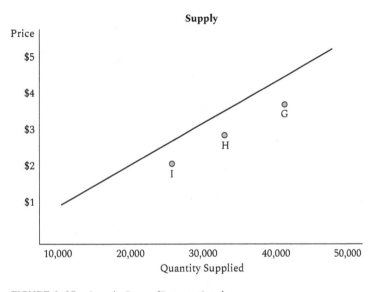

FIGURE 4-48 Supply Curve (Expectations)

The opposite is true. When times look bleak in the days, weeks, months, or even years ahead, producers will likely reduce output/supply/production of their goods for fear that many of those goods will have no buyers. You as a pizza shop owner may feel inclined to scale back your capacity to produce. Having a high capacity for output is expensive. You must have a lot of building space, equipment, and workers ready for production. If things look bad in the future, you will likely not maintain so much of it.

This is bad news for workers who could lose their jobs as a result of a drop in supply/output/production. Pessimism can kill an economy! Such a drop in output or supply would shift your supply curve to the left from Point X to Point Z as seen in figure 4-50.

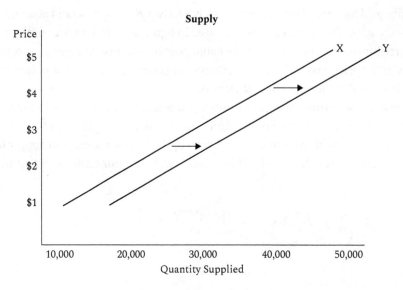

FIGURE 4-49   Supply Curve Shift Right (Expectations)

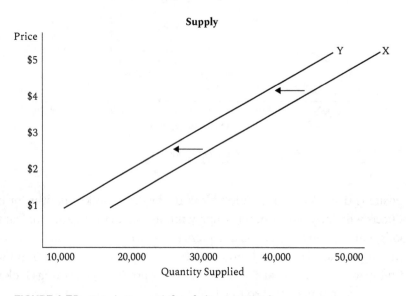

FIGURE 4-50   Supply Curve Shift Left (Expectations)

NUMBER OF SELLERS

Let's look at supply from the market standpoint. As population increases, more people are available to offer their services and goods. This can increase supply. In other words, you will likely have more pizza suppliers entering the market and more workers available to run those pizza shops as population increases.

The market supply curve for pizzas would then shift to the right.

The opposite is true. When population declines, there are fewer producers and therefore less supply/output and more bad news for both consumers and workers, as it means that there could be fewer goods available, higher prices, and fewer jobs.

OTHER GOODS

When we discussed other goods in the context of demand, we referred to things such as substitute goods and complementary goods. If the prices of complementary and substitute goods change, your demand will change, and thus your supply will likely change accordingly to meet increases in demand, or you may adjust supply downward if demand declines.

In the context of supply, however, there is another way to define "other goods." You can also think of other goods as goods that are appearing to be more profitable than what you are now producing. Suppose, for example, you learn that the profits derived from the production of burgers is far greater than that of pizza and/or those profits can be obtained with a lot less work and stress. At that point, you may choose to stop producing pizzas altogether and begin to make burgers. Your supply of pizza would then become nonexistent, as would your supply curve for pizza.

SUMMARY OF DETERMINANTS OF SUPPLY

- Price changes move supply along the supply curve.
- Other determinants of overall supply will shift the supply curve, and they are as follows:
  o Technology
  o Factor costs
  o Taxes
  o Regulations
  o Subsidies
  o Expectations
  o Number of sellers
  o Other goods

Figure 4-51 is a summary of the shifts of demand and supply curves when their determinants change as we have discussed in this chapter.

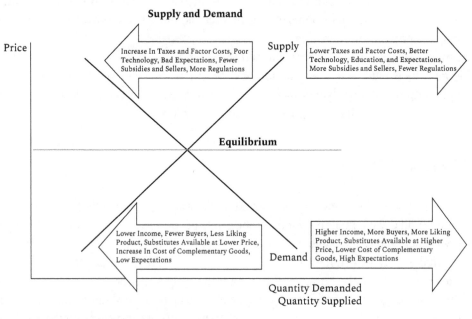

Supply and Demand

Price

Increase In Taxes and Factor Costs, Poor Technology, Bad Expectations, Fewer Subsidies and Sellers, More Regulations

Supply

Lower Taxes and Factor Costs, Better Technology, Education, and Expectations, More Subsidies and Sellers, Fewer Regulations

Equilibrium

Lower Income, Fewer Buyers, Less Liking Product, Substitutes Available at Lower Price, Increase In Cost of Complementary Goods, Low Expectations

Demand

Higher Income, More Buyers, More Liking Product, Substitutes Available at Higher Price, Lower Cost of Complementary Goods, High Expectations

Quantity Demanded
Quantity Supplied

FIGURE 4-51 Summary of Supply and Demand

The chart in figure 4-51 displays a new term that is important to understand: *equilibrium*. **Equilibrium** exists where the supply and demand curves intersect. The price level at that point would be called the **clearing price**. It is the price that will set quantity demanded equal to quantity supplied for goods and services. Producers are able to find buyers of everything they make, and there are enough goods and services to go around for all buyers. Buyers experience no shortages and sellers experience no surpluses. A **surplus** exists when sellers have more goods than they can sell. Surpluses are not good for producers, as producers must either reduce their price to sell their surplus goods or, in some cases, dispose of them if they are the type of goods, such as food products, that won't last longer than a few days.

Shortages exist when the quantity demanded of any goods or services exceeds the quantity supplied of them. Shortages usually cause higher prices (as discussed earlier), and if prices rise to the point that many cannot afford the goods, shortages then require consumers to manage without the things they want or need.

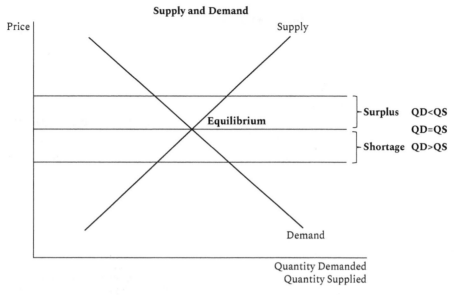

FIGURE 4-52   Shortages and Surpluses of Supply and Demand

Surpluses will exist when prices rise *above* equilibrium. When prices get that high, producers are motivated to produce more, but consumers will buy less. Shortages will exist when prices fall *below* equilibrium. When prices get that low, producers are less motivated to produce, but consumers will demand or buy more. It is at this point that Adam Smith believed that our economy can self-correct. If, for example, producers have large surpluses, as shown at the surplus level in figure 4-52 where QD (quantity demanded) is less than QS (quantity supplied), they will lower their prices, reluctantly, to get people back into their stores, restaurants, and showrooms to buy up those goods that are not selling.

As the prices are lowered, supply and demand do not typically stop exactly at equilibrium. It takes time for the demand to change or respond to a price change. Some people don't even know that prices have fallen, and even if they do, they don't just run out and buy things to take advantage of those price reductions unless they really need or want the goods that are now on sale.

Therefore, as prices fall below equilibrium, a shortage eventually ensues, as shown somewhere around shortage level in figure 4-52 where QD (quantity demanded) is greater than QS (quantity supplied). Shortages cause prices to rise, and thus demand will bring the price levels back up toward equilibrium.

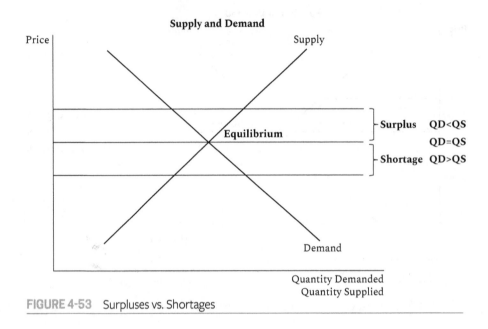

FIGURE 4-53 Surpluses vs. Shortages

This back-and-forth, up-and-down process will continue naturally in many cases. Sometimes it takes a few weeks or months, while in other cases it could take years to go through one complete cycle.

DEMAND CURVE VARIATIONS

There are times that demand curves don't resemble a straight line because of the nature of the industries in which they operate.

HIGH-PRICED-ITEM DEMAND CURVES

Goods and services that are high in price will often generate a demand curve that has more of a stair-step appearance. High-priced goods are not necessarily luxury goods. A car is a high-priced good, but many cars are not luxury cars.

Why do high-priced items create a stair-step curve?

Let's look at cars for an example. If a car at a local car dealer is priced at $15,000, there is not likely going to be higher sales or greater demand for those cars if the price is only lowered by one dollar, or even one hundred dollars. There is a certain point to which the price of the car must fall before anyone changes their demand for them. In figure 4-54, notice that the car dealer sees no sales until the price of the cars is lowered to $14,600 per car. If the dealer lowers the price by an additional $100, there are no more cars demanded. Even after lowering the price by another $100, the demand for those cars remains at one, because drops in increments of $100 usually aren't enough to motivate anyone to start buying more and will have a very small impact upon a monthly car payment. Once the price is lowered to $14,000, more buyers are now interested. That $600 drop is what it took to attract another buyer. The cost of high-priced items must be lowered significantly to see a change in demand of even one item. If the car dealer wishes to sell a third car, once again a price change of only $100 is not adequate to make that happen. In any case, demand leaps from one point to the next on the *x* axis and the line is not continuous; hence, the curve will have a stair-step appearance with gaps between each line.

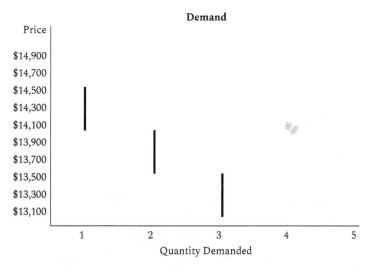

FIGURE 4-54   Demand Curve (High-Priced Items)

DEMAND CURVES FOR GOODS REQUIRING MINIMUM QUALITY

Demand for goods and services that require a minimum amount of quality will also see a different type of demand curve. If the price gets to be too low on a product or service, people begin to become skeptical of the quality of the product, and they will not buy it. For example, medical services that are too low in price are not likely going to see much demand, because people don't want the quality of their health care compromised. Lower prices for such services will scare customers away and reduce demand (figure 4-55). Initially, as prices for medical services fall, demand will increase to a point, because those who could not afford the medical care and didn't truly need it before, could now get the medical care they want. However, demand will only increase to a point, until the price gets so low it begins to remove people's confidence in the quality of the service. These are the reasons that the demand curve is initially sloped downward but then is bent backward for products or services requiring high quality.

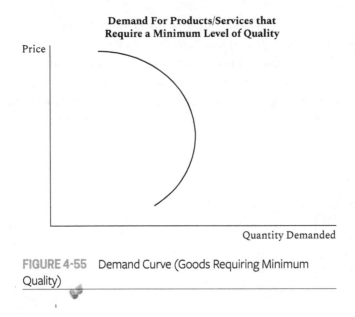

FIGURE 4-55 Demand Curve (Goods Requiring Minimum Quality)

DEMAND CURVES FOR LUXURY GOODS

Luxury items are things that many people own, except that they have features and attributes that add to their price as symbols of status. For example, a car is something people of all income groups own, but a luxury car is one that has high-priced, expensive attributes that are used more for status than necessity. The demand curve for such luxury goods is different as well. Depending upon the type of luxury item, there are many combinations that can exist.

During bad economic times when income falls, many would argue that the demand curve would be the same as any other demand curve, except that it may be almost flat. Why? Because when income falls, many more will begin to buy only necessities or things that meet food, shelter, clothing, or medical needs.

On the other hand, if the economy is stable, some argue that the curve could become almost a straight, vertical line. Why? Because luxury items are usually desired by two groups of people: those who want to show their wealth and their ability to be able to buy expensive items, and those who are not very wealthy but only want to appear that they are wealthy. Those who are indeed wealthy are used to paying more for goods for the purpose of letting everyone know that they are rich and have paid top dollar for their possessions. For example, if Cadillac would significantly lower their prices to the point that everyone could afford a Cadillac, it would no longer be a status symbol. Luxury items lose their value when they lose their status of being expensive. Lower prices for such goods cheapens them in the eyes of many. As prices for them fall, the quantity demanded of those goods by wealthy people will also fall. On the other hand, those who only want to appear wealthy are looking for deals, and the quantity demanded by not-so-wealthy people will increase as the price for luxury goods falls. Some argue that if you put their demand schedules together, you will see that generally they cancel each other out. Therefore, the demand schedule could look something like what you see in figure 4-56.

Price	Quantity Demanded	Quantity Demanded Wealthy	Total Quantity Demanded
$50	1	5	6
$40	2	4	6
$30	3	3	6
$20	4	2	6
$10	5	1	6

FIGURE 4-56   Demand Schedule for Luxury Goods

Therefore, the curve of this demand schedule is a vertical line (see figure 4-57).

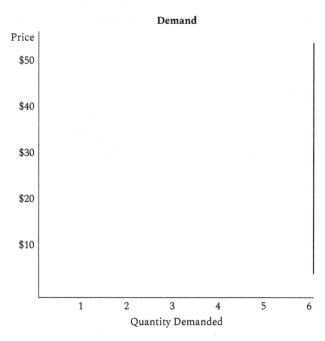

FIGURE 4-57   Demand Curve for Luxury Goods

CHAPTER 4 REVIEW

QUESTIONS TO THINK ABOUT

1. Describe the different determinants of demand and which way they will shift the demand curve under given circumstances.
2. Describe the different determinants of supply and which way they will shift the supply curve under given circumstances.
3. What determinant of demand does not shift the curve?
4. What determinant of supply does not shift the curve?

TERMS TO KNOW

Aggregate demand
Aggregate demand curve
Aggregate supply
Clearing price
Complementary goods
Demand
Disposable income
Equilibrium
Factor costs
Firm's demand
Firm's supply
Full employment GDP
High-priced goods
Income effect
Individual consumer's demand
Inflation
Inflationary gap

Law of demand
Law of supply
Luxury goods
Macro equilibrium
Macro equilibrium GDP
Macro failure
Market demand
Market supply
Personal income
Recessionary gap
Shortages
Subsidy
Substitute goods
Substitution effect
Supply
Surplus

CHAPTER FIVE

Making Sure We All Have What We Need

THERE ARE A few things, among others, that make our government and politicians particularly nervous.

One of them is high prices for things we need. If prices for something like rent or food become too high, constituents complain to their political leaders that they cannot afford the necessities of life. They will insist that government fix such social problems. Therefore, politicians will try to resolve them by imposing things such as **price ceilings** to keep prices for such things low and affordable. They set limits on how much anyone can charge for such things.

On the other hand, low prices for things we need can also become a problem if no company can make any profit at those low prices. When that happens, with no profits to be made, the product or service becomes unavailable as firms refuse to provide them. At that point, constituents will be unhappy again, but now because needed products are unavailable. As a result, the government may impose **a price floor** to keep prices artificially high so producers will continue to produce such things we need.

In the past, however, price floors and price ceilings have usually backfired. Understanding the laws of supply and demand and their determinants will help you to understand why they backfire.

Let's look at price ceilings for rent (or rent ceilings) first.

In big cities, there is usually a reduction in the number of housing units available each year due to fires, demolition (when apartment buildings are purchased for parking lots and economic development or when they are condemned due to poor maintenance), and many other reasons. Hopefully, there is someone to build new housing units somewhere to replace those lost units.

When the government imposes rent ceilings, however, many of the lost units are never replaced, because those who would normally provide housing are less motivated to create new ones. If they can't charge the rent they need, units simply won't be built. Therefore, the supply of housing units declines (or shifts to the left). The government will usually try to set the rent ceiling at the equilibrium price, but when they do, and when the supply curve shifts left, we instantly have a shortage as seen in figure 5-1. Remember, when a curve shifts, the old curve ceases to exist. Notice that the rent price is now below the equilibrium price. Remember also that when prices of products go below equilibrium, there is a shortage, because the quantity demanded of the goods becomes greater than the supply of them. How does a market take care of itself when there is a shortage? As mentioned earlier, prices will rise, thus lowering demand and removing the shortage. But the price ceiling forbids housing providers to raise rents when there is a price ceiling! Therefore, the rent ceiling (meant to make housing more available to people by making it affordable) actually makes things worse by creating a housing shortage.

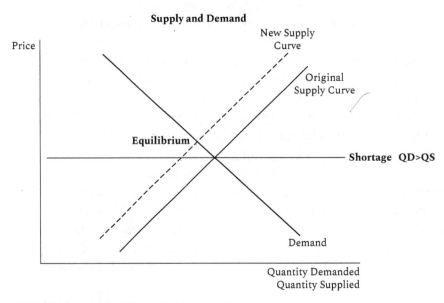

FIGURE 5-1   Supply and Demand (Price Ceilings)

Now let's look at price floors for milk.

When a price floor is imposed, the price will likely be set by the government, again, at equilibrium. Many milk producers who were once discouraged by the low market prices of milk will now be encouraged to get back into the business and to supply it again once the price floor is in place. That will shift the supply curve to the right. In doing so, the government has now created a surplus as seen in figure 5-2. Remember, when prices go above equilibrium, you will have a surplus, because the quantity demanded will be less than the quantity supplied. Suppliers/producers are once again discouraged, but now it is because they cannot continue to be profitable when there is always a surplus in their market. Government's action in cases such as these, even though they are with good intentions, actually make the problems worse.

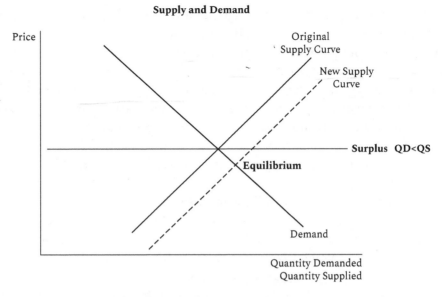

Supply and Demand

FIGURE 5-2   Supply and Demand (Price Floors)

UTILITY

Something that we must factor in as we talk about supply and demand is the concept of utility. Lower prices often create a higher quantity demanded, assuming that the benefit derived from such purchases remains constant. Unfortunately, this is not reality. Continued consumption of a good or service usually causes a reduction of benefit, or what is often called **utility**.

Whenever we spend money, we have many things from which to choose. The typical consumer will try to buy a combination of goods and services to maximize the benefits they derive from them. They will also attempt to do so with the limited amount of money available to them. In other words, when consumers make a purchase, they would like to receive the maximum utility per dollar spent.

Suppose, for example, you are on a very limited budget, and you can only spend $15 on a given evening. Also assume that you only have to choose between the purchase of a slice of pizza and a soft drink.

The total utility is the sum of **utils**, which are units of utility. Economists attempt to quantify the utility you receive, only to show how consumers try to receive the maximum utility per dollar spent.

If you buy more pizza, that leaves you less money to use for buying soft drinks. The opposite is true, as buying more soft drinks leaves you less money for buying pizza. As mentioned earlier, the more that there is consumption of an item, benefit or utility will decline. Figure 5-3 is aimed at showing you what kind of utility you might receive as you continue to purchase more and more pizza, and thus fewer soft drinks or vice versa. Notice that as more pizza is purchased, the change in utility, or the **marginal utility**, which is your overall change in utility with each purchase, is going down. If you choose, therefore, to buy more soft drinks, your marginal utility for pizza will be higher but it will be lower for soft drinks. Notice in figure 5-3 that the quantity purchased of pizza is the inverse of the quantity purchased of soft drinks, because one may be inclined to buy more of one thing as they buy less of the other. In either case, the marginal utility is falling as purchases of one of them increase. Each time a purchase of one is made, you can add up the price, which must always equal $15, because that is the maximum (in this example) that you can spend. You can also add up the total utility for each possibility. To find the utility per dollar spent, you can divide the total utility by the total dollars spent.

Look for a moment at Possibility C. If you buy two slices of pizza and three soft drinks at a cost of $3 each, your total dollars spent is $15 ((two slices of pizza + three soft drinks) * $3 each). If you add the total utility of 88 for the two slices of pizza to the total utility of 225 for the three soft drinks, you would have a total utility of 313 utils. The total utility of 313 utils divided by $15 will give you utility per dollar of 20.87.

In this example, therefore, it may be best for you to buy that combination of Possibility C of two slices of pizza and three soft drinks. Why? Because you are getting the maximum of utility, and the utility per dollar spent in that possibility is at its highest.

With a Budget of $15 For Only Two Activities
Cost Of A Slice of Pizza = $3
Cost Of A Soft Drink = $3

| Possibility | Pizza | | Total Utility | Marginal Utility | Soft Drink | | Total Utility | Marginal Utility | Total $ Spent | Total Utility (Both) | Utility Per Dollar |
	Quantity	Total Paid			Quantity	Total Paid					
A	0	$0	0		5	$15	291	31	$ 15.00	291	19.4000
B	1	$3	50	50	4	$12	260	35	$ 15.00	310	20.6667
C	2	$6	88	38	3	$9	225	44	$ 15.00	313	20.8667
D	3	$9	121	33	2	$6	181	64	$ 15.00	302	20.1333
E	4	$12	150	29	1	$3	117	117	$ 15.00	267	17.8000
F	5	$15	175	25	0	$0	0		$ 15.00	175	11.6667

Maximization of Total Utility Within Budget @ 2 Pizza Slices and 3 Soft Drinks

FIGURE 5-3   Marginal Utility Table

Obviously, the average person doesn't do math to this depth when they make simple purchases such as these, but they still try to make purchases that make utility at its highest per dollar spent. Thus, your quantity demanded may go up or down based upon the satisfaction or utility you give your customers in conjunction with the prices you charge.

Another concept that you may consider is what some refer to as **consumer surplus**. Buyers receive a consumer surplus when marginal benefit exceeds price. Have you ever made a purchase, thinking that you got a great deal or a bargain? That's what you want your customers to feel. This will also increase your demand if you can give your customers that feeling, even if your price doesn't change.

CHAPTER 5 REVIEW

QUESTIONS TO THINK ABOUT

1. What are some of the economic myths of this chapter?
2. How effective are price floors and rent ceilings, and why?
3. Has American society been experiencing a huge problem with the rich getting richer and the poor getting poorer?
4. Has any government regulation been good for the country? Has any been bad for the country?

TERMS TO KNOW

Consumer surplus
Marginal utility
Price ceilings
Price floors

Rent ceilings
Utility
Utils

CHAPTER SIX

Elasticity

NOW THAT WE know that higher prices cause a lower quantity demanded (and vice versa), the question now becomes, how much will demand change when you change your prices? With some products, a small change in their prices causes a huge change in demand, while other products' price changes cause a very small change in demand. This chapter studies these changes in demand with changes in prices as well as other determinants of demand.

What does it mean to be elastic? Many think of it as something that stretches or is flexible and readily reacts to change. If I pull an elastic piece of clothing material, it will change in size. If it's not elastic, pulling on it will likely not change its size, and in fact, it might even tear.

The same thing can happen with the purchase of goods and services. If demand for a product is **price elastic**, it means that it will change a lot when price and/or some of the other determinants of demand change. If demand for a product is **price inelastic**, it means that it will change very little when price and/or some of the other determinants of demand change.

ELASTICITY OF DEMAND

Suppose for a moment that there was only one telephone company in the world, and you are now paying $20 per month to use it. Would you stop using the telephone service if the price per month went up to $40 per month? How about $50 per month? How about $80 per month? How about $100 per month? Some would still keep using their phone service even if the price gets very high. Why? Because many feel that telephone service is a necessity. If someone is breaking into your house, or if it is on fire, it's not likely that you would email the police or fire department for help. Therefore, a *huge* change in the price would cause only a very *small* change in demand. In other words, the **price elasticity of demand** for those things is **relatively price inelastic**. That typically happens for things of necessity and/or that have only one or only a few producers making them available.

On the other hand, some products are **relatively price elastic**, because a *small* change in their prices causes a *huge* change in their demand. Then we would say that their **price elasticity of demand** is **relatively price elastic.** For example, if you go to a gas station (Gas Station A) that has a competitor right next door to it (Gas Station B), you may choose to buy gas at Gas Station A because the gas station next door (Gas Station B) is charging a price that is a few cents higher. The gas station that raises their price only a few pennies will likely see a huge drop in business; thus, their price elasticity of demand is relatively price elastic.

If you raise your price, as we stated in the law of demand, you will likely sell fewer units. However, selling fewer units isn't always bad. It doesn't always mean that you will bring in less money.

Suppose you are a business selling prescription pharmaceuticals with which you have a patent and thus no competitors are selling it. Let's also assume that your sales figures are as represented in figure 6-1. Notice that if you raise your price by 50 percent from $20.00 per bottle of medication to $30.00 per bottle, you will sell one less unit, as your quantity demanded would fall from 18 to 17. However, your **total revenue** (your quantity demanded times your price) is actually going up. In this case, it increases from $360 to $510. Your **marginal revenue** (the change in overall revenue with each unit sale) is actually increasing as you raise your price and reduce your quantity demanded. In this case, your marginal revenue is $150 ($510–$360). You would be working less and yet you would be bringing in more money. As a producer, it would be very good for you to be in that position! Everyone would like to work less and be paid more.

Also notice that if you lower your price to get more business, perhaps from $100 per bottle of medication down to $90 per bottle, you would sell one more bottle (quantity demanded jumps up from 10 to 11), but you will actually begin to bring in less money. Total revenue would fall from $1,000 to $990. Your marginal revenue would actually be decreasing (or changing by minus $10). It would not be wise of you to lower your price under those circumstances. Doing so would make you work harder for less money, and yet many companies do so without realizing it! In this example, your prices are relatively price inelastic.

Price		Quantity Demanded	Total Revenue	Marginal Revenue by RAISING Prices	Marginal Revenue by LOWERING Prices
$100.00	X	10	$1,000.00	$10.00	
$90.00	X	11	$990.00	$30.00	$(10.00)
$80.00	X	12	$960.00	$50.00	$(30.00)
$70.00	X	13	$910.00	$70.00	$(50.00)
$60.00	X	14	$840.00	$90.00	$(70.00)
$50.00	X	15	$750.00	$110.00	$(90.00)
$40.00	X	16	$640.00	$130.00	$(110.00)
$30.00	X	17	$510.00	$150.00	$(130.00)
$20.00	X	18	$360.00		$(150.00)

FIGURE 6-1   Demand Schedule (Inelastic Product)

Therefore, if your price <u>elasticity of demand is relatively inelastic,</u>

1. <u>more work brings in less money</u> (by lower prices), <u>which is not using your resources economically</u>; and
2. <u>less work brings in more money</u> (by raising prices), <u>which is a very economical use of your resources.</u>

Now suppose you are selling the medication represented in figure 6-2, selling more of the generic medication with which there are many competitors, such as aspirin. As you lower your price, you will likely sell more aspirin *and* you will bring in more money, but only to a given point. Therefore, economists would say that your price elasticity of demand is relatively price elastic. When this is the case, you need to be careful that you don't raise prices because your quantity demanded, and your dollar sales, will decline. Instead, you may want to lower your price to have more demand and more sales revenue.

Also notice that if you lower your price too far, your marginal revenue will start to become negative as well, just as it did for the product that was relatively price inelastic. Figure 6-2 shows that you would not be wise to lower your price below $5 per bottle. If you did, once again you will be working harder to produce more while bringing in less money, because your marginal revenue at a price of $4 is minus $1. Again, this is not an economical use of your time, and yet many firms do this without realizing it!

Price		Quantity Demanded	Total Revenue	Marginal Revenue by REDUCING Prices
$9.00	X	1	$9.00	
$8.00	X	2	$16.00	$7.00
$7.00	X	3	$21.00	$5.00
$6.00	X	4	$24.00	$3.00
$5.00	X	5	$25.00	$1.00
$4.00	X	6	$24.00	(1.00)
$3.00	X	7	$21.00	$(3.00)
$2.00	X	8	$16.00	$(5.00)
$1.00	X	9	$9.00	$(7.00)

FIGURE 6-2   Demand Schedule (Elastic Product)

Therefore, if your price <u>elasticity of demand is relatively elastic,</u>

1. <u>less work brings less money</u> (<u>by raising prices</u>), and
2. <u>more work brings in more money</u> (by lower prices) <u>to a point, but eventually income will decline.</u>

So, where do you stand? How do you know if you are selling a product or service that is relatively price elastic or relatively price inelastic? If you study the outcomes of your price changes and the impact that they have on your demand, you can actually figure it out mathematically.

Price elasticity of demand is equal to the percent change in your products' quantity demanded divided by the percent change in your price as shown here:

> **Price Elasticity of Demand = % Change in Quantity Demanded / % Change in Price**

If your quantity demanded changes at a faster rate than the change in your price, this is a clear indication that your demand is very sensitive to your price changes. The opposite is also true. If your quantity demanded changes at a slower rate than the change in your price, this shows that your demand is not very sensitive to your price changes.

When you begin to do the math, you must make a slight change, however. Referring to figure 6-1 again, if you raise your price by $10, from $20 to $30, you would have increased your price by 50 percent. However, if you lower your price by $10 (from $30 back down to $20), you would not have lowered your price by 50 percent but rather by only 33.3 percent. When we calculate price elasticity of demand, we want to know what price changes will do to demand, whether we are raising or lowering prices. That's the reason that we must refine the formula for elasticity. Economists believe, therefore, that the formula should be refined as follows:

Price Elasticity of Demand = % Change in the Average
Quantity Demanded / % Change in the Average Price

If your price elasticity of demand is greater than one, it is relatively price elastic; if it is less than one, it is relatively price inelastic. Why? Because when a fraction is greater than one, that is an indication that the numerator is larger than the denominator. Thus, as stated earlier, if the demand rate of change is greater than the price rate of change, the fraction will exceed one.

Let's return to our prescription pharmaceutical firm example from figure 6-1. Please notice that if we apply the elasticity formula to that demand schedule, you would get the result seen in figure 6-3.

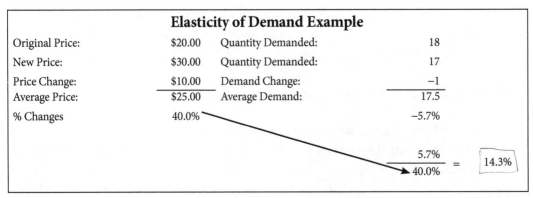

Elasticity of Demand Example

Original Price:	$20.00	Quantity Demanded:	18
New Price:	$30.00	Quantity Demanded:	17
Price Change:	$10.00	Demand Change:	−1
Average Price:	$25.00	Average Demand:	17.5
% Changes	40.0%		−5.7%

$$\frac{5.7\%}{40.0\%} = \boxed{14.3\%}$$

FIGURE 6-3   Price Elasticity of Demand Example

The average price is the same as any average. You would find the sum of your observations and then divide that sum by the number of observations. In this formula, there will always only be two observations: the original price and the new price. Therefore, if you add $20 to $30 you would get $50. If you divide $50 by two, the average price would be $25. The same would be true for demand. If you add 18 bottles sold to 17 bottles sold, you would get 35 bottles sold. When you divide 35 by the two observations, you would get an average demand of 17.5 bottles.

Now let's complete the formula calculation. The percent change price is equal to $10 divided by $25 or 40 percent. The percent change in demand is equal to minus 1 divided by 17.5 which is minus 5.7 percent. Please remember that we must *always, always* use the absolute value when we find the percent changes! The elasticity calculation is meant for increases or decreases in price or demand, therefore always remove the negative numbers! Also, it is imperative that you remember that the average percent change in demand is always the numerator in this formula, and the average percent change in price is always the denominator! Therefore, when we divide the average percent change of demand (5.7 percent) by the average percent change in price (40 percent), you would get 0.143, or 14.3 percent.

So, in our example, are your prescription pharmaceuticals relatively price elastic or inelastic? Since 0.143, or 14.3 percent is *below* one, we say that it is relatively price inelastic.

There is another way we can use these numbers.

If your price elasticity of demand is relatively price inelastic: A 1 percent price decrease will increase quantity demanded by *less* than 1 percent; therefore, your total revenue will decrease.

If your price elasticity of demand is relatively price elastic: A 1 percent price decrease will increase quantity demanded by *more* than 1 percent; therefore, your total revenue may increase (to a point).

Another way of stating what these numbers mean in this example is that for every 1percent change you have in your pricing, your demand only changes by 0.143, or 14.3 percent.

What if your calculation had given us a number that is *equal* to one? Then your price elasticity of demand would be **price unit elastic**: A 1 percent price decrease will increase quantity demanded by 1 percent, thus your total revenue would remain unchanged.

Returning to our example, if the change in price would have reduced quantity demanded from 18 to 12 instead of 17, price elasticity of demand would then be 100 percent (or 1) as shown below in Figure 6-4.

Elasticity of Demand Example				
Original Price:	$20.00	Quantity Demanded:		18
New Price:	$30.00	Quantity Demanded:		12
Price Change:	$10.00	Demand Change:		−6
Average Price:	$25.00	Average Demand:		15
% Changes	40.0%			−40.0%
			$\frac{40.0\%}{40.0\%} =$	100.0%

FIGURE 6-4   Price Elasticity of Demand Example

When that happens, revenue is unchanged; thus, it doesn't help or hurt your dollar sales by changing your prices as seen in Figure 6-5.

Price	Quantity Demanded	Total Revenue
$20.00	18	$360.00
$30.00	12	$360.00

FIGURE 6-5 Showing No Changes in Revenue with Unit Elasticity

In this case, it may be wise of you to go ahead and raise your price, even though you would sell fewer goods. If you reduce your output, it would likely cost you less money to produce, yet if you get the same amount of money while producing less output, you will get more profit by working less.

You, as a consumer, also have price elasticity. While some consumers may continue to purchase your prescription meds as you raise your price, others may not, either because they can't afford them, or they may find another source to satisfy that need. Every person is different.

If your price elasticity of demand as a consumer of a good or service is relatively price elastic: A 1 percent price decrease will compel you to increase your purchases of the good by *more* than 1 percent.

If your price elasticity of demand as a consumer of a good or service is relatively price inelastic: A 1 percent price decrease will compel you to increase your purchases of the good by *less* than 1 percent.

CROSS ELASTICITY OF DEMAND

So far, the calculation of elasticity has given you as a producer some idea as to what pricing strategy you should use. Depending upon whether your product's price elasticity of demand is relatively price elastic or inelastic, your price changes will have a large impact on your dollar sales and profits. You have some control over what you decide to charge your customers, and this information will help you to decide what your pricing strategy should be.

The question now becomes: how much impact do the other determinants of demand have on your demand that you *cannot* control? This is referred to as **cross elasticity of demand**. It is a measure of how sensitive your demand is to a change in the price of substitute goods or complementary goods, even though the price *you* charge is unchanged.

The formula for finding it is absolutely the same. The only difference in doing the math is that you would then track the change in the complementary good or substitute good prices, and then track what they do to *your* demand. In figure 6-6, you can see that a change in your competitor's price from $30 to $25 has a huge impact on your demand, changing it from 18 medication bottles sold to 10 bottles. The cross elasticity is 314.3 percent or 3.143, which is greater than one, thus your cross elasticity of demand is relatively price elastic. While you can't control what your competitors' prices are, you may have to change some of your other business strategies, either by matching the price change of your competitors or promoting your product as being better.

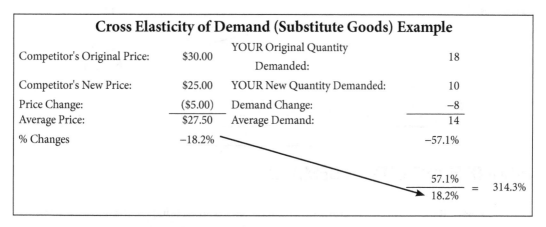

Cross Elasticity of Demand (Substitute Goods) Example

Competitor's Original Price:	$30.00	YOUR Original Quantity Demanded:	18
Competitor's New Price:	$25.00	YOUR New Quantity Demanded:	10
Price Change:	($5.00)	Demand Change:	−8
Average Price:	$27.50	Average Demand:	14
% Changes	−18.2%		−57.1%

$$\frac{57.1\%}{18.2\%} = 314.3\%$$

FIGURE 6-6   Cross Elasticity of Demand (Substitute Goods)

Returning to the medicine example, what would happen if the copay costs of doctor visits goes sky-high in your market area? You would likely see a decrease in the demand for your prescription drugs, because people can't buy your meds without a prescription, and people would be less likely to get prescriptions if they don't visit their doctors. That would clearly make doctor visits a complementary good (or service) for your product. Sadly, fewer people would be visiting their doctors if the price of doctor visits is out of their reach; thus, you would sell fewer prescription meds. For example, suppose the average copay fees for local doctor visits were to increase from $25 per visit to $40 per visit, causing a decline in your hourly sales of medicine to drop from 18 to four. After using the very same formulas, you can see in figure 6-7 that your cross elasticity for demand would be relatively price elastic as it will be 2.758, or 275.8 percent, which is well above one.

Again, you can't do much about it. Changes in doctor visit copay prices are beyond your control. This may only change your promotional strategies, or you may choose to lower your price as a result to make up for the lost sales.

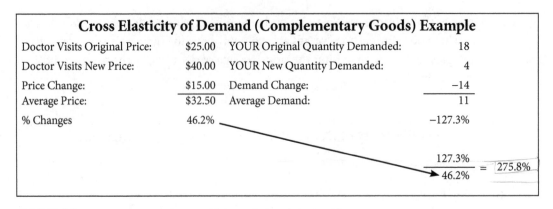

FIGURE 6-7   Cross Elasticity of Demand (Complementary Goods)

INCOME ELASTICITY OF DEMAND

Income elasticity of demand measures how sensitive your product demand is to a change in the disposable income (income after taxes) of the people living in your market area. Once again, the formula is virtually the same.

One more time, let's return to our pharmaceutical example to see what kind of impact income will have on your business. In figure 6-8, you will see that if household income in your market area were to rise by $120 per week (from $980 to $1,100), your sales would be greatly increased from 18 to 25 bottles of medicine, thus it would be relatively elastic as your price elasticity of income would be 282.2 percent, or 2.822, which again is greater than one.

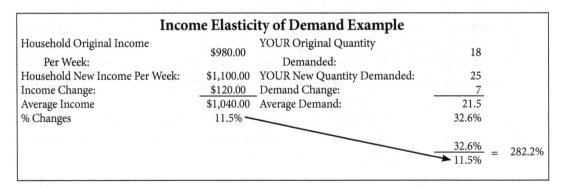

FIGURE 6-8   Cross Elasticity of Demand (Income)

Knowing if your income elasticity of demand is or is not highly elastic is also helpful to predict your change in demand when income changes. For example, if your income elasticity of demand is relatively elastic, it opens the door for you to consider what to do if you must once again engage in marketing strategies should there be a decline in income in your market area.

PERFECT PRICE ELASTICITY OF DEMAND (INFINITE)

There are some industries that have a flat demand curve. This is called **perfect price elasticity**. It usually happens in industries that are very highly competitive, or what are called **pure competition** (which is also discussed later in this textbook in more depth). One example of such an industry is farming. Farmers typically do not have the option of telling their customers what they are going to charge them. Instead, they are told what they will be paid on the day they take their goods to market for sale. There is usually a central location where farm products are purchased, and for the farmers, sales are on a take-it-or-leave-it basis. They can either accept the price offered at the market, or they can take their goods back to their farms and wait and hope that they will be offered more money on another day.

Suppose you are a corn farmer. You take your corn to market, and you are told that you will be paid $3 per bushel. If you accept that price, you can sell an infinite amount of corn (see figure 6-9), and that is why they say that your price elasticity of demand in that case would then be infinite.

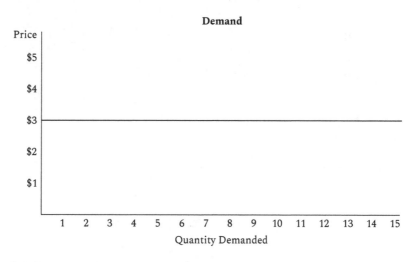

FIGURE 6-9 Demand Curve (Perfect Price Elasticity)

However, if you insist that you want more than $3 per bushel, even if you declare that you will take nothing less than $3.0000000000001, you will sell no corn; thus, your quantity demanded will go to zero. Of course, you would not likely insist on taking less than the $3 per bushel that the market is offering to pay you; hence, your demand curve will be flat.

The demand curve for you as a farmer is flat, but demand is likely going to be different than that of the entire farming industry. The corn industry as a whole, for example, will still have a downward-sloping demand curve, because consumers will still buy *less* of it if the prices get to be too high and *more* of it as corn prices fall.

PERFECT PRICE INELASTICITY OF DEMAND

You may be in an industry where prices don't change demand. Very few industries experience this, but there are some that come close. Such industries have a vertical demand curve; thus, their price elasticity of demand is equal to zero, and therefore they experience perfect **price inelasticity of demand** (see figure 6-10).

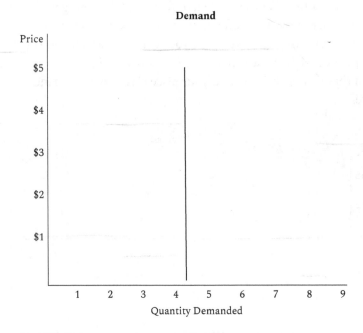

FIGURE 6-10   Demand Curve (Perfect Price Inelasticity)

For example, the medical field has had shortages of qualified people in this country, which drives prices up. People need medical services, and they will continue to demand them even if the price goes higher and higher. Because of the income effect, mentioned earlier, it is still not likely, however, that the curve in the medical field will be perfectly vertical. You will have some who will still need and want the medical services, but they won't demand it because they would have no means for purchasing it.

UNIT PRICE ELASTICITY OF DEMAND

If you have unit price elasticity of demand, as mentioned earlier, your elasticity will be equal to one. Thus, the curve is downward-sloping, and you will have a demand change that will move directly with the change in price and should be at about 45 degrees.

DETERMINANTS OF PRICE ELASTICITY OF DEMAND

So, what makes your firm or industry more likely to be price elastic or price inelastic? The first determinant is the closeness and availability of substitutes. As mentioned before, if you have very few or no competitors, it is much more likely that you can raise your prices more often without the fear of losing business to another firm; thus you have price inelasticity. On the other hand, if there are many similar substitutes of your product or service, you will see a huge change in demand when you change your prices as competitors and other firms meet or beat your prices; thus you have price elasticity.

A second determinant is the need or desire for the good or service. It doesn't matter if you are the only producer or one of few producers of a good or service if the product you're selling is not needed or wanted very much. In the example given earlier, many feel that a phone is very much needed, and if there is only one producer, people will pay the higher price to get it. They won't like paying the higher price, but they will feel as if they have little choice. With other products, if they are perceived as nonnecessities or even as luxury goods, in time higher prices will reduce their quantity demanded.

Third, the time elapsed since a price change will have an impact on price elasticity. If you raise your price, you may see very little change in demand at first, because it takes time for people to find out about your price change, to find substitutes, and to then change their buying behavior.

Fourth, loyalty makes a difference. If you raise your prices, even when your competitors don't, the level of loyalty your customers have to you may also keep them from finding other ways to meet their consumption needs. Conversely, if your customers have very little loyalty to you, they will quickly purchase your competitors' goods and services if your prices get to be too high.

Finally, the proportion of income (or a budget) spent on the good is also a factor. If you get a price increase from your sanitation company for hauling your trash away, a change from $20 per month to $25 per month, a 25 percent increase, may not be such a budget buster for you, and you may not likely seek another firm to take care of this for you. You might do so, however, if your income is very low, causing even a $5 per month increase to become a problem for you.

ELASTICITY OF SUPPLY

Price elasticity of supply measures the sensitivity of supply based upon a change in what the market price is paying suppliers or producers. This is not something that you need to know in order to set a business strategy. It is more useful to institutions such as government when they fear that lower prices in an industry could cause a shortage of those goods. Government doesn't typically get concerned unless the industry provides vital goods or service to our society.

To calculate price elasticity of supply, the procedure and interpretation of the calculation are virtually the same as it would be for calculating and interpreting the price elasticity of demand. In figure 6-11A, you can see that a change in your average market price of medicine goes from $35 to $45. Suppose it would motivate you to increase output or supply of medicine from 18 bottles to 28 bottles per hour. If so, your price elasticity of supply would be 1.739, or 173.9 percent. This would indicate that your price elasticity of supply would be relatively price elastic, because it is greater than one. A price change therefore would indeed motivate you to change your output.

Knowing how much you would change supply as a result of market price changes doesn't help you as much as knowing if your price elasticity of supply is or is not highly elastic in your *entire market*. Higher prices can motivate you to raise your own supply, but if the entire market is also raising supply that could mean that your market is getting saturated with all of your products. A saturated market (or a glutted market) can bring prices down in the long run and can make it much more competitive, less profitable, and difficult for producers.

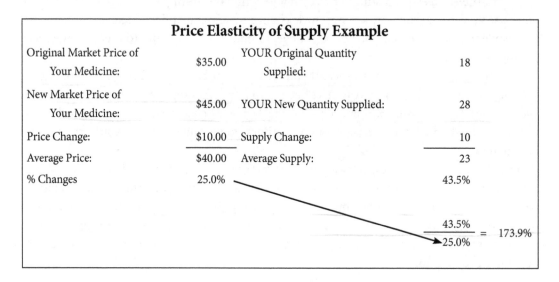

FIGURE 6-11A   Price Elasticity of Supply

PERFECT PRICE ELASTICITY OF SUPPLY (INFINITE)

If you are likely to produce more and more goods and services, even if the price you are paid remains the same, you are practicing **perfect price elasticity of supply (infinite)** as seen in figure 6-11B.

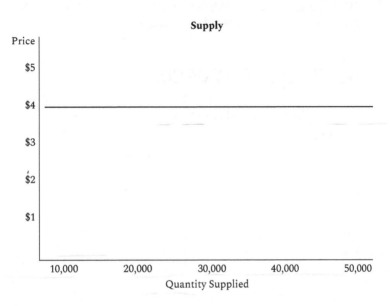

FIGURE 6-11B   Supply Curve (Perfect Price Elasticity)

Why would you do that? As mentioned earlier, if you are a corn farmer, you may not have a choice. If price remains the same, you will likely produce as much as you can as long as you make a profit from each bushel of corn you produce. On the other hand, you may just be experiencing bad times. During a recession, deep recession, or depression, the supply curve is likely to be flat, because you will likely be producing far below your output capacity. For example, if your factory is getting very little business, you are still paying for the occupancy and possession costs of your building and machinery. If they are idle during bad times, it will cost you dearly. Therefore, you and many producers are not likely to insist on getting a higher price with higher output or demand. Your requiring a higher price to produce will not likely occur until your factory or operation is getting close to producing at full capacity. When you get to that point, it may become more stressful and expensive to operate, because you may have to consider paying out more money to add capital equipment and floor space for production, to say nothing of having to hire more workers or paying overtime wages to your workers.

Also, as mentioned earlier, another reason that supply curves are relatively flat during bad times is that suppliers to producers are also likely seeing bad times. Those suppliers may be willing to keep their prices lower in order to keep your business. Therefore, your factor costs may go down. If so, your profits per unit of output may rise slightly as you increase output due to your suppliers' lower prices. As a result, you may continue to increase production without price changes, because your profits per unit will in fact be rising as if prices were rising

UNIT PRICE ELASTICITY OF SUPPLY

If you have **unit price elasticity of supply** being equal to one, your supply curve is going to be upward-sloping and you will have a supply change that moves directly with the change in market price. It will likely be at about a 45-degree angle.

PERFECT PRICE INELASTICITY OF SUPPLY

If you have **perfect price inelasticity of supply**, the elasticity is equal to zero, and thus the curve is vertical (figure 6-11C).

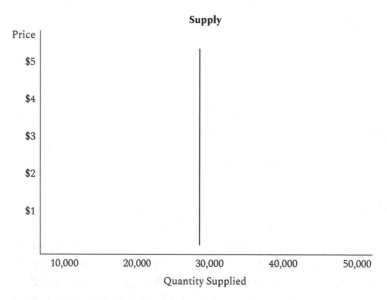

FIGURE 6-11C   Supply Curve (Perfect Price Inelasticity)

This shows, therefore, that your supply remains the same with any price change. When would that happen? It can happen when the economy is booming or when you and other companies are operating at full capacity. It doesn't matter that the buyers in the market are offering you more money; you still can't supply their needs because you have no more resources with which to do it.

Once again, the medical field has this problem. If you own a medical facility. and you want to increase the supply of your doctor's office services, you can't just run out and hire another physician at the spur of the moment. You would have to hire physicians with qualifications to fill your needs. It takes years for physicians to acquire such qualifications, and those willing to become physicians can only obtain those qualifications if there is a medical school available to educate them. In most other industries, when prices go sky-high, businesses find a way to produce goods in those industries to cash in on those prices. But the medical field isn't one in which this would likely happen.

SUPPLY CURVES BASED UPON TIME

If market prices rise quickly, sometimes producers are unable to change their supply of goods and services in order to respond quickly enough to cash in on such times. Why? Because their ability to increase output is a slow process, and/or they may already be producing at full-capacity output. For example, if a factory's business is booming, it would take a while to increase output capabilities by buying more capital equipment and hiring more workers. Thus, their **momentary supply curves** may be vertical, which would indicate that any market price increases would not change their output or supply. The momentary supply curve shows how much supply may change, if it will change at all, on a momentary basis (figure 6-12A). On the other hand, some businesses may not be doing much business, and/or they could easily make a few phone calls and get their operations to increase output within hours, thus having an upward sloping momentary supply curve (figure 6-12B). This would show that market price changes would indeed change supply or output.

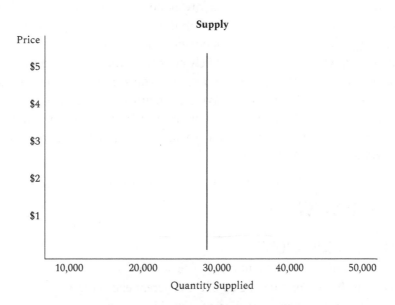

FIGURE 6-12A   Inelastic Supply Curve (Momentary, Short/ Long Run)

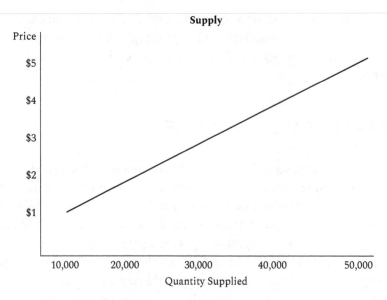

FIGURE 6-12B   Elastic Supply Curve (Momentary, Short/Long run)

The **short-run supply curve** shows the changes, if any, of your supply curve on a short-run basis, which usually is from a few days to a year. If your short-run supply curve is vertical (as shown in figure 6-12A), it's because you can't respond in any way to a price change within that time frame. If it's upward sloping (as shown in Figure 6-12B), your circumstances may make it possible to be able to change output during those months.

The **long-run supply curve** shows the likely change of your supply curve on a long-run basis. That is typically longer than one year. Again, if you are in the medical profession, it is likely that you have a vertical supply curve as seen in figure 6-12A because of your inability to increase the size of your medical staff even as prices soar. In the long run, you may be able to add staff over a period of several years, and thus your long-run supply curve could then begin to slope upwards as figure 6-12B illustrates.

CHAPTER 6 REVIEW

QUESTIONS TO THINK ABOUT

1. Can you calculate the different types of elasticities?
2. What is the benefit of knowing all of the different elasticities?
3. Under what circumstances of elasticity should you raise price or lower price?
4. Why do the different demand curves have the shape they have with various types of elasticity?

TERMS TO KNOW

Cross elasticity of demand
Elasticity of demand
Income elasticity of demand
Long-run supply curve
Marginal revenue
Momentary supply curves
Perfect price elasticity
Perfect price inelasticity
Price elasticity of demand

Price elasticity of supply
Pure competition
Relatively price elastic
Relatively price inelastic
Short-run supply curve
Total revenue
Unit elastic
Unit price elasticity of demand

Efficiency and Social Interest

THE MORE WE produce, the more our needs in society will be met. If, for some reason, businesses choose to cut production, shortages ensue, prices rise, and society suffers. Among other things, this chapter studies what producers do that may cause shortages and why. We also discuss government's feelings and actions toward these things.

One way to know if there is a chance that society's needs for goods and services are being met is to find out if we are using all our resources effectively and efficiently. **Allocation efficiency** is in effect when this happens. This is something we discussed earlier with the production possibilities curve. Perfect allocation efficiency exists when you can't produce one more of a product without giving up the production of another. Remember, when we satisfy the need of a person, we make that person's life better. When we are unable to satisfy a need for a person, that person is going to experience a difficult time. Another way to express the idea of allocation efficiency, therefore, is to say that it exists when you cannot make one person better off without making another person experience a difficult time.

Let's explore in more depth why it is that we cannot have allocation efficiency or why we often choose not to have it. Let us explore why we intentionally fall short of producing with allocation efficiency, and thus have many people in our society going with unmet needs.

DECREASING MARGINAL BENEFIT

The added value of using or consuming one more unit of a good or service is its **marginal benefit**, thus driving the amount of money that a person is willing to pay for the purchase of one more unit of that good or service. The **principle of decreasing marginal benefit** states that marginal benefit will decrease the more that a given item is consumed. People simply get tired of things the more they consume or use them, even if they are good things.

Marginal benefit for a good or service is expressed in one of two ways. First, it is expressed as the number of substitute goods one is willing to forgo to consume it. For example, if I am selling pizza, how many hamburgers would people forgo in order to eat one more of my pizzas? If that number is high, it means that the marginal benefit for my pizzas is high. But after a while, when my customers become bored or tired of the pizzas I offer, they will not be so willing to forgo the purchase of burgers, and I will lose business to all of the burger restaurants. Second, marginal benefit of a product can be expressed in terms of the dollar value of other goods and services that people are willing to forgo to consume it. Returning to my previous example, if consumers in my market area are willing to forgo the consumption of $1 million in burgers this year in order to consume my pizza, the marginal benefit of my pizza perceived by my customers is very good. However, if they are willing to spend more on burgers and forgo only $500,000 worth of burgers this year, then my marginal benefits from my pizza are dropping.

As the quantity supplied of my pizza increases, the dollar value of other items that people are willing to forgo to get yet one more pizza decreases. Why? Because of what was said earlier, the more I supply, the more quickly people tire of my product. Then, people are less willing to pay for my pizzas, then the value of my pizzas is diminished, and thus people are less willing to forgo hamburgers.

As people are willing to spend less for pizzas and more for burgers, my marginal revenue is going to go lower because I may have to lower my price to get people to buy my pizzas. Therefore, decreasing marginal benefit often decreases marginal revenue.

MARGINAL COST

Recall that one definition of **marginal cost** is the opportunity cost of producing one more good or service. It is also the change in **total costs** for producing one more item.

Typically, the marginal cost of a product will initially decline and then rise as the quantity produced increases. Why? Opportunity costs go up because people are likely tiring of the product and likely paying less for it. If this is the case, resources could be better spent somewhere else. Dollar costs of production will also rise in the long run as output increases due to a principal called the **law of diminishing returns,** which is also discussed in greater depth in a later chapter.

Therefore, if your marginal revenue is likely falling while your marginal cost is going up, there is a point where you need to stop producing. Figure 7-1 shows that you should not produce beyond that of the fifth unit of production. Why? Because you will be working harder and longer to do so while taking a cut in pay. It will cost you more to produce that sixth good than you will be getting in revenue. Therefore, one reason that producers choose not to use all their resources to obtain allocation efficiency is because it is not economically wise to work harder for less profit. People work harder for less pay all the time and don't realize it, but financially, it is one of the worst economical moves you can make. Perhaps it would be efficient if you chose to continue to produce more products in order to use up all your resources, giving you **allocation efficiency**, but it would not be giving you **financial efficiency**.

As you study figure 7-1 again, it also shows that you should not stop short of producing five units of your product. Why? Because if you do, there are profits that you could otherwise be earning that you are throwing away. This would also be financially inefficient.

Before moving on, therefore, it is extremely important to remember one thing. As we have just demonstrated, in order to maximize profits, you must set production at the level where marginal cost is equal to marginal revenue. This is the basis for what is called the **production decision,** and it will be our battle cry many times in this book.

Marginal Revenue and Marginal Costs

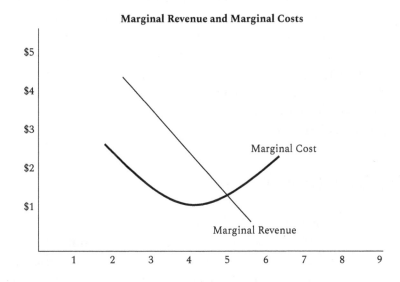

FIGURE 7-1   Marginal Revenue and Marginal Cost Intersection

Therefore, if marginal benefit (and therefore marginal revenue) exceeds marginal cost, you should increase production. If marginal benefit (and therefore marginal revenue) is less than marginal cost, you should reduce production. If marginal benefit (and therefore marginal revenue) is equal to marginal cost, maintain that level of production. That would be financially efficient, but it may not give you allocation efficiency in the use of all your resources.

One way to avoid this problem would be for you to find another product that you can produce in addition to what you're producing now, where marginal benefit, and thus marginal revenue, is going up and not down.

UTILITARIANISM

Utilitarianism contends that we should strive for the greatest good or happiness for the greatest number of people. The philosophy may insist that producers become efficient to give society as many products and services possible so that society will not be lacking in any product or service. However, this idea is not factoring in the concept of financial efficiency. Some say that the competitive market is not fair if the result isn't fair. They argue that if society is deprived of needed goods and services because business owners want to be competitive to the point of maximizing profits, some portion of our society will have to do without needed goods or services. But is it practical to force producers to increase output, even if it means it hurts their profits or when it is done in a way that is not economical? This is the question that many ask, and people often urge our government to force the production of certain needed goods and services regardless of the impact it has on profits.

It is important to note here that, contrary to what many contend, most profits are not evil. Most will agree that profits obtained by the exploitation of workers and the environment, or profits that are obtained in ways that are immoral, unethical, or illegal, are indeed evil. However, most profits are not obtained in this way. Many profits create needed jobs while other profits are often donated to the poor and the needy. If there are no profits, businesses close. When businesses close, there are no jobs. When there are no jobs, inefficiency, poverty, and many other social issues become rampant.

These issues have been and will continue to be hotly debated within each society.

THE LEGAL ENVIRONMENT

Should our government force firms to do things that impede profit maximization?

The government can and has done things to keep producers from denying society the products or services that they need. For example, the government has passed and implemented laws that do not allow people to unfairly dominate a market. Those laws will also be discussed later in this textbook.

Government can also make sure that private property is transferred from one party to another by voluntary exchange only. There are times, however, when the government exercises **eminent domain**, by which they can force a person to sell their land to them if it is needed for government purposes, such as building a highway or building government and military facilities.

As mentioned before, the legal environment must have a balance. It must not under tax nor over tax. It must not under regulate nor over regulate. If overregulation occurs, firms move out of our country, taking their jobs with them. If a firm threatens to leave because the government insists on safe and livable working conditions and fair wages, then such a firm would not be missed if they left the country. Few people would want to work for terrible pay in a place that has horrible or unsafe working conditions.

Many of the things put in place by government to create equity and fairness have aggravated the problem, creating obstacles to efficiency. They usually result in overproduction or underproduction such as price ceilings and price floors, which were discussed earlier.

Regardless of what government does to manage the economy, there will always be those who will be financially hurt by any given government action. The best possible policy in the world is never going to solve everyone's financial or social problems. Government, therefore, must strive to minimize the financial woes and social problems as much as they possibly can if they can't remove them altogether.

Other government actions that have created inefficiency include taxes. **Taxes** cause the prices paid by buyers to rise and the prices received by sellers to decline. They shift supply curves to the left, reducing the amount of resources used and driving up prices, further causing underproduction. Taxes also reduce demand when they artificially raise prices above the value of the goods sold. However, taxes are a necessity if we want the basic services that the free market cannot provide; therefore, if we must tax, we must not tax beyond the level that is needed. **Subsidies** decrease the prices paid by buyers and increase the prices received by sellers, thus increasing supply and lowering prices of goods and services. While this helps us in our own economy, these subsidies are not usually available to producers in other countries. Therefore, subsidies paid to producers here in America cause surpluses in other countries as our producers sell their cheaper goods overseas, making it difficult for farmers overseas to compete. As a result, they exit the market, and inefficiencies in those countries begin to occur.

Quotas are often set by government (particularly in farming). They also hurt efficiency as they encourage underproduction. They keep producers from producing the max in the use of resources. So why does government do this? One thing that people need to understand is that government wants to make sure that we get all of the things we need and at a reasonable price.

Food production is a great example of what they try to manage. If production of food is high, just as when there is a large supply of any product (as mentioned earlier), the prices the market is willing to pay are reduced. When this happens, farmers cut production if they can't get the prices they need, even if they are receiving subsidies. This can create a shortage of food. Therefore, government wants to make sure that food production in the world is balanced. They don't want it to be too high, because the lower prices force farmers to get discouraged and cut production, and they don't want it to be too low, because this will cause shortages.

Keeping production from getting too high in order to prevent cuts in production sounds like a contradiction, but this in fact is what government does. Therefore, they set quotas that producers are not to exceed. Suppose you have a farm, and you are told that you can't plant on all of your tillable land because there is a production quota imposed by the government. The unused land still costs you to own it. You will still have to pay property taxes, insurance, labor (to maintain it), and much more for the land. When this happens, you would lose money on it because you can't generate revenue by producing goods with it, while it still costs you to own it. Hence, the government will pay you an amount comparable what you would have been paid had you planted on it. In other words, you are paid *not* to produce.

Government certainly doesn't want production to be too low either, as shortages cause more people to go without food and/or pay higher prices for it. Thus, they are working to keep production balanced where it will maximize food availability at an affordable cost.

Whatever the case, some of these actions cause underproduction and thus cause a lack of allocation efficiency.

Reduction of monopolies is often a major objective of government, as monopolies often choose to engage in underproduction and create shortages in order to maintain high prices and thus high profits for their goods and services.

External costs, or **externalities,** are those borne by a third party who does not cause, nor benefit from, those costs. For example, if you live across the street from a factory that you do not work for or whose products you don't benefit from, and if that factory is polluting the ground water, you will likely have high medical bills because of that factory's activity even though it gives you no benefit. Government therefore passes laws to outlaw pollution to protect society from such conduct.

Public goods and **common resources** are also provided and/or protected by government in order to ensure that we have all we need.

Public goods are goods consumed by all, even by those who don't pay taxes. Examples include national defense and emergency services. Competitive markets produce too few of these goods because they cannot get adequate profits from them.

Common resources, such as the air we breathe, the water we drink, and the fish in the ocean, are owned by all of us, and government strives to make sure that they are all safe and available to the public.

Whatever the case, as we choose to engage in the competitive markets, some of our decisions may be great financial decisions but may harm society. This is when government may step in to try to remedy the social ills caused by such decisions. Whether government is effective enough or is overstepping its boundaries in doing so is often debated.

For a healthy society, we must attempt to achieve a level of satisfaction for its people that is acceptable without costs that are beyond that of the benefits. These costs are often known as **marginal social costs,** which would be the cost of one person to help another. **Marginal social benefits** are the added benefits to society as a result of these actions. Efficiency is at equilibrium, therefore, at the point where marginal social benefits are equal to marginal social costs.

CHAPTER 7 REVIEW

QUESTIONS TO THINK ABOUT

1. At what point should production be set when you know the marginal cost and marginal revenue of your operation? Why?
2. Why does the government dislike monopolies?
3. Has taxing the rich to give to the poor been an effective tool to help society? Why or why not?

TERMS TO KNOW

Allocation efficiency
Common resources
Decreasing marginal benefit
External costs
Externalities
Financial efficiency
Law of diminishing returns
Marginal benefit

Marginal cost
Marginal revenue
Marginal social benefits
Marginal social costs
Public goods
Total costs
Utilitarianism

Read Ch. 8, 9, 10, 11

Two hours reading

CHAPTER EIGHT

Organizing for Production

NOW THAT WE have considered the use of resources for our own benefits and for the benefits of society, in this chapter we now turn to making decisions that would help us to properly start, own, and/or maintain a business for profit.

OPPORTUNITY COSTS AND PROFIT

If you are considering the purchase of a business or starting a new one, this is the chapter for you. These are some things to strongly consider.

Suppose you have an opportunity to buy a business. Also suppose that, according to the accountant of that business, it is currently making $50,000 per year, and those profits are to continue for the foreseeable future. Also assume that the cost of buying the business is $100,000. Finally, assume that you could get a job, with your current skill and knowledge, that pays $45,000 per year, but you would have to give up that job to buy this business. Should you do it?

Probably not. Why? Because while your **accounting profits** may be decent, they do not account for your opportunity costs. Accounting profits are just what they sound like. They are the profits that your accountant says you make when your costs of doing business are subtracted from your dollar sales. But what about the opportunity cost? In this example, you are throwing away a job that pays $45,000 per year in order to make $50,000 per year in this business. The economist would say that you are really only making $5,000 in **economic profits**, which are accounting profits minus your opportunity costs. What you would be doing in a sense is buying a job. What if you could put your $100,000 in some other investment that was getting perhaps a 5 percent return. That would give you a return of $5,000 per year. But if you use that $100,000 to buy this business, you would be having to forego the $5,000 investment return.

In actuality, therefore, the economic profits are now at zero! In other words, economic profits are zero unless your accounting profits exceed opportunity costs.

These incomes that you are forgoing are often referred to as **implicit costs**. They represent money that you can't have because of your accepting this "opportunity" to buy or start a business. This is what happens when business ownership requires you to use your time and your own capital assets (such as your own building, equipment, or financial resources). They are costs, even though no one will send you a bill for them and even though you pay no money out of pocket for them.

On the other hand, **explicit costs,** such as rent, utilities, and wages, are in fact paid for with money. They are the costs that accountants use while figuring out your accounting profits.

Sometimes accountants will also calculate what is called **depreciation** as they determine your costs of doing business. This is an estimation as to how much the value of your capital equipment and tangible assets have declined. This applies to any capital equipment, or anything that has the potential to lose value by wear and tear, by the passing of time, or by obsolescence. The federal government created one way of estimating the amount by which assets depreciate based upon the time an asset has been owned by an organization. One that has been used over the years is called the MACRS (modified accelerated cost recovery system). It categorizes all the different types of tangible assets you own, and it will give you a percentage by which organizations estimate those assets will lose their values. Once again, economists take issue with this. They believe that such things only lose value when their market value (or whatever the market would pay) for such things declines. This is called **economic depreciation**.

To put this all together then, you can begin to think about **economic costs**. After this discussion, therefore, you can figure out that it is equal to the sum of your explicit costs, plus your implicit costs.

$$\text{Economic Costs} = \text{Explicit Costs} + \text{Implicit Costs}$$

Some might say that any decent amount of profits should be enough for owning a business because "being your own boss" is better than working for someone else and that there is value in that. This may be true, but owning a business often requires more hours and stress than working as an employee elsewhere.

Therefore, when you are faced with making a decision as to whether to start a business or to buy one, all of these things are extremely important to consider! If you were starting a new business with the same circumstances, the same guidelines would apply.

TO ACHIEVE MAXIMUM PROFITS

In addition to the things that have already been discussed, once you are in business you must make sure that you do the following things.

First, as mentioned before, you must decide what and how many goods and services you will provide. You don't want to produce things that are not likely to give you future economic profits. Obtaining economic profit is more likely to happen if you offer a product or service that the public truly needs or wants. Also, you must set your output at the point where marginal costs are equal to marginal revenue.

Second, you must also decide what techniques to use to produce them. Something that will be discussed in a later chapter has to do with the cost of production. You must use the right combination of labor and capital for production. Too much or too little of either can cause you to have costs that are higher than necessary. When that happens, you must then raise your price to maintain a given level or margin of profit. If your higher price is chronically higher than that of your competition, and if your customers don't perceive that the quality of your product justifies your higher price, this can put you out of business.

Once you have established the techniques and processes you will use for production, you must always be looking for ways to make them better. This is called **process improvement**. For example, if you are taking 10 steps to accomplish a given task, it is always best to look for ways to reduce that process down to fewer steps, without reducing the quality of your product or service.

Sometimes the process may become so outdated or convoluted that the process has to be completely scrapped, removed, and replaced. This is called **process reengineering**. It is often very difficult to do this as it is very expensive, and it takes cooperation and approval from a firm's staff.

More successful firms also spend a great deal of time when they decide how to organize, compensate, and manage those who make things happen in the organization. The old cliché that states no organization is better than its weakest employee is true. Great performance from workers is more likely to exist in your firm if they are motivated to do a great job and if your process of communication and support is organized in a way that they are productive rather than frustrated.

Production of goods and services is worthless without buyers. You must also decide, therefore, how to best market your product. Marketing is not just advertising and selling. Marketing also involves making sure that you are always offering what the public wants and that the public is satisfied about every part of the experience of doing business with you, from the attention and efficiency with which you serve them to the quality of the product or service you sell them. Those who do marketing will need to work with the accounting, production, and engineering departments of your firm to make sure that products do what the public wants, in the time frame that the public wants them, and for the price they are willing to pay. Marketers will often do research and will advise you as to whether your product is even needed or desired by the public before the process of making them available even begins.

Also, you must decide whether you will make or buy your products. Sometimes it is better to buy your goods from another firm that can produce them more efficiently and effectively rather than to manufacture them yourself. You can profit by keeping a significant portion of the sale price while leaving the manufacturing tasks to others who have more experience and who have a well-oiled production process to make the products fit the needs of the market.

Other things that can enhance profitability include **technological efficiency** and **economic efficiency**. Technological efficiency is needed as it permits firms to produce a greater amount of output with fewer inputs. When technological efficiency is not available, it is still important that you keep your costs down. Economic efficiency exists if you as an organization are using all your resources to the max, thus eliminating any kind of inefficiency or waste.

FIRM CONSTRAINTS

In the midst of production, you will often find yourself unable to control certain aspects of your business, and your lack of control of them can put constraints on your success. While they can't be controlled, sometimes you may be able to manage them.

One of them is technology. Years ago, technology was used primarily to cut costs and increase output in order to get ahead of the competition. Those days are now gone. It is no longer used to get ahead, but it is now required for your business's survival. If your competitors' use of technology makes it so they can produce more products, less expense products, and/or better products, you must either match their technology or close your doors. You can't control what the competition does with technology, and in some cases, you may not even know the technologies they are using. It's crucial that you know what new technology is available in order to keep from falling behind. Sometimes you need certain technology that doesn't exist, at which time you must create your own.

Technology does not only apply to production. It can also be a part of the product you offer. The features of your product must be those that your customers demand. For example, if you sell computers or cell phones, they must have the latest technological features that are expected by the public.

Another constraint is information. It is critical to obtain it, internally and externally. Internally, you must know things about your own firm, such as costs, trends in sales, product returns for refunds, customers' satisfaction or dissatisfaction rates, and so on. Fortunately, you have some control of that, but you need to have the technology to find information in a timely fashion. Externally, you will need to know things such as the status of our economy, things that your competitors are doing, attitudes of the customers in your market, and much more. Such information is the type over which you have less control, not only how much information to which you have access, but the timeliness and the accuracy of it. Information is of no use if it is either late or inaccurate.

Finally, firms are constrained by markets. Markets determine the behavior of the consumers and the competition, and they can change in an instant. Market behavior has a huge impact on your firm. It is often unpredictable and without reason. Managing it is very difficult at times. Many products and services offered today did not exist five years ago, and because of market behavior between what consumers want and what producers offer, many of these products will not exist five years from now. Once again, you must be in tune to what consumers want or no longer want.

THE PEOPLE PROBLEM

If you have an organization, where every worker is honest, motivated, skilled, efficient, effective, and easy to work with, you have a good thing going. Very few organizations, however, can boast of such a workforce.

So, how do we get there? There are several ways to get close to such an ideal organizational system.

First, many organizations create a combination of **command systems** and **incentive systems**. A command system is a hierarchy of management with various levels of power and authority. It must be designed so that your workers are held accountable. It works to ensure that workers are honest and productive, and they must answer to a manager in their organization. However, workers also need guidance and support from their managers and supervisors. Therefore, a command system is also set up to make sure that everyone knows who answers to them and to whom they answer. It is best to set it up in a way that there is an atmosphere of cooperation between the different levels of the organization. Workers must have a clear idea as to what their jobs are. They must know full well what the exact structure of the command system is.

An incentive system is one that compensates workers for better performance. Compensation doesn't always have to be monetary. You can compensate them with competitive wages and benefits, as well as positive feedback for their performance and enthusiasm for taking care of their needs.

THE AGENCY PROBLEM

The **agency problem** is also referred to as the **principal-agent problem**. Every employee or supplier to an organization is, in one way or another, considered to be a representative for it, and therefore they are considered to be an **agent** for it or the person in charge. The person they represent is called the **principal**. The principals can also be the owners or the stockholders of the firm. If an agent or representative does something wrong or bad, the principal or the organization must live with it. The agency problem therefore exists when the agents put their own agendas ahead of the agendas of the principals. This happens when agents underperform; make serious, costly mistakes; or even steal from the firm. Thus, the firm must protect themselves from such conduct.

But how? There are several ways to cope with the agency problem, but they are broken down into two categories. The first is the **utilization of market forces**. To a large extent, workers don't want to lose their jobs. Their fear of dismissal compels them to work harder and better to avoid being fired; thus, they will be inclined to perform and to stay out of trouble. Even a **chief executive officer (CEO)**, who is the top-ranking manager of an organization, can fear dismissal. Chief executive officers can be ousted by a **board of directors** of a firm (those elected by the shareholders to make major decisions on their behalf), or they could be removed if a firm is taken over by another. Takeovers don't likely happen as much if a firm is being run well, but if a top manager leads the firm down a path that does not maximize profits, and thus reduces the value of the corporation's stock, a firm is often vulnerable to a takeover by outside firms or investors. Such firms or investors would buy the corporation at a low price, with the belief that they could run the company better and thus they would get the stock price to go up. If this happens, the existing managers are usually the first be dismissed. Managers don't want that to happen, and they will usually work hard to make sure that it doesn't.

Unfortunately, the fear of dismissal is not enough to prevent the agency problem, as it has been rampant in many organizations for many decades. Organizations have been the victims of theft and underperformance since the beginning of time. So, what then are some of the other options to fight this problem? Other options will usually cost money; thus, they are called **agency costs**. Such costs could include **monitoring expenses**, where employees are watched in every way possible, by audits or even video cameras, to make sure that there is no theft or underperformance.

Restructuring of the command system is another tool. The system may be set in a way that those who are supposed to watch out for theft and bad performance simply don't do their jobs, and a great deal of it is then permitted. Therefore, restructuring of the command system on a regular basis, by moving managers around from department to department, keeps workers more refined in their conduct. In doing so, when theft or poor performance is going on under one manager who has chosen to permit it or overlook it, the new manager to replacing the old one is more likely to spot it, report it, and/or stop it. Another reason that such restructuring can help is that poor performance and theft often follow managers to their new departments when they are moved. Thus, if a department sees better performance under a new manager, and the department to which the former manager is transferred begins to show bad performance, it gives management a reason to investigate, correct, and, if necessary, ultimately remove such managers.

Incentive pay, which is compensation to workers based upon performance, can also help. Examples of incentive pay would be to permit workers to be given a **percent of the profits**. If they perform honestly and better, they will be rewarded for that by sharing in the profits they help to generate. They can also be given **bonuses** if they reach certain levels of performance or if the firm reaches certain levels of profit. Bonuses can also be given if the firm's stock price reaches a certain level. For reasons we will discuss in more detail later, more profits (after taxes) make a firm's stock price rise as long as the firm isn't taking bigger risks to get those profits.

Another tool for dealing with the agency problem is stock options, often known as **employee stock option plans (ESOPs)**. Ownership of **stock options** doesn't give workers or anyone ownership of stocks. It just gives workers the right to buy or sell them at today's stock price within a certain time frame. If people buy a stock option with the right to sell the stock at today's market value within so many days, this gives them an opportunity to make a profit when and if the price goes higher during that time. Such an option is referred to as a **call option**. For example, if you are given the right to buy perhaps 100 shares of the stock of the firm that employs you at today's market price, you can make a lot of money later if the stock price goes up. Suppose you are told that you have the right to buy your firm's stock at its current market price of $50 at any time: now, twenty years from now, or anytime in between. If your performance in managing the firm gets the stock price up to perhaps $100 per share in a few years, you can still buy it cheap at $50 per share and then sell it for $100 per share when the price reaches that point. This gives workers a great incentive to maximize their loyalty to the firm and to give it their best performance. Better performance improves profits, and better profits improve a firm's stock price. Beware of employees who buy **put options**. They are given the right to sell your firm's stock at today's market price at any time. If your stock price goes down significantly lower than today's price, they would make a chunk of change by selling the stock at that point. This gives workers an incentive to hurt the firm. It has the same effect as **selling short**. Selling short takes place when workers borrow stocks from someone and then they sell them to a third party with the understanding that they must buy them back from that third party in a given period of time. They can buy it back from that third party at the price the stock happens to be the day that they buy it back. For example, if I borrow $50,000 worth of stock, I initially pay nothing for it. If I then sell you that $50,000 worth of stock and then the value of the stock falls to $5,000, I would make the difference—$45,000 in profit on the day I buy it back from you at that $5,000 price. Beware of workers who also sell your stock short or buy put options for your stock, therefore. They are likely to do things that will hurt the firm to get the stock price down in order for them to cash in. There are laws that prevent workers from trading your stock if they have inside information on the day of making such trades that they are not legally allowed to use to their advantage.

Fidelity bonds are also used by many firms' shareholders for protection. Fidelity bonds are offered by firms who promise to pay shareholders a certain sum of money in the event that workers do in fact make major, costly mistakes or engage in theft. It is like an insurance policy to make sure that managers and workers never do anything that could dramatically reduce the value of a firm's stock.

Contracts are also used to avoid the agency problem. Contracts for workers spell out exactly what each is expected to do and what they are not to do. They spell out levels of achievement required of workers and managers during given time periods, making it easier for them to know what is expected of them, but also giving an employer justification of dismissal if the workers fail to honor those contracts.

MANAGING TASKS

Sometimes workers do not perform to their full potential because management does not properly delegate tasks to them and/or communicate those tasks to them.

On far too numerous occasions when I, as a consultant, analyzed the tasks performed to produce the final product by a given firm, I discovered that the people in those firms made several common, fatal mistakes.

First, as mentioned earlier, they had been requiring workers to take 10 steps in a process that really only needed four steps, and each step took much more time to accomplish than necessary. Process improvement was used to correct this. In some cases, there were entire procedures that could even be completely eliminated. Still other times, the existing processes that weren't going to be removed had to be completely redesigned. Process reengineering took care of that.

Second, workers weren't completely sure what tasks they were required to do. Management did not clearly communicate the tasks to them.

Third, some tasks were not getting accomplished while at the same time some tasks were being performed twice by different people.

In addition to process improvement and process reengineering, management must take a clear inventory of what the goals of the firm are, the objectives needed to accomplish those goals, and who will carry out those objectives, making sure that no required task is neglected and that there will be no overlap of duties between workers. Once you have done this, you must make sure that all workers are on board with the tasks at hand and that the tasks are clear to them. Anything short of this is not an economical use of your resources. This must also be done on a regular basis. Organizations change, therefore the goals, objectives, and tasks needed will change too.

CHOOSING A FORM OF OWNERSHIP

There are three major forms of ownership of a firm.

The first is called a **sole proprietorship**. This exists when you start in business without seeking other investors or partners to join you in the venture. Anyone can become a sole proprietor by deciding one day they will sell a particular product or service and then by just going out and starting the business.

As a sole proprietor, you will have a few advantages. First, you will have the ease of entry into the business, as there are no legal formalities in the startup. Suppose, for example, that you wanted to start your own maintenance firm. If you get on the phone and start offering your services today to people whom you feel need you, you are in business. Another advantage is that you can run things the way you like, because you have no partners or investors to whom you must answer. Also, your profits are taxed only once, as opposed to other forms of ownership. This is called **single taxation**.

Becoming a sole proprietor also has it disadvantages. For example, you would have unlimited liability. This means that if things go badly for you, and you find your firm owing more money than it has in assets or capital, your creditors can then begin to take some of your personal belongings from you in order to sell them to pay those debts. They could take your life savings, your home, your cars, or anything of value that you own. Another problem is that there is death of the company at the death of the sole proprietor. If you die, the company dies with you. When that happens, your workers are out of a job. Could you perhaps put in your will who with inherit the firm if you die? Yes, but the firm still dies and then reopens the next day as a new business. So, what's the problem? Well, for one thing, many wills are contested, and your firm could be closed for a long time until the estate is settled. If you close a firm for a long enough period of time, it can kill it. Also, many firms won't lend you money if they know that you could die and leave all of your debts unpaid. Another disadvantage of being a sole proprietor is that the transfer of ownership of your firm is not legally possible. If you want to sell it, the new owners would only own your good name and whatever else you want to sell them, but the original firm will cease to exist. Another thing to consider is that as a sole proprietor, you can't raise money unless you borrow from a financial institution, an individual, or from yourself by using your existing savings. Therefore, you would also have limited funds for startup and expansion, either because of lenders who are reluctant to do business with you or because you can't issue stock for expansion as a corporation can. You also have limits on your intellectual resources. Additional owners can bring a great deal of knowledge to the table, and that knowledge can be crucial to keeping your business afloat.

Another form of ownership is a **C corporation**. General Motors and Microsoft are examples of C corporations. These are the ones in which most citizens in our country have ownership when buying stocks for their retirements or for their children's college funds. Before discussing the advantages and disadvantages of starting one, it is important to have some background information about them.

First, when you start a company, you may not have enough financial resources to do so, and you may have to find investors. Suppose you figure out that you need $50,000 to begin your corporation. One option you would have would be to sell 5,000 shares of stock at a price of $10 each. To sell those 5,000 shares, you may choose to find 100 people, each of whom would buy 50 shares from you. In any case, they would only pay you $10 for each of those shares of stock if they expected your company to be profitable enough to give them a good return on their $10. Suppose that each year that you are in business you were able to net $100,000 in profits after taxes and that you paid all of that profit out in dividends to your shareholders for each share that they own. If you do the math, that would be giving a $10 return to each shareholder, per year, for their $10 investment. That would be a 100 percent return on their investment per year. If the firm's risk is moderate or relatively reasonable, the shareholders would be ecstatic! This would be a fantastic return on their money, as many stocks typically get a much lower return rate than that. With returns like this, there are others who would then be willing to pay them for their stock, far more than $10 each. For example, if I paid them $40 for each of their shares of stock, a $10 return in dividends is still a 25 percent return ($10/$40 = 25%), which is still very good for a firm that has moderate or reasonable risk. Hence, the value of the stock rises with the rise of its net profits after taxes. This rise in stock price or value is called a **capital gain**.

So, how does one sell their stock to others? If you are a **public corporation**, anyone can freely buy the stock from any one of the existing stockholders (or shareholders) of the firm, whereas a person owning stock in a **close, closely held**, or **closed corporation** cannot sell their shares of stock to anyone without the approval of all of the other stockholders of the firm.

Chief executive officers will keep their jobs as long as the wealth of company stockholders is strong, because stockholders will derive their wealth from the value of a company's stock. If the value of the stock goes down, so too does their wealth, just as it would if the value of a savings account for some reason was reduced. The board of directors, who represent the stockholders, would likely vote the CEO out of the firm if this happens. The job of all managers and employees, therefore, is to maximize the wealth of the stockholders. If you become a public corporation (or if you go public), you will likely have an **initial public offering (IPO)**. Those who buy your stock directly from the firm when it initially goes public take big risks, because the company might fail. On the other hand, they can reap the benefits if your firm prospers. This is also called the **primary market**. If any of the owners of the IPO stocks wish to sell their shares, they will sell to the **secondary market**. Whenever those stocks are sold, no matter how many times and no matter how many people buy them, those stock sales are always considered to be in the secondary market.

There will be more about corporations and stocks in a later chapter.

Now, what are the advantages of a starting a corporation? First of all, they have limited liability, hence if your firm goes under and you can't pay your debts, creditors can't take your personal property to pay those debts. Second, there is no death of the firm at the death of any one of the stockholders or owners. If one of them dies, they can leave the stocks to an heir in their estate, but the corporation doesn't miss a beat—unless, of course, the stockholder that died was running the entire firm. If this is the case, the firm will still live and flourish as long as the new manager hired to run the firm is capable of doing so properly. The corporation will also maintain all of its rights to patents, copyrights, and all assets. It will also continue to be responsible for all liabilities and binding contracts from before. Third, corporations have more opportunities for raising funds. As mentioned earlier, in addition to borrowing from lenders, stocks can be issued to give the firm what money it needs to operate or expand. Finally, more owners mean that more intellectual resources will be available, thus better decisions may be made.

So, what is the downside of owning a corporation? For one thing, you can't just wake up one day and start a C corporation. There are lots of legal steps you must take, in addition to finding investors, while remaining in compliance with the law. Second, you lack control. In a sole proprietorship, you can do whatever you want, but in a corporation, you must often clear major decisions with the stockholders, or with the board of directors, or with anyone to whom the board of directors has delegated that authority. Finally, your profits are taxed an infinite number of times. Remember, shareholders are the owners. They are paid in dividends, and dividends are derived from profits after taxes. Therefore, the profits they receive have already been taxed before they receive dividends. Then, the dividends are taxed when they are paid to the stockholders. At that point, the same profits have been taxed twice. In some cases, other corporations own stock in other corporations. Thus, if a corporation receives dividends, those are taxed again when they pay them to *their* stockholders, and this can continue infinitely.

There are some smaller types of corporations where these things are not the same. For example, you can start a **limited liability corporation (LLC)**, in most states, by just filling out a simple form and sending it to state officials with a nominal fee. One of the biggest reasons that people choose to own a corporation (or incorporate) is to have limited liability. In an LLC, you get the advantage of having limited liability, while still being taxed only once, and with ease of entry into the business, as does a sole proprietorship. If it's so great, then why doesn't every firm become an LLC to avoid the double taxation? The answer is that it is only permitted for smaller firms. There is a limit to how big the firm is if they want to remain an LLC in most states. Also, owners of an LLC are called members, not stockholders.

S corporations are similar to LLCs except that shares of stock can be sold in an S corporation, while they cannot be sold in an LLC. Also, S corporations do not pay federal tax; instead, they divide profits among their shareholders, as well as any losses. You can also form an S corporation with *you* being the only stockholder, thus you would not have to answer to anyone besides yourself.

What about **partnerships**? A partnership is a noncorporation firm with multiple owners (or partners). Each owner is usually required to make some kind of contribution to the firm to become a part of it and to thus share in the profits. Their contributions could be money invested or personal assets (such as office furniture or a car), or they can simply contribute their good name, their time, and/or their knowledge. The value of each partner's contribution or investment is evaluated, and it will thus determine the degree to which each partner is compensated during the course of the firm's operations. The more profits that a partner contributes to the partnership would, obviously, likely give them a higher percent of the profits. Partnerships have similarities to both corporations and sole proprietorships. For example, there are still few formalities required by law to start one, although it is very unwise to create one without having a lawyer draw up a contract that declares who owns what, and what the duties and rights of each partner will be. Such a contract should also put in writing the amount of compensation that each partner is entitled to receive based upon what they contribute. If you start one with a friend or family member, you may be inclined to feel that you trust each other and that no contract is needed. However, this is very foolish and naïve. Many friendships and families have been destroyed over the years when they get into a partnership. Without a contract, it becomes very messy when the partnership is disbanded. There is also single taxation of partnership profits. The disadvantages of partnerships include unlimited liability. A **limited liability partnership (LLP)** can remove liability from some of the partners, but at least one of the partners must have the unlimited liability and few would want to have that burden. You also have control issues, because it always happens when there is more than one owner. Thus, again, you can't just do what you want. There is also a limit to the funds you can raise. To expand the business, you must either have partners put in more money, or borrow from an institution or someone willing to grant you a loan, or you must bring in more partners with money. Finally, death of any one of the owners ends the partnership, and a new contract must be renegotiated. This can become very complicated if there are a lot of partners involved with a firm. Sometimes, the estate of the deceased partner will require the surviving partners to pay the estate some money for the value of the deceased partner's portion of ownership. Thus, surviving partners are encouraged to become beneficiaries of a life insurance policy of the deceased partner before their death.

A summary of these advantages and disadvantages are listed in figure 8-1.

	Advantages	Disadvantages
Sole proprietorship	1. Ease of Entry 2. Control 3. Single Taxation	1. Unlimited liability 2. Death of the company at the death of the owner or at the transfer of ownership 3. Limited funds for startup or expansion 4. Fewer intellectual resources
Partnerships	1. Easier to enter than a C Corporation but formalities of a contract are recommended 2. Single taxation	1. Lack of control 2. Unlimited liability 3. Limited funds for startup or expansion 4. Death of the company at the death of an owner or at a change in ownership
C Corporations	1. Limited liability 2. No death by death/ease of transfer of ownership 3. Unlimited fund for startup or expansion 4. More intellectual resources	1. Formalities in entry 2. Lack of control 3. Multiple-taxation

FIGURE 8-1   Advantages and Disadvantages of Different Ownership

CHAPTER 8 REVIEW

QUESTIONS TO THINK ABOUT

1. Are accounting profits the best to consider when deciding if your profits are enough? Why or why not?   No
2. What are the ways to maximize profits?
3. What are the main things over which firms have no control and thus are constrained by them?   Tech, Info, Market
4. What method(s) do you feel you should use to address the agency problem? Why?
5. What form of business ownership do you prefer? Why?

TERMS TO KNOW

Accounting profits
Agency costs
Agency problem
Board of directors
Bonuses
C corporation
Call options
Chief executive officer - CEO
Command systems
Depreciation
Economic efficiency
Economic profits
Employee stock option plan (ESOP)
Explicit costs
Fidelity bonds
Implicit costs
Incentive pay

Incentive systems
Initial public offering (IPO)
Limited liability corporation (LLC)
Limited liability partnership (LLP)
Monitory expenses
Primary market
Principal-agent problem
Process improvement
Process reengineering
Public corporation
Restructuring
Secondary market
Single taxation
Sole proprietorship
Stock options
Technological efficiency
Unlimited liability

CHAPTER NINE

Markets in the Competitive Environment

HOW MUCH COMPETITION do you have? You can answer that question in one of several ways. It can depend upon how much your firms' sales are in comparison to the size of your market, or you can tell by some of the characteristics of your market's competitors. This chapter will give you a better understanding of the intensity of competition you may be facing or the lack thereof. Less competition is always better for you as a business owner, but not so much for consumers. Business owners are more profitable if there are only a few competitors in their markets because they can often charge a higher price. On the other hand, with fewer competitors in a market, consumers have fewer choices and must often pay higher prices for the goods they need.

LEVELS OF COMPETITION

There are four major levels of competition that we will study. Figure 9-1 shows the different extremes in a competitive continuum. A **monopoly** exists if you are the only firm or producer in the market, or if you are the only one that has any relevant sales. You *are* the market. It is very difficult to remain a monopoly, however. If you have cornered the market on a product or service that has a significant amount of profits, there will be people who will take many measures to quickly become your competitor. They will want to tap into those profits. You can prevent that by what is referred to as **barriers to entry**. Barriers to entry to your market by others keeps them out of the market and could include things such as a patent or a copyright you may have on the product you are selling. It could also be the fact that you started your business with a lot of money invested, which many could not raise to match your stature. For example, it's difficult to start up a car manufacturing firm to compete with existing firms because, up front, you need a high scale of volume of sales in order to keep your prices competitive. This is called **economies of scale**, which is something that will also be discussed later in this textbook.

There have been firms that had more than 98 percent of the market's business, and, in some cases, they were considered monopolies as well, even though they did not have 100 percent of the market's share of sales. Why? Because the other 2 percent of the market had sales that did not materially impact that of the monopoly. For example, there was a time when Microsoft had the overwhelming majority of the market share in their industry, but not 100 percent. However, many people in those days still felt that they were a monopoly.

An **oligopoly** has very few relevant competitors. One type of oligopoly is called a **duopoly**, which has only two competitors. When this happens, any time one of the competitors takes steps to increase their business and to get a greater share of the market's business (or **market share**), it will have a significant impact on the market because there are so few players within it. This will almost always bring retaliation from the other few competitors. In 1980, for example, when Chrysler Corporation became the first major automaker to offer a two-year, 20,000-mile warranty, the other automakers were significantly affected by the offer because there are so few auto manufacturers. As a result, Ford, General Motors, and the foreign auto manufacturers retaliated with their own similar warranties. One of them offered a three-year, 30,000-mile warranty, and then another offered a four-year, 40,000-mile warranty. Chrysler then offered a five-year, 50,000-mile warranty. This process continued until car manufacturers began to offer 10-year, 100,000-mile warranties, and this is the standard that is common today. Anytime an oligopoly gains market share, when the retaliation of the other competitors takes place, in almost every case the market share gain is only temporary, and market shares in the industry in the long run remain basically the same.

Then there are those firms who are in a market that is considered **monopolistic competition**. This sounds like a contradiction in its own right. So, how can a firm be considered monopolistic and still have competition? The answer is that there are many firms in markets where people buy things or services from them because they feel that those firms have something unique to sell. The market has lots of competitors, but they get their business because their products and services have qualities that cannot be found elsewhere. For example, there are many, many restaurants, and the restaurant market is very competitive. Yet, people go to certain restaurants because there is something unique about them that cannot be found anywhere else, perhaps the atmosphere, the desserts, their steaks, their service, or whatever intrigues their customers. When you enter the market, change your prices, change your services, or leave the market, there may be some who notice, but the market is so large that not much will change, and few will care. However, the main thing to remember here is that your customers will still likely perceive a difference between you and your competitors, and that difference gives you a quasi monopoly on that trait your firm may have.

As you can see, as we move from right to left of this continuum, the number of competitors in these markets is increasing dramatically.

The last of the four major levels of competition is that of **perfect/pure competition,** or **perfect competition**. This exists when your market has so much competition that you will have absolutely no impact on the market when you enter it, change your strategies, or exit it. Please note in Figure 9-1 that all markets, therefore, are imperfect with exception to that of perfect or pure competition.

Another attribute of those working in a perfectly or purely competitive market is that your customers will not perceive any difference between you and your competitors. You will also be in a position where you can't even set your prices. Instead, you will be told what you will be paid rather than being asked what you will charge. Therefore, you will be considered a firm that is a **price taker** and not a **price maker**. A good example would be that of the farming industry as was discussed in an earlier chapter. When you sell your corn, you will likely have to take it to a central market. It is there that you will be told what will be paid for it. It is on a take-it-or-leave-it basis.

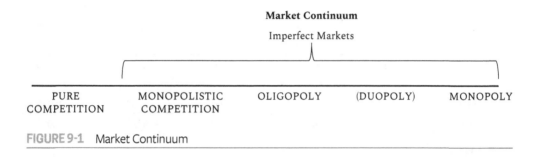

FIGURE 9-1   Market Continuum

Those are the characteristics of the different levels of competition. Now, let us discuss the mathematical way of figuring out what type of market it is in which you operate.

THE TOP FOUR-FIRM CONCENTRATION RATIO

Suppose you operate in a market that is described in figure 9-2. As you can see, Market/Industry 1 has all of the sales of the industry, so that's an easy one. It would be a monopoly. As mentioned earlier, some will argue that if the total sales of Market/Industry 1 would have been 98 percent, it would still be considered a monopoly.

Market/Industry 2 would likely be an oligopoly. Why? Because in this example, the sales for the top four firms of its industry is $3,950,000,000, while the entire industry has total sales of $5,850,000,000. If you divide the total sales of the top four firms by the industry's total sales, you will see that those top four firms' sales represent 68 percent of the entire industry. This is called the **top four-firm concentration ratio**.

Top Four-Firm Concentration Ratio = Total Sales of
The Largest Four Firms/The Industry's Total Sales

A case like this, indicates that the industry has very few competitors besides that of the largest four firms. Any time you calculate this ratio, if the percent of sales of those top four firms is greater than 60 percent of the industry, you likely would be in a market described as an oligopoly.

Top Four Concentration Ratios				
	Market/ Industry 1	Market/ Industry 2	Market/ Industry 3	Market/ Industry 4
	Monopoly	Oligopoly	Monopolistic Competition	Pure or Perfect Competition
Sales (000,000) Firm 1	4,000	2,500	450	7
Sales (000,000) Firm 2	–	900	375	7
Sales (000,000) Firm 3	–	350	200	4
Sales (000,000) Firm 4	–	200	195	2
Total Sales of the Largest Firms	4,000	3,950	1,220	20
Remaining Firms	–	1,900	2,500	9,000
Industry Total	4,000	5,850	3,720	9,020
Four-Firm Concentration Ratio	100%	68%	33%	0.22%
		>60%	<=60%	<1%

FIGURE 9-2   Top Four Concentration Ratios

Now take a look at Market/Industry 3. Total sales of the top four firms of that industry are $1,220,000,000. After dividing those sales by the total sales of the industry of $3,720,000,000, the ratio would be 33 percent. If the ratio is at or lower than 60 percent, while still being greater than 1 percent, it is likely that you are operating in a market that would be described as monopolistic competition. Finally, when the ratio goes below 1 percent, many economists believe that you are then operating in a pure, or perfectly competitive market, as you can see in Market/Industry 4 in figure 9-2.

Knowing what type of competitive market it is in which you operate is very important because each competitive market has their own demand curve, which will be explained in more depth later. It is also important because it will help you to understand what pricing strategies you should use. For example, if your firm is an oligopoly and if you reduce your prices, you will bring retaliation from other competitors as was discussed earlier, while monopolies don't have to deal with that.

HERFINDAHL-HIRSCHMAN INDEX (HHI)

Another thing to be concerned about is the government. They don't like monopolies. Why? For the reasons mentioned earlier in this book. First, they create shortages and a lack of options for our purchasing public. Second, monopolies, or firms that are very close to being monopolies, often create higher prices in their markets. Third, monopolies create hardship on those trying to enter certain markets, and that keeps many from being able to enjoy their fair share of the American dream. As mentioned earlier, many free-market societies have little or no middle-income families, with nearly 98 percent of the country living in poverty while the remaining 2 percent live as billionaires. Laws that prohibit monopolies, it is believed, have been effective to keep the problem of having no middle-income families from happening here in the United States. The laws that prohibit anyone from conspiring to create monopolies, limit competition, or limit society's choices in making a purchase are called **antitrust laws**, which were discussed briefly in an earlier chapter. To violate such laws is a criminal act. More on that later.

If the government feels that your industry is changing in a way that its competition is dramatically decreasing, they may scrutinize it and maybe even stop it from happening. The United States Department of Justice is always watching industries to see if they are monopolies in the making.

Acquisitions and mergers of firms are obviously a major means for reducing competition. While some use the terms interchangeably, there really is a distinct different between them. A **merger** takes place when two firms come together to form a new entity, often with a new name and a shakeup in management. Once the merger takes place, the two original companies cease to exist. Firms will often do that, not necessarily to monopolize a market, but to become stronger by sharing resources and customers. An **acquisition** on the other hand exists when one firm takes control of another, often without a change in the makeup of either firm. It can happen when one firm acquires anywhere from 51% of another firm's stock, all the way to acquiring all of a firm's assets. When this happens, both firms usually continue to operate with the same names as separate companies. In many cases, the public is unaware that the acquisition has occurred. Another difference between the two events is that mergers are usually executed with full cooperation and acceptance by the two firms that merge, while some acquisitions are done in a way that is not so friendly. Some acquisitions are called **hostile** to the firm that is acquired. Some firms don't want to be acquired, but when there is freedom for others to buy their stock, a firm can buy up the majority of its shares without the approval of the current shareholders or current management.

The government uses what is called the **Herfindahl-Hirschman Index (HHI)** to determine this. The calculation is a simple sum of the square of the market shares. If the sum of the square of the market shares is below 1,500, then your industry is considered to be highly competitive, and they will not be concerned. However, when the number falls between the range of 1,500 to 2,500 it would be considered a moderately concentrated market, which means that it isn't highly competitive, yet it isn't really gravitating toward monopoly either. Such industries are watched closely by the government. In such industries, any future mergers that would raise the HHI by 200 points or more will again be given heavy scrutiny.

Any industry that is considering mergers among their competition will automatically be challenged if, after the merger, the HHI would go above 2,500, because it would be considered highly concentrated or noncompetitive, and such an effort would be stopped by the government unless there were circumstances that would justify such a merger.

Let's try an example. Suppose you are in an industry with the market shares shown in figure 9-3.

Firm	Market Shares as a Percent	Percentages Removed	Market Shares Squared
Company 1	23.5%	23.5	552.25
Company 2	19.2%	19.2	368.64
Company 3	14.6%	14.6	213.16
Company 4	11.9%	11.9	141.61
Company 5	8.3%	8.3	68.89
Company 6	7.5%	7.5	56.25
Company 7	6.3%	6.3	39.69
Company 8	5.5%	5.5	30.25
Company 9	3.2%	3.2	10.24
Totals	100.0%	100.00	1,480.98

FIGURE 9-3 Herfindahl-Hirshman Market Share Ratios Squared

The first thing to do is remove the percentages. Otherwise, the numbers get very small and difficult to calculate and interpret. Second, square those nonpercentage numbers. Third, add up those squared numbers. In this example, the sum of the squares of the market shares of this industry would be 1,480.98 as seen in figure 9-3. Therefore, this industry is one that the government would not likely worry about, as its HHI is lower than 1,500. If a merger were to be attempted by two of these firms that would give the same results, the government would not likely take any measures to prevent it.

OTHER THINGS TO KNOW ABOUT COMPETITIVE MARKETS

It is important to understand that the lines between oligopoly, monopolistic competition, and pure competition are often debated. For example, many argue that the fast-food industry experiences monopolistic competition because there are so many restaurants out there. However, when McDonald's, Wendy's, or Burger King make changes, the others "ante up," or retaliate to gain back market share that was lost when the changes were first made. For example, Wendy's was among the first to install a drive-through at their retaurants many years ago, but it didn't take long for the others to do the same. When one of them added kids' meals and value meals, so too did the others. Thus, while they were in a very competitive market, they were still showing characteristics of an oligopoly.

It's also important to know that you don't have to be a major corporation to be a monopoly or an oligopoly. It really depends upon what kind of market you are in. A **regional market** is one that is limited in scope, such as restaurants, gas stations, or grocery stores. People aren't likely to be able to buy such products and have them shipped to them, thus their market potential is likely going to be limited to customers who live within about a thirty-minute drive or less from their operations. Groceries, restaurants, or gas stations that are small could in fact then have a monopoly if they are the only ones operating in a given, limited region. This is very unlikely to happen, however, as these types of firms have very few barriers to entry to their markets, and in a short period of time competitors are likely to set up shop near them.

Monopolies and oligopolies in **national markets**, those that sell across the United States but not beyond our borders, would likely have to be a much bigger firm. Monopolies and oligopolies in **global markets**, those that sell across the United States and beyond, would also likely need to be larger firms to have such a status. Why? Because the potential for having competitors is far greater, and only a very large firm could get to the point that it would discourage others from trying to compete with them.

Also, markets don't always correspond to industries. While your firm as a whole may not be a monopoly, it may operate in many markets and have a monopoly on given product lines but not on others. For example, pharmaceutical firms may have a patent on, and therefore a monopoly on, given types of medication they sell, but they may also be in a highly competitive market if they sell aspirin or other medicines in which the market is very crowded with many competitors.

When opportunity knocks, and it appears that a new market is emerging with very little competition, many firms quickly and often change to that market. When the market gets too crowded to the point that they can't make the economic profits they need or want, they will exit the market, hence many firms regularly move from one market to the next.

CHAPTER 9 REVIEW

QUESTIONS TO THINK ABOUT

1. Go online and see if you can to find the data you need to calculate the status of given markets by use of the top-four concentration ratio and the Herfindahl-Hirschman Index (HHI).

TERMS TO KNOW

Antitrust laws	Monopoly
Barriers to entry	Oligopoly
Duopoly	Price maker
Herfindahl-Hirschman Index (HHI)	Price taker
Market continuum	Pure competition or perfect competition
Market share	Top four-firm concentration ratio
Monopolistic competition	

Output and Costs

IN THE PREVIOUS chapters, we discussed the concept of costs. In this chapter, we will determine the different types of costs and how they are calculated.

SHORT RUN VS. LONG RUN COSTS

First, when studying production and relationships between output and costs, you must determine whether the production or output is taking place in the *short run* or in the *long run*. Output in the short run is usually considered to have taken place within one year, while a time frame that lasts approximately one year or longer is considered to be the long run.

Another important thing to know is that, in the long run, the quantities and the amount of availability of some resources are varied. Why? For example, if I need a builder to increase the size of my factory, it may take over a year to find that contractor who is suitable, as they may be taking a great deal of time on other existing projects. Once the builder is chosen, it will then take time for them to complete the work. People who provide you with the things you need often need many months of lead time before they can provide them to you. In the short run, therefore, you are limited to a certain number of supplies and suppliers. For the same reasons, firms often have constraints on how much technology they can add in the short run as well.

COSTS

There are three major types of costs. **Fixed costs** are those that do not change as you get more business or as you have more output. An example of this would be rent. Most landlords don't lower your rent when you have a decline in business, nor do they raise your rent when your business is good. Rent does change, but typically not because of a change in your output and sales volume. Another example of fixed costs is capital equipment. It is costly to have machinery, whether you own it or lease it.

When business declines, it's not likely that you can "lay off" your equipment like you can an employee. You must still pay the costs of owning that equipment even if it is idle.

In colleges, you have salaries of teachers and administrators as well as building costs. Whether you have two students enrolled or two thousand students enrolled, you must still pay those basic costs.

In the long run, there are no fixed costs, because fixed costs are those that do not change by a change in volume. In the long run, persistent and exceptionally higher volume requires additions of plant and capital equipment, which increases costs of things such as rent and salaries, and the cost of owning the capital equipment.

Figure 10-1 shows that if your business reaches a certain point to where you cannot continue to operate in your smaller, current location or with your current capital equipment, you may have to expand and get a bigger place with more equipment, which would raise those rent and equipment costs. When you make your move to do so, those costs would jump up to the level that the new landlord would charge and to what you would pay for the added equipment. This would create a stair-step effect as shown in figure 10-1. The same thing is true if your business is getting so bad that you don't see it ever improving again. Then it would be time to downsize. If you sell off much of your equipment and move to a smaller place, your rent and equipment costs would abruptly fall to the next, lower level, also as shown in figure 10-1. When rent, capital equipment costs, and costs such as these begin to rise or fall abruptly, there will be a breakpoint in your fixed costs. Why? Because if they jump from perhaps $1,000 per month to $2,000 per month, the coordinate on the

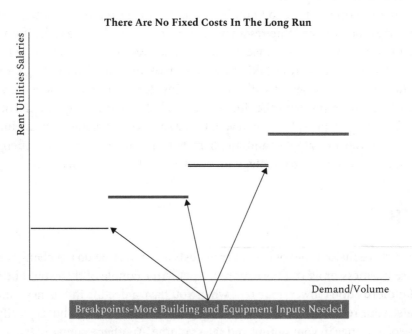

FIGURE 10-1 There are No Fixed Costs in the Long Run

graph would be separate. Once the costs change, they will begin to remain unchanged as long as more expansion or downsizing is not required.

Variable costs are costs that *do* change with a change in your output and sales volume. They comprise things including, but not limited to, **direct material** and **direct labor**. For example, if you sell frozen pizzas, your cost of dough, sauce, cheese, pepperoni, and whatever else you put on your pizza would be examples of direct material, which are materials that are directly used as a part of the substance of your product. Your costs of those direct materials will go up if you must buy more to keep up with demand and production. But if business hits the skids, you won't need to buy as much, and those costs will go down. Direct labor is what you pay for wages of those who are directly involved with production of your pizzas. If business is down, you will ask some of your workers to stay home until business gets better, thus your labor cost will also decline. If business increases, you will call those workers back to work, and your labor costs will then rise again.

Another cost would be **mixed costs**. Mixed costs are those that have a combination of both fixed and variable costs. For example, utilities may be fixed as you heat your building and as you keep lights on in your building regardless of whether you have no customers or if business is booming. However, as business increases, you may be using more heat, as more people are going in and out of your building and allowing heat to escape. You may also see your electric bill go up if you use machinery during production. Added business requires you to run that equipment more, and your electric bill would rise. Therefore, part of your electric bill would be considered fixed costs, while the rest of your electric bill would be considered variable costs, hence it would be a mixed cost.

Whenever you own a business, you never know how high your costs will be unless you have some idea as to what your sales volume will be. Why? As mentioned earlier, it's because your variable cost will rise as your sales do. The good news is, you *do* know what your cost minimum will be. This will be your fixed costs. Remember, these are the costs you will have even if you have no sales.

OUTPUT TENDENCIES

If you are producing a tangible good, you will likely be inclined to add labor or capital resources to your production process as your demand increases. As you produce, you will experience what is known as **marginal physical product**. This is the increase in the total output or production of your firm's product that results from a one-unit increase in the quantity of a resource, which could be either labor employed or the use of capital equipment, with all other inputs remaining the same. As output increases to meet demand, you will likely see your marginal physical product initially rise. However, if you don't add the right combination of labor and capital, you will likely see your marginal physical product begin to fall due to **the law of diminishing returns** as seen in figure 10-1. Marginal physical product is found by the following formula:

$$\text{Marginal Physical Product (MPP)} = \text{Total Output after Adding an Input} - \text{Previous Quantity of Output}$$

Why does the marginal physical product go up? When you add another input, such as a worker, two heads are better than one, and two people working together can help make things run smoother. When you add more capital equipment, the existing workers can become more productive. Why, then, does marginal physical product later begin to decline? In regard to hiring more workers, as more people begin to get involved with production, without adding working space and/or capital equipment, two things will happen. First, personalities can start to become an issue, and efficiency and effectiveness are usually strained when this happens. When people get together to work, it becomes necessary to have harmony between them, but that does not always happen. Second, if you get more people into a room without proportionately adding capital equipment or space, you will have some workers sitting and waiting for equipment to become available. This, too, can add to the tension. It can also happen if you add capital equipment without adding workers. Assuming you still are working in the same space, if you add more equipment without hiring workers, initially you will get an increase in marginal physical product as more than one set of equipment may be a little helpful. However, over time the unused equipment will get in the way in your limited work area, and efficiencies will once again begin to occur.

For example, suppose we return to the business of making frozen pizzas that you sell around the world. Also assume that each unit of capital equipment is composed of a prep set that slices the pepperoni and then slices the pizza when it is assembled, and has a means of wrapping and boxing the pizza for shipping. Figure 10-2 shows what could happen in your making frozen pizzas as you increase the number of workers without adding the capital equipment inputs (the pizza prep sets), or what could happen if you add prep sets without adding workers.

Let's now assume that you are going to focus on adding workers without adding capital equipment. Therefore, we will use the numbers in the highlighted row of figure 10-2 that has only one capital equipment input per day (the pizza prep set). Figure 10-3 shows you mathematically, using the formula given earlier, how marginal physical product is equal to 25 and 35 in Scenarios B and C. Marginal physical product is not applicable to Scenario A because it is the first scenario and there is no production. Figure 10-3 also shows you graphically what would happen to your output and how it changes as you continue to hire workers without adding capital. Notice that the law of diminishing returns is in full force because marginal physical product goes up at first and then begins to decline as predicted.

Capital Equipment Input/Day Pizza Prep Set	Labor Input Workers/Day									
	0	1	2	3	4	5	6	7	8	9
0	0	0	0	0	0	0	0	0	0	0
1	0	25	60	75	87	97	105	112	115	114
2	0	27	64	79	91	101	109	116	119	118
3	0	28	66	81	93	103	111	118	121	120
4	0	28	65	80	92	102	110	117	120	119
5	0	28	65	80	92	102	110	117	120	119
6	0	28	65	80	92	102	110	117	120	119
7	0	28	65	80	92	102	110	117	120	119
8	0	28	65	80	92	102	110	117	120	119
9	0	28	65	80	92	102	110	117	120	119

FIGURE 10-2   Labor Input Workers/Day with Capital Equipment Input/Day

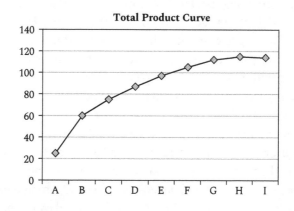

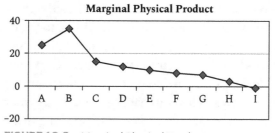

FIGURE 10-3   Marginal Physical Product

Marginal Revenue = sales go up by 1

Now look at figure 10-4. It is very revealing. There are several important observations that you must note. First, each worker hired will bring in additional revenue for you. This is called **marginal revenue product**. It is found by the following formula:

how much more rev. I bring by hiring another worker

$$\text{Marginal Revenue Product (MRP)} = \text{Marginal Physical Product (MPP)} \times \text{Product Price}$$

For example, in Scenario B, the added 25 pizzas produced by hiring Worker 1 (or the marginal physical product from Worker 1) will bring $9 each to the firm or a total of added revenue of $225 ($9 × Column [4]). The 35 added frozen pizzas produced after hiring Worker 2 in Scenario C will have a marginal revenue product of $315 ($9 × 35 additional pizzas produced).

Suppose each worker is paid $11.25 per hour (or $90 per day, assuming that each worker puts in eight hours of work each day). Therefore, you would be foolish to hire Worker 6 (as shown in Scenario G), because Worker 6 will only bring you marginal revenue product of $72 (eight pizzas × $9), but that worker will be paid $90. You are losing $18 by hiring that worker. When you think about it, you are only breaking even on Worker 5. One could argue, then, that if we don't add any additional capital equipment to this operation, our capacity for output is 87 (as shown in Scenario E), because we would be very unwise to produce more than that.

It is also very important to note here that while we would not hire a worker with a marginal revenue product less than the wage paid to that worker, we must also consider the direct material that would be utilized for the production of that worker's output. Many do not factor in the material, but it is actually very relevant here. If you hire an additional worker, you will incur the cost of their wage, but you will also pay more for direct material. That is because there is output you now have with that worker that you would not have had otherwise. With that added output, material is used that also would not have been used and/or purchased without having hired that worker. Therefore, the **hiring decision** should be to not hire a worker if the marginal revenue product that they generate by their productivity is less than the **marginal cost by worker**. The **marginal cost by worker** does factor in the direct material used for production. Therefore, the hiring decision should now be to hire no one after hiring worker number 3. That is because worker 4 will generate a marginal revenue product of only $108 with a marginal cost per worker of $114. Hiring worker 4 would cause the firm to lose money.

Please notice that as output goes up, initially, the growth rate of that output is large. But then it begins to slow down after you hire additional workers due to the diminishing returns (see the chart in the upper right of figure 10-3). It is important to note, therefore, that when marginal physical product rises by hiring a new worker, productivity is better. When the marginal physical product begins to fall (as seen in the chart in the lower right of figure 10-3), this means that productivity is getting lower. When this happens, your costs will rise. When you are able to get **more** output from a given number of workers, assuming that their wages remain the same, your labor costs **per unit of** output will *fall*. On the other hand, when you get **less** output from a given number of workers, assuming that their wages remain the same, your labor costs **per unit of** output will *rise*. Marginal revenue product and labor costs, therefore, are inversely related. Thus, now that we know what your output will be like, we can begin to get a flavor for what your costs will be.

Figure 10-4 is an extension of figure 10-3. Let's now make a few more assumptions in order to find other information. Suppose that it costs your frozen pizza firm $100 per day (or about $3,100 per month) for rent and other fixed costs. Also assume that it costs you $2 in direct material to produce one pizza (supplies for pizza crusts, cheese, sauce, toppings, and packaging for each frozen pizza you sell). Finally, let us continue to assume that you are paying each of your workers $11.25 per hour, or $90 per day in direct labor. What, then, would your costs be if you have only one worker?

Remember, your fixed costs remain the same regardless of how many workers you have or how much business you have. That will be $100. Next, with only one worker, you will produce 25 frozen pizzas; therefore, your variable cost will be $50 for the direct materials (25 pizzas × $2) and $90 for the direct labor. Your **total variable costs** would then be $140 ($50 + $90). Thus, total variable costs, shown in Column [6], are found as follows:

$$\text{Total Variable Costs (TVC)} = \text{Cost of Added Direct Labor (DL)} +$$
$$(\text{Direct Material (DM) Cost} \times \text{Quantity of Units Produced})$$

Please note, therefore, that the added cost of direct labor is found by taking the number of workers employed (shown in Column [2]) and multiplying it by the $90 wage. Also, the direct material cost is found by multiplying the total output, found in Column [3], by the cost of direct materials used per unit of output.

Now let's calculate the total costs. Figure 10-4 shows you that this is obtained by adding Column [5] to Column [6]; thus, **total costs** (shown in Column [7]) are found by the following formula:

$$\text{Total Costs} = \text{Fixed Costs (FC)} + \text{Total Variable Costs (TVC)}$$

Each time you hire a new worker, your costs will rise. Let us now assume that Worker 2 (in Scenario C) has been hired. Figure 10-4 will remind you that it is assumed that it would give you an output of 60 frozen pizzas per day. As already stated, fixed costs will remain unchanged. This would make your total variable costs rise to $300 ($90 × two workers) + ($2 in direct material variable costs × 60 units produced).

Notice now how we have the issue with **marginal cost by worker.** This is found as follows:

$$\text{Marginal Cost by Worker} = \text{Added Direct Labor (DL) Cost} + (\text{Added}$$
$$\text{Direct Material (DM) Cost} \times \text{Marginal Physical Product})$$

It can also be found by:

$$\text{Marginal Cost by Worker} = \text{Total Cost (TC) With the Most}$$
$$\text{Recent Worker} - \text{Previous Total Cost (TC)}$$

After hiring your Worker 2, your total costs have risen because of the rise in your variable costs from your direct labor in addition to the direct materials from the added items produced by that worker. The amount is $160 ($90 in added direct labor cost + the cost of the added direct material of $2 × the 35 added frozen pizzas produced). Using the other approach, the total cost from Scenario B (in Column [7]) is $140. In Scenario C, total cost rises to $300 or by $160.

Now we come to **marginal cost per unit of output (MC)**, which is one of the most important of these costs. Why? Because, as we have already stated in Chapter 7, the way to maximize profits is to set production at the point where marginal cost (per unit of output) is equal to marginal revenue. In order to make that happen you must know how to calculate marginal cost per unit of output. In figure 10-4 you can see that you can find this by dividing Column [8] by Column [4]. So, the marginal cost per unit of output is found by the following:

Marginal Cost Per Unit of Output (MC) = Marginal Cost by
Worker/Marginal Physical Product (MPP)

It is very important to note here that the marginal cost per unit of output is the only one of these output costs that will use marginal physical product as the denominator. The remaining calculations after that in Columns [10] through [12] will use total output as their denominators. This is why they are color coded in red. They are grouped by that color to draw attention to this fact in figure 10-4.

Next, we will calculate the **average fixed cost (AFC)**. It is important to know this because the AFC shows how much of your rent and other fixed costs are applied to each unit of output produced. It will always decline, unless you continue to produce to the point where your marginal physical product becomes negative. Figure 10-4 also shows you that this is obtained by dividing Column [5] by Column [3], thus is found by the following formula:

Average Fixed Cost (AFC) = Total Fixed Cost (FC)/Total Output

Another cost that is important to compute is **average variable cost (AVC)**. This will let you know what your average costs are of things such as direct labor and direct material. Among other reasons, AVC is helpful to know because it can help you to see whether or not your operation is efficient. If your AVC is on the rise, it may be a sign that workers are losing their efficiency and effectiveness, and/or your material costs from vendors could be on the rise. It could also indicate that workers are wasting those direct materials. To calculate AVC, you can divide the total variable cost by total output. In figure 10-4, therefore, this would mean that you would divide Column [6] by Column [3].

And now, for another important calculation we have **average total cost**. Once again, this will help you discern whether your efficiency and effectiveness are holding, while simultaneously factoring in fixed costs. Average total cost is found in figure 10-4 by dividing Column [7] by Column [3]. In other words,

Average Total Costs = Total Cost/Total Output

[1]	[2]	[3]	[4]	[5]	[6]	[7]	[8]	[9]	[10]	[11]	[12]	[13]
Scenario	Workers (Given)	Total Output (Given)	Marginal Physical Product (Scenario B Output -A Output etc.)	Fixed Cost (Given)	Total Variable Cost @$90 Labor + $2 Material Per Unit of Output ([2]*$90)+($2*[3])	Total Cost [5]+[6]	Marginal Cost By Worker (Scenario B Total Cost-A Total Cost)	Marginal Cost Per Unit of Output [8]/[4]	Average Fixed Cost [5]/[3]	Average Variable Cost [6]/[3]	Average Total Cost [7]/[3]	Marginal Revenue Product $9 × [4]
A	0	0	N/A	$100	$0	$100	N/A	N/A	N/A	N/A	N/A	N/A
B	1	25	25	$100	$140	$240	$140	$5.60	$4.00	$5.60	$9.60	$225.00
C	2	60	35	$100	$300	$400	$160	$4.57	$1.67	$5.00	$6.67	$315.00
D	3	75	15	$100	$420	$520	$120	$8.00	$1.33	$5.60	$6.93	$135.00
E	4	87	12	$100	$534	$634	$114	$9.50	$1.15	$6.14	$7.29	$108.00
F	5	97	10	$100	$644	$744	$110	$11.00	$1.03	$6.64	$7.67	$90.00
G	6	105	8	$100	$750	$850	$106	$13.25	$0.95	$7.14	$8.10	$72.00
H	7	112	7	$100	$854	$954	$104	$14.86	$0.89	$7.63	$8.52	$63.00
I	8	115	3	$100	$950	$1,050	$96	$32.00	$0.87	$8.26	$9.13	$27.00

FIGURE 10-4 Total Costs, Marginal Cost by Worker, Marginal Cost per Unit of Output, Average Fixed Cost, Average Variable Cost, Average Total Cost

ECONOMIES OF SCALE

There is a very important thing to note here. Marginal costs per unit of output are similar to average variable cost and average total cost in that all of them will fall initially and then rise due to diminishing returns. We like it when costs fall, but how do we keep them from rising? In other words, how do we prevent diminishing returns?

To prevent or reduce diminishing returns, you must take whatever measures you can to put the level of your labor and capital inputs in balance. Remember, diminishing returns are often the result of having too many inputs of labor and not enough capital inputs and/or having too many inputs of capital and not enough labor inputs. This does not mean that they must equal, but they must not be out of balance. For example, if you have 2 idle or underutilized workers who both need to use 1 machine between them to keep up with demand and to remain efficient, then a machine should be obtained for their use to keep the labor/capital input combination in balance. In the same way, if you have 1 idle or underutilized machine that you need to utilize to keep up with demand and remain efficient that require 2 people to operate it, then you should hire the 2 workers to do so in order to be in balance.

When your marginal physical product falls and thus your costs begin to rise, you need to add the necessary capital equipment or labor input to stop the diminishing returns. In figure 10-5 you can see at Point A that this firm added the necessary inputs, which brought average total cost down. But then after more time passes, as demand and thus output increases, and as more workers are added without a proportionate or appropriate addition of capital equipment, the diminishing returns are back. At that point (Point B), the addition of added capital is needed again. More added inputs then compel average total costs to decline again. Figure 10-5 shows only three examples of this, but there is no limit to how many times it can be done in order to keep ATC going down and down and down, depending upon your firm's circumstances.

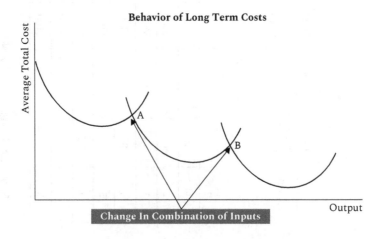

FIGURE 10-5 Economies of Scale

If you are able to do so, you are experiencing **economies of scale**. Economies of scale exist if your high scale of demand and production volume make it possible for you to make costs decline (or obtain economies) by the use of a firm's technology and/or other added capital and labor inputs that lead to a falling long-run average total costs as output increases. This process must continue as long as you can lower your average total costs by doing so. We want to keep average total costs at a minimum, as you can see with the curve to the right of Point B in figure 10-5, where the curve eventually dips to its lowest point. This is often possible because a firm may centralize the production of its products into one facility rather than producing in many small ones. Or, business can just be booming so much in one factory, that they simply expand it with these added inputs to keep average total cost falling.

Unfortunately, some firms aren't always able to make this happen. Sometimes, in spite of their efforts to keep average total costs on the decline after adding inputs, their average total costs decline, but never below a certain point. This is called **return to scale** or **constant return to scale** (figure 10-6).

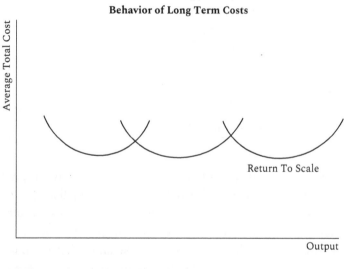

Behavior of Long Term Costs

FIGURE 10-6   Return to Scale

This can be caused by several circumstances. First, it may be that you can't seem to make your large or centralized plant or factory any more efficient than many smaller ones. Your volume may be just too low to reach your lower ATC objectives. It could also be because the market is limited in the area where your industry is located, and you can't seem to get the volume high enough to be able to make ATC fall as you would like. Restaurants, for example, are limited in the volume of sales they can make because people will only use their services if they are within a certain distance from them. Another cause can be issues within your operation that need to be resolved, such as office politics or top-heavy management. For many firms and industries, there is a limit to how much the addition of inputs can get

ATC to decline. The process of adding inputs to reduce ATC can sometimes simply run its course.

As a factory continues to attempt to reduce average total cost, it may even fail to achieve constant returns to scale. It may even get to the point where ATC will actually continue to rise in spite of attempts to use the appropriate combinations of labor and capital equipment inputs. This is called **diseconomies of scale** (figure 10-7).

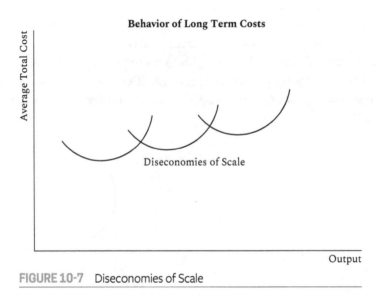

FIGURE 10-7   Diseconomies of Scale

At this point, many of the firm's management and workers are simply exploited to the max, where they are just losing their ability to be effective and efficient. It is usually accompanied by a lack of morale and a lot of burn out among managers and employees (Gregory 2005). There are some industries that also may have this problem because of experiencing an even smaller market potential. For example, physicians, photographers, and psychologists who have a small practice are limited to the number of hours they can work. They won't have a scale of volume that can readily utilize much in the way of added labor and capital equipment. They will see very little ability to keep average total costs going down with added inputs.

Figure 10-8 gives an idea of what can happen once a firm goes from enjoying economies of scale, to constant returns to scale, and then to diseconomies of scale.

Regardless of your circumstances, the goal of getting average total cost to fall is something that you must still try to achieve in order to be competitive in your market.

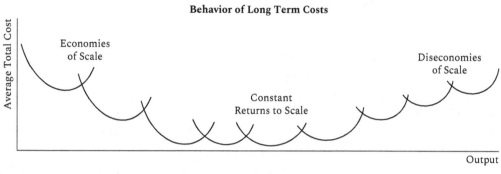

FIGURE 10-8 Behavior of Long-Term Costs

THE SHUTDOWN DECISION

There are some firms whose slow seasons are so slow that it may be in their interest to shut down until the busy season returns. For businesses such as ski resorts or summer camps, the decision is easy because you can't have a ski resort opened in the summer if there is no snow. You can't run a summer camp when, in fact, there is snow. In some cases, however, the decision is not so easy.

There are two problems you will have during a slow season. First, with your lower volume of sales, you can't buy your materials or goods in the higher quantities that would give you discounts. When you buy things on a larger scale, many vendors will give you a lower price per unit, but this is less likely to happen when business is slow and when you are thus buying fewer of such things. Second, you often have to lower your price to entice people to use your product or service during the off season. Therefore, you have two strikes against you: you have to charge lower prices and your variable costs are higher, thus squeezing your profit margin per sale, sometimes to the point of being negative or losing money on each sale. Many vacation spots have been found to do this. This is why we have spring break in America. Hotels in the southern, warmer climate lower their rates to get students to come down and spend their money in the spring when business for them is slow.

Therefore, economists recommend that you shut down your operation only if your total variable costs exceed total revenues. In other words, you must shut down if the price you must charge for each sale is lower than the variable cost you will pay for each sale.

Some may wonder why a firm should stay open at all during slow times. There are two reasons. First, closing your firm during the slow season could get your customers out of the habit of using your firm, especially if competitors remain open. However, the biggest reason is that you will always have to pay fixed costs, even if you are closed. During a shut down, you will likely still have to pay your property taxes, rent, insurance, and even some utilities. When you close your business during the winter, for example, you can't turn off the heat because pipes will likely freeze and burst.

If you still have to pay fixed costs, the sales you make (as long as they bring in revenue that exceeds variable costs) will pay for at least some of those fixed costs. For example, suppose you have fixed costs of $1,000 per month for your building. If you sell your goods for $6 each and your variable costs are $4 each, this would give you what is known as a **contribution margin** of $2 for each sale. Contribution margin is equal to your sale price minus your variable cost. In this case, that would be your sale price of $6 minus your variable cost of $4. You can take that $2 to begin to pay toward those fixed costs for each sale you make. Suppose you sell 400 items. If you multiply 400 times that $2, this would be $800 you can pay toward that $1,000 fixed cost. While your firm would still take a loss of $200 for the entire operation, as well as the cost of your time in keeping the operation open, it is better than losing the entire $1,000.

Therefore, continue to operate as long as total revenues are in excess of total variable costs in order to pay toward fixed costs.

CHAPTER 10 REVIEW

QUESTIONS TO THINK ABOUT

1. Explain why there at no fixed costs in the long run.
2. Using your own numbers, create your own scenario in a grid to calculate the major types of short-run costs.
3. What would you do if your firm could take advantage of economies of scale?
4. Describe what circumstances would make it better for you to shut down your operation during slow seasons.

TERMS TO KNOW

Average fixed cost (AFC)

Average variable cost (AVC)

Constant return to scale

Direct labor

Direct material

Diseconomies of scale

Economies of scale

Fixed costs

Law of diminishing returns

Marginal cost by worker

Marginal cost per unit of output (MC)

Marginal physical product

Mixed costs

Return to scale

Shutdown decision

Total variable costs

Variable costs

CHAPTER ELEVEN

Demand Curves, Marginal Revenue, Supply Curves, and Production Decisions of Each Competitive Market

IN PREVIOUS CHAPTERS, we have stated on many occasions that when you make your **production decision** you must set production at the point where marginal cost is equal to marginal revenue. This is an important concept to remember and by which a firm must operate. The problem is that each competitive market has unique attributes that must be considered in order to apply this principal. Those attributes and what you can do about them are the focus of this chapter.

PURE COMPETITION

In chapter 6, we discussed the concept of perfect or pure competition where the demand curve is flat because the sellers are not able to set their own prices. Instead, they must take the market price that is offered. As a result, the price they are paid will always be the same as their marginal revenue. Why? Because marginal revenue is the change in total revenue of your firm with the sale of one more of your goods. In the case of farming, for example, if you will be getting the same price for each unit of production, the marginal revenue will always be equal to the price. Therefore, the demand curve and the marginal revenue curve for a perfectly or purely competitive firm will be one and the same, as shown in figure 11-1. So, wherever the marginal cost curve intersects the demand curve, it is simultaneously intersecting the marginal revenue curve, and it is there that you should set production to maximize profits (see figure 11-1). In this case, the farmers should produce 5 bushels of corn.

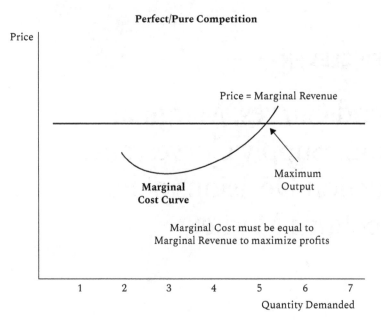

FIGURE 11-1 Perfect/Pure Competition Demand and Marginal Revenue Curves

Another thing that is unique about these firms is that their short-run supply curves and their marginal cost curves are also one and the same. Why? First of all, we repeat the major microeconomic proverb that to maximize profits, you must set production at the level where marginal cost is equal to marginal revenue. Suppose the farm represented in figure 11-2 produces corn, and that the price of corn rises. In this example, suppose the price has jumped from $3 per bushel of corn to $4. In figure 11-2, you can see that the demand curve would then move upward. Therefore, the new output should be set at six bushels of corn instead of five, because that is where the marginal cost curve and the marginal revenue curve now intersect. One way to look at this is that the price, being the same as marginal revenue, must be at least equal to marginal cost; hence, the marginal cost will determine the lower limit for an acceptable price. Thus, wherever the farmer sets production becomes the level of supply for the corn.

Therefore, the marginal cost curve is in fact the short-run supply curve for a perfectly competitive firm.

There is something else that is very important to note here. When the price charged by a firm changes, it will typically move demand along the demand curve. With pure or perfectly competitive firms, this does not apply, because price remains constant at all levels of demand. This is the only time that price alone will shift a demand curve.

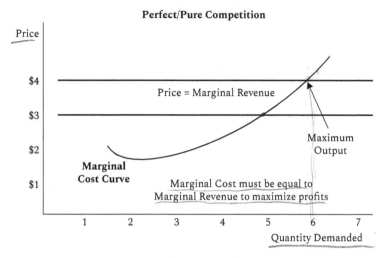

FIGURE 11-2 Perfect/Pure Competition Demand and Marginal Revenue Curves with Higher Prices

MONOPOLIES AND MONOPOLISTIC COMPETITION

With firms operating as monopolies or in markets with monopolistic competition, their marginal revenue curves are not the same as their demand curves—unlike what we saw earlier with firms that experience pure competition—because their demand curves are both downward sloping. Instead, the demand curve and the marginal revenue curve for these firms are split (see figure 11-3A). While the demand curve for monopolies and firms with monopolistic competition are the same shape, in many cases the monopoly's demand curve will likely be steeper because firms with less competition will usually experience price inelasticity.

As discussed in chapter 6, your marginal revenue tends to fall as your prices drop if you are not a firm that is purely or perfectly competitive as shown in figure 11-3A. The graph is reflecting the numbers shown in the upper left of that figure. Notice that the marginal revenue declines as the price drops by $1 per unit of demand. Marginal revenue eventually becomes negative; thus, the marginal revenue curve will fall below the *x* axis.

There is a false assumption that many make about monopolies. Many feel that if you are the only game in town, you can charge as much as you want for your goods. This is not true. Why? First, there is always a limit to how high you can set your prices. The income effect will keep people from buying your goods if your prices get to be too high. Second, you still have to have value in the product. If you are a monopoly in the cell phone business, for example, people are not going to pay $2,000 for your cell phones per month, because the value of any phone is just not that high. Most importantly, you really don't

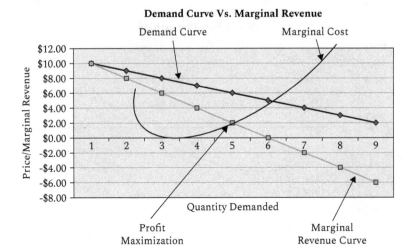

FIGURE 11-3A Monopoly and Monopolistic Competition Demand and Marginal Revenue Curves with Higher Prices

want to set prices too high, because you want your demand to be at a level where marginal cost is equal marginal revenue. If your price is too high, you may not accomplish this. In this case, as seen in figure 11-3A, if you set your price at $10, your quantity demanded would only be one unit, which does not maximize profits. The quantity demanded of five is what you need to do, because it is at this point that the marginal cost curve intersects the marginal revenue curve.

It is important to note here that every demand curve has its own accompanying marginal revenue curve. In the case of perfect or pure competition, the marginal revenue curve is the same as the demand curve as mentioned earlier. In the case of a monopoly or firms with monopolistic competition, the curve protracts out as the demand curve is no longer flat and as it begins to become steeper.

Figure 11-3B will show you that if the demand for a firm becomes perfectly inelastic, the marginal revenue curve eventually separates from the demand curve and will eventually only be a small point (Point X). This is because if you lower your price when your demand is perfectly inelastic, quantity demanded does not change. All you would do is reduce your marginal revenue by the amount at which you lower your price times the quantity demanded. In this example, when price drops by $1, the quantity demanded of 10 does not change. When price drops by an additional $1, the quantity demanded of 10 still does not change, but the revenue falls by $1 x 10 units of sale. In other words, marginal revenue is negative $10 each time there is a price decrease.

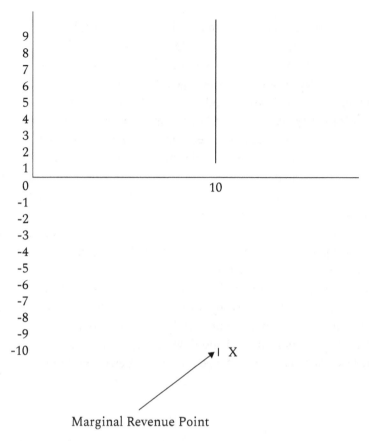

Marginal Revenue Point

FIGURE 11-3B Perfectly Inelastic Competition Demand and Marginal Revenue Curves with Higher Prices

OLIGOPOLIES

Oligopolies are much different. Why? Because they have two demand curves. In order to understand why, you have to recall that any actions that oligopolies take to increase demand will likely be met with swift action from their few competitors to counter those measures. As a result, they will have a demand curve that will reflect demand *before* their competitors' retaliation and then another curve that will reflect demand *after* their competitors' retaliation. Let's use the automotive industry as an example. Suppose one of the major automakers is charging $15,000 for one of their economy cars. Notice in figure 11-4 that such a price would give them a demand of one million cars. Now suppose they wish to lower the price to $12,000. Figure 11-4 will also show you that the price drop to $12,000 would cause the quantity demanded of their cars to jump from one million cars to 1.7 million cars, which is Point A in figure 11-4. Initially, the greater sales in cars would be good news. However, that level of increase of the quantity demanded would not last, because their competitors will likely ante up and meet that price drop. Quantity demanded would then slowly start to decline. This is why economists often say that the quantity demanded for oligopolies is sticky. They say this because demand initially goes up as prices decrease, but they slowly fall back, just as something sticky in your hand will come back to you if you throw it away. When this happens, the quantity demanded will not drop to its original level of one million cars. Why? Because even if the competition meets the firm's lower car prices, more cars will be purchased in the entire industry. More people could afford cars if all car makers lower their prices, and so quantity demanded would be higher for all car producers. In this example, when the retaliation of competitors kicks in, demand will fall back some, perhaps to Point B (between 1.5 million and 1.7 million cars).

Let's now assume that this same automaker decides to lower prices again. Demand will increase again and could likely jump to Point C, but it will then pull back again (to about Point D) once their competitors retaliate again.

After studying figure 11-4, it is now clear that you could connect the coordinates for quantity demanded before retaliation by competitors (Points A and C), and this would give you the demand curve for this automaker. But now there is a second demand curve. This curve is created by connecting the coordinates B and D, which represent sales after all of the retaliation by competitors has taken place. These two curves will intersect at Point X.

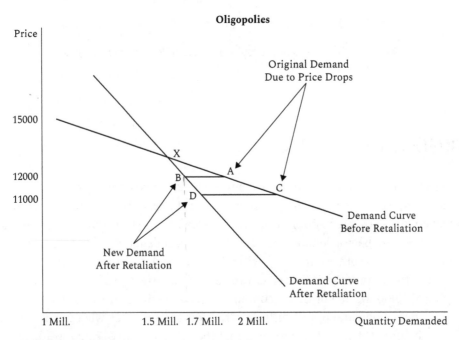

FIGURE 11-4   Oligopoly Competition Demand Curves

If you extract the demand curve where the two curves intersect at Point X, it will be kinked as you can see in figure 11-5, hence demand curves for oligopolies are kinked.

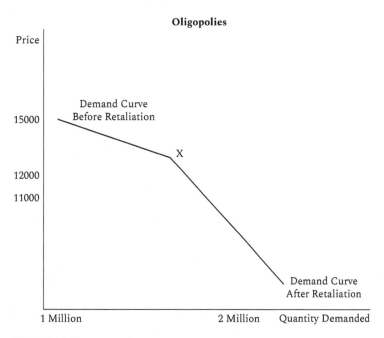

FIGURE 11-5 Oligopoly Competition Demand Kinked

The oligopoly demand curve is actually an integration of two curves that result from retaliation.

Now recall that every demand curve has its own, separate marginal revenue curve. Figure 11-6 shows the marginal revenue curves that could accompany each demand curve. This is a very important point. With two marginal revenue curves, you must now decide which one to use when you are looking for the intersection of the marginal cost curve with the marginal revenue curve when making the production decision. With oligopolies, therefore, the marginal revenue curve is also kinked and, in some cases, could have a gap. In this case, the red line in figure 11-6 shows where a gap in the two marginal revenue curves could exist. At that point, marginal revenue stops at Point L and then starts up again at Point M.

If we extract the marginal revenue curves, as we did the demand curves, you can see that together, they are also kinked. As you well know, marginal cost curves can be at different positions depending upon what combination of labor and capital you have. If the marginal cost curves are above or below the gap, the production decision as usual remains at the point of the intersection as you can see in figure 11-7. If the marginal cost curve falls anywhere inside that gap, the production decision would remain the same even if it moves up or down. This is because at the point when there is movement up or down inside the gap, marginal revenue is

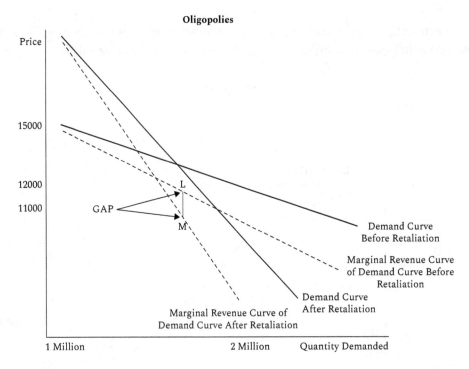

Oligopolies

FIGURE 11-6 Oligopoly Competition Demand and Marginal Revenue Curves Before and After Retaliation

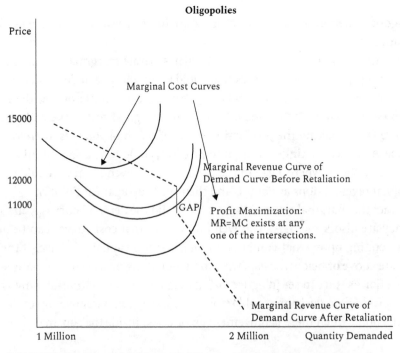

Oligopolies

FIGURE 11-7 Oligopoly Competition Marginal Revenue Curves before and after Retaliation with Marginal Cost and the Marginal Revenue Gap

unchanged. Movement inside the gap up or down does not move you anywhere, right or left, on the X axis (also seen in figure 11-7).

If the marginal cost curves move by changing the combination of inputs to attempt to get economies of scale, as mentioned earlier, they could intersect at different points of the combined marginal revenue curves, as also seen in figure 11-7. As long as those curves stay out of the gap, they will change the production decision, hence changing production to a new desired level of output.

CHAPTER 11 REVIEW

QUESTIONS TO THINK ABOUT
What strategies would you use to maximize profits in each of the major competitive markets? Why?

TERMS TO KNOW
Pure competition demand curve
Pure competition marginal revenue
Oligopoly demand curve
Oligopoly marginal revenue curve

Monopoly and monopolistic competition demand curve
Monopoly and monopolistic competition marginal revenue curve

Oligopoly

Regulation and Deregulation of Competition

NOW THAT WE have some ideas regarding the different levels of competition, this chapter will now look at how government regulates such competitive markets.

REGULATIONS

Not all regulations are bad. There are some that actually help businesses and markets to operate on a more even playing field. Therefore, there are times that people and firms actually ask for or demand regulations. This is referred to as **capture theory,** in which producers feel that regulation is in their interest. Politicians and government are usually ready and willing to supply the regulations that people or businesses seek or demand.

Government is also concerned about whether society gets all that it needs, including, but not limited to, food, shelter, clothing, and medical services. One way for this to happen is for government to make sure that our resources are used to the max, preventing any unnecessary shortages. This is called **social interest theory**, where government and society strive to make sure that efficient allocation of resources takes place.

One thing that can prevent the maximization of resources, and therefore create shortages, is limited competition and choices for the American public. As discussed earlier, monopolies are an example of this. Monopolies reduce competition and choices for consumers. Therefore, government attempts to dramatically reduce or even prevent them from coming into our economy. The government's actions in the past toward the prevention of monopolies has to some extent accomplished some social benefits. The first is that everyone has a better chance to have equal opportunity in a market. As also discussed before, the American dream is in danger if only a few firms have all the resources and capital and if others are unable to tap into markets that are dominated by huge monopolies. Second, government wants to make sure that there is

avg fixed cost ↓ when our prices stay stable

AT&T

ample supply of needed services, especially those needed by society. Monopolies prevent this, especially when they limit their output as they set marginal cost equal to marginal revenue. Third, by preventing the proliferation of monopolies, pricing is not as likely to be exploitive. Available resources don't do society any good if they are unaffordable.

A **natural monopoly** exists in a competitive market or industry when one firm can supply the entire market at a lower price than two or more firms can. This is often because their marginal cost is constant and fixed costs are large. A good example of this is in the telecommunications industry. Before the 1980s, AT&T owned and managed all the telecommunications networks in the United States. In 1984, the government forced it to break up, and the networks were opened and made available to competitors. Before that point, it was actually less costly for people to have only one telephone service which used one telephone network. Otherwise, a person would have had to own two phones to be able to use the service of each competitor. The cost of two phones is likely going to be higher than that of one. The government is okay with such situations where one provider keeps prices lower, but they still regulate those providers to make sure that needed services and goods are at the disposal of all and remain affordable

ANTITRUST LAWS

In order to prevent firms from conspiring to create monopolies, **the Sherman Act of 1890** was passed, making it a crime to conspire, or even attempt, to monopolize or restrain trade or commerce in the United States and/or any other foreign nations. It was authored in large part by **Senator John Sherman** of Ohio.

Laws such as the Sherman Act and other similar laws that followed its passage are called **antitrust laws** because corporate trusts are groups of businesses, corporations, and conglomerates that were put together over the years to acquire a large market share in a given market. It is this law that made unions illegal for many decades until the **Wagner Act of 1935** was passed. The courts felt that unions were attempting to monopolize the labor market (which will be discussed later). The laws are not enforced unless a firm's attempts to monopolize substantially reduce competition.

The problem was that the Sherman Act lacked teeth in many areas. Restraint of trade and removal of options and choices for the American consumers continued for many years in spite of the law. Firms that dominated many markets were still increasing their market shares even without buying up the competition. For example, one practice that took place was something called **predatory pricing,** where firms didn't buy up the competition in order to dominate a market. Instead, they crushed the competition by dramatically lowering their prices to levels that the competitors couldn't possibly match. Large firms could do this for two reasons. One reason is that they had a lot of money, and thus they could afford to lose money for a while from lower prices, just long enough until the competitors had to close their doors. Second, these firms usually raised prices in other locations of their operations that were not in the same market area as the competitors they were trying to destroy. This is called **price discrimination,**

FVK

as these firms charged higher prices to one market area while charging lower prices to others for the purpose of engaging in predatory pricing. Another thing that was happening was that representatives of big manufacturers of important and popular products sold in retail stores were going to the owners of those retail stores and demanding that their competitors' products be removed from the stores' shelves. If the stores didn't comply, the producers would no longer sell them their products. These products were popular and important products to those retailers, and thus they had little choice but to comply. This is called **exclusive dealing**. **Price fixing** also began to take place. Again, without buying out competitors and gaining a monopoly, some firms still managed to get the high prices they sought when they would band together to agree to keep prices artificially high, thus causing a lack of options and choices to the public. It also bothers government when consumers are forced to buy things that they don't want. It doesn't limit choices as a monopoly would, but forcing the hand of consumers is still something that can cause problems. **Tying agreements** are examples of this. These require people to buy something they don't want in order to be permitted to buy something that they do want. For example, if you are a new car dealer, you will be out of business if the car manufacturer you represent stops selling their cars to you. If then the manufacturer forces you to buy car models that are of low quality and unpopular in order for you to continue receiving the cars that you *do* need, a tying agreement has been imposed. All of these practices restrain trade and/or give the public fewer choices, and they were not addressed by the Sherman Act. Therefore, the government had to pass laws to prohibit them.

The Clayton Act of 1914 (and its two amendments, **the Robinson-Patman Act of 1936** and **the Celler-Kefauver Act of 1950**) was passed as a supplement to the Sherman Act to address these issues. It also created the **Federal Trade Commission (FTC)**, which is often nicknamed the "Fair Trade Commission" and charged with enforcing these antitrust laws.

In addition to what has already been stated, the laws also prohibit things such as requirement contracts (making a firm buy all of its needed items from one firm), territorial confinement (preventing a buyer from reselling outside a specified area), acquisition of a competitor's shares or assets (where the HHI is used), and becoming the head of a company's competing firm.

Those who do the things that are prohibited by these laws will only be challenged or charged with a crime by the government if their actions substantially change, disrupt, or impact their markets in a negative manner.

CHAPTER 12 REVIEW

QUESTIONS TO THINK ABOUT

1. Why does government feel the need to enforce antitrust laws?
2. Do you agree that they are needed?

TERMS TO KNOW

Capture theory

Celler-Kefauver Act of 1950

Clayton Act of 1914

Exclusive dealing

Federal Trade Commission (FTC)

Natural monopoly

Predatory pricing

Price discrimination

Price fixing

Robinson-Patman Act of 1936

Senator John Sherman

Sherman Act of 1890

Tying agreements

Wagner Act of 1935

CHAPTER THIRTEEN

A Closer Look at Labor

AT THIS POINT of the textbook, we will now take a closer look at three of the four different factors of production: land, labor, and capital. This chapter focuses specifically on labor.

Labor markets vary between different companies and industries, and even different sectors of the country. In many cases, workers must negotiate wages and employment conditions directly with their employers. Other workers are employed in a union shop, where a union organization will do all of the negotiating and bargaining for all of a firm's employees.

Sometimes a firm is a major employer in a geographical area where they hold a great deal of power. If workers in that area don't give them the service needed at a pay rate that the employer can live with, that employer may choose to move to an area where labor is cheaper and better. This is what some refer to as a **monopsony**. While a monopoly exists in a market where there is only one seller, a monopsony exists when there is only one buyer. They are not very common, but in a sense, large, major employers can be the only buyers *of* labor in a specific labor market. In some cases, most of the workers in an area like that are represented by a union, which becomes the only seller of the labor. Some would call this a **bilateral monopoly** when an arrangement exists when there is only one buyer and one seller in a market.

With labor, in given areas, it can be argued that a major employer could be a single buyer or one of very few buyers of given skills, thus giving the buyer (the employer) the advantage over the worker. Such employers will determine the wage rate and will pay the lowest it possibly can while still being able to attract productive labor.

SUPPLY AND DEMAND FOR LABOR

Just like there is a supply and demand curve for goods and services, there is also a supply and demand curve for labor. They too can have equilibrium, shortages, or a surplus. Figure 13-1 is an example of what the curves could look like.

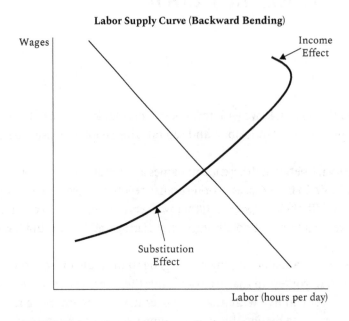

FIGURE 13-1 Labor Supply Curve (Backward Bending)

With the supply and demand of goods and services, the Y axis represents the prices of those goods. With the **labor demand curve**, we use wages in place of price as our independent variable on the Y axis. If wages required by workers increase, either because of minimum wage laws (more on that later) or because workers demand a certain level of pay before they will apply for given jobs, then the demand for labor hours will decrease. Employers simply can't make the profits they seek if the wages of their workers are too high, thus they either reduce their staff or move the operation altogether to an area where wages are lower (more on that later as well). It's important to note here that workers are only hired if business is good and if employers are in need of people to help produce the products demanded of the company. This is called **derived demand**. It means that the number of workers hired, or the number of labor hours demanded of workers, is derived from the amount of business a firm has. The demand for labor hours will only rise if businesses need their help to keep up with production to meet demand.

There are those who believe that more machinery, automation, and technology put people out of work. In reality, there are more jobs in our society today than there would be if we did not use machinery, automation, and technology. There are three reasons for this. First, machinery, automation, and technology aren't free. When businesses purchase machines, computers, and software, they create jobs in the companies that produce and sell them. Second, many American firms would have closed their doors by now without technology and machinery. We are in a global economy, and firms in other countries use them all the time. If we don't match their use of these things, costs of foreign competitors will be well below ours and we could never compete. Finally, businesses obtain technology not to put people out of work but to make them more productive. They want to get more units produced from the same number of workers, not the same amount of output from fewer workers. More output per worker keeps costs down so that your employer can stay in business.

It is also important to note here that not only do economists tell us that technology creates more, and not fewer, jobs, but those jobs pay more than the jobs of yesteryear. Using this technology requires skill that makes workers eligible for higher pay. Many workers who lose jobs to technology often lose them when they refuse to learn the skills needed to operate the technological capital equipment that is being used.

Supply of labor hours by workers is also very similar to that of the supply of goods and services, with two very important differences. First, wages are again put on the Y axis in place of price. Second, there is a point when the **labor supply curve** will bend backwards. Why? Figure 13-1 illustrates what happens when hourly wages rise to a certain point at which people will supply fewer labor hours to employers. For example, if you would be paid more and more per hour to work, you may gladly work extra hours to earn more income. However, there are those who will want to begin to take it easy and work less if hourly wages get very high. Especially with cases of older workers who are nearing retirement, they may want to begin to enjoy the benefits of their pay and work fewer hours. If their wage is high enough, they may put money aside, thus they would not then need as much money to live. They can also work fewer hours and still make a handsome living while enjoying life. This is called the **income effect**. This income effect is completely different from the income effect that was discussed in chapter 4, which explained the downward slope of the demand curve for goods and services.

The other part of the supply curve slopes upward until it reaches the point of the graph where it begins to bend backward. It slopes upward just like that of the supply curve for goods and services, but for a different reason. This is due to what is known as the **substitution effect**. This also must not be confused with the substitution effect that explains the demand curve for goods and services. This part of the curve is upward sloping as people will supply more hours of work as the wage per hour increases. This is due to the high opportunity cost of leisure that exists when higher wages are offered to workers. People have no remorse or guilt trips when they loaf if wages are low. But when wages in a given labor market go up, it becomes too costly to sit around and not cash in; therefore, workers will begin to substitute leisure for a high-paying job.

Each worker has their own labor supply curve, and the supply curve of the labor market is a combination of each of those curves. The labor hours that you are willing to supply at different wage rates may be much different than what others will supply.

LABOR DEMAND CURVE SHIFTS

Just as with supply and demand curves of goods and services, the labor supply and demand curves shift as well. Suppose a local employer has anywhere from 75 to 125 jobs to fill (or anywhere from 3,000 to 5,000 labor hours needed per week) while promising a wage of $14 per hour. If wages required by workers would fall to $13 per hour, the quantity demanded of labor hours would increase to 4,000 (or about 100 workers). If wages required by workers would fall to $12 per hour, the quantity demanded of labor hours would increase to 5,000 (or about 125 workers). Figure 13-2 shows what the demand curve for that firm would be for labor hours. A change in wages required by workers will move the quantity demanded of labor hours along the labor demand curve, just like prices will move the quantity demanded along the demand curve of goods and services.

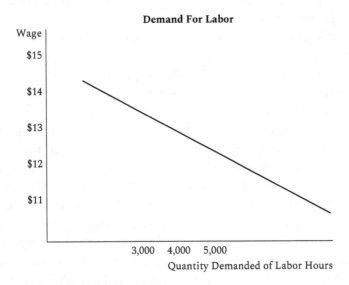

FIGURE 13-2   Demand for Labor

THE BOOMS AND BUSTS OF EMPLOYERS

Now suppose that this employer is now paying $14 per hour and business starts booming. Figure 13-3 shows that even if the wage they require does not change, the demand for labor hours will likely increase, going out, perhaps to Point A. If the current wage is $13, the increase in the employer's business could make the demand for labor hours increase out to Point B. In the same way, if the current wage is $12, the increase in the employer's business could make the demand for labor hours increase out to Point C.

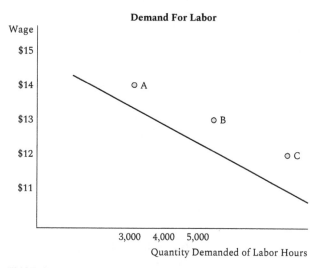

FIGURE 13-3   Demand for Labor (New Points)

If you connect coordinate points A, B, and C, you will have a new labor demand curve, thus the labor demand curve will shift out to the right when employers get a boost in demand for their products or services (figure 13-4). In chapter 4, the concept of how and why curves shift was explained in depth, and therefore we will not repeat the continuous repetition of that concept with each change in the determinants of demand of labor.

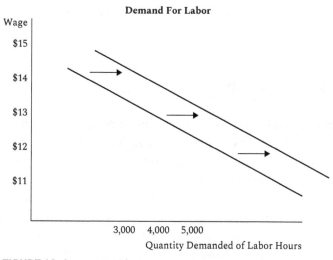

FIGURE 13-4   Demand for Labor (Shift Right)

Obviously therefore, if business dramatically declined (or goes bust) for the employer, the demand for labor curve would shift to the left (figure 13-5).

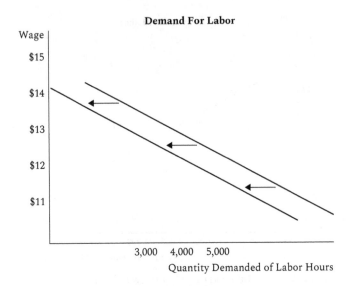

FIGURE 13-5   Demand for Labor (Shift Left)

ECONOMIC TIMES

It is important to note here, therefore, that economic times will drive the supply and demand for labor. A recession will shift the curve left, because bad economic times will cause businesses to lose their need or demand for labor. A booming economy, therefore, will obviously shift the curve to the right.

NUMBER OF EMPLOYERS

Another thing that can shift the labor demand curve out or to the right is the number of employers in a given vicinity. As more employers seek to locate in those areas, demand for labor hours will shift out or to the right, while other areas where employers close or vacate will see their labor demand curve shifting left.

Businesses are inclined to move to areas where they feel that labor costs, taxes, and regulations are suitable to them. Many local governments often create what is called an **enterprise zone**, where regulations and taxes are lower for new businesses that wish to locate there. When taxes are lowered to entice an employer to move to a given town or county, they are called **tax abatements**. They are offered with the hope that the added tax revenue collected by government from the added income from those working there will pay for those abatements. In some of those cases, the tax abatements offered are only in place for a finite period of time. If civic leaders continue to be successful toward enticing firms to locate in their community, the labor demand curve will shift outward. The opposite is also true. If firms leave communities in search of better opportunities to save in labor costs and taxes, the demand for labor curve in those labor market areas will shift to the left.

THE MARGINAL REVENUE PRODUCT OF LABOR

If an area tends to have a large number of skilled workers, there will likely be a large demand for labor in that area, even if workers require a higher wage. As mentioned earlier, you don't want to pay a worker more than the revenue (or the marginal revenue product) that they generate for your firm. Higher-skilled workers will be more likely to make that happen. Therefore, if organizations in your area steadily increase the skills of workers by aggressive training and education initiatives, the labor demand curve is likely to shift outward again in that area.

LABOR SUPPLY CURVE SHIFTS

Using the same principles of this text that describe the shifting of supply curves with goods and services, with reductions being reflected by shifts to the left and increases reflected by shifts to the right, let us look at what causes shifts of the labor supply curve.

As with the labor demand curve, wages will move quantity of labor hours supplied along the labor supply curve. However, there are determinants of labor supply that will shift the curve.

ATTITUDES OF LABOR TOWARD LEISURE, INCOME, AND WORK

When leisure is more popular, the labor supply curve will shift to the left as people would rather relax than to work and earn income as shown in figure 13-6.

However, if the need for work and income and the attitude toward them put a better value on them, or if the value of leisure is diminished, more people would look for jobs. The labor supply curve would then shift out, or to the right as shown in figure 13-7A. There are geographical areas, for example, that are popular for those who wish to retire. The attitude toward leisure in those areas is very positive and not very good toward work. Retirees often need jobs to keep them active, but not jobs that are stressful, require physical strength, or require long hours. As those attitudes persist or grow in such areas, the labor supply curve there will continue to shift to the left.

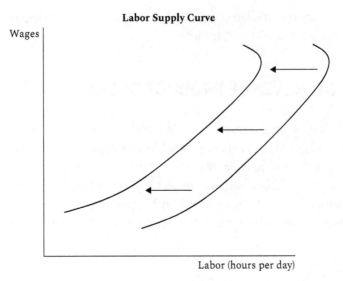

FIGURE 13-6   Labor Supply Curve (Shift Left)

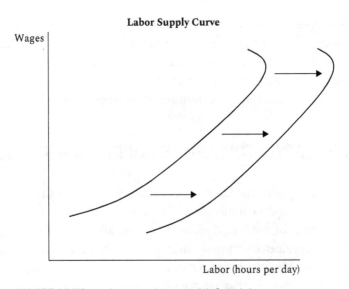

FIGURE 13-7A   Labor Supply Curve (Shift Right)

WEALTH

As people become wealthier, they can live off of their wealth. This is obviously what happens when people take many years to build a retirement with their savings and investments. Again, there are geographical areas that are popular for those who wish to retire. The people who live in these areas rely heavily on their wealth, and it is a major determinant of labor supply in those areas. As their wealth increases, fewer people look for work, and the labor supply curve will shift left (refer again to figure 13-6). The opposite is true. During bad economic times, or when government raises corporate tax rates, the value of stocks will decline in value and in the dollar amount of dividends they pay. Dividends are derived from net profits after taxes of corporations around the world. When that happens, retirees, or those depending upon dividends from their already-accrued wealth, will have to seek work when dividends from retirement accounts decline. In the meltdown of the stock market in 2008 and 2009, there were many retirees who had to find jobs just to buy groceries as their income from their stocks fell, as did the value of those stocks. Some lost their retirements altogether. The labor supply curve shifted to the right during that time (refer again to figure 13-7A). Some retirement accounts are set up to pay out a fixed amount of income to retirees regardless of the volatility of the stock market. Many retirees choose to settle for those lower income amounts in order to maintain stability in their retirement incomes, thus the labor hours supplied of these retirees aren't changed by the stock market.

GOVERNMENT RELIEF

During the 1960s and 1970s, government programs for the poor, such as welfare, unemployment benefits, and social security, were very high. When people lost their jobs, they had some breathing room, and many did not immediately seek new employment. When such benefits increase, the labor supply curve will likely be shifted left (figure 13-6).

Therefore, when government spending on these programs was reduced over the decades, the supply curve for labor shifted out or to the right. In 1995, Congress passed the **Welfare Reform Act**. It limited the time that workers would be eligible for welfare and required welfare recipients to find work within a certain period of time. This shifted the labor supply curve out or to the right (once again referring to figure 13-7A).

EXPECTATIONS

Supply for labor can be affected by the expectations of income, consumption, and prices of the labor force in the future. For example, if people expect that income or compensation for their labor will decrease, they may want to supply less of their time to the labor market because they don't expect ample compensation for their work, thus the curve would then shift to the left (figure 13-6). If workers feel that employers are likely to be paying more for the foreseeable future, they will likely be willing to supply more labor hours, and thus the labor supply curve will shift outward, or to the right (figure 13-7A).

If workers expect that they will do less consumption in the near future, they may want to supply less of their time to the labor market, because they simply would not likely need the added income. This will shift the labor supply curve to the left (figure 13-6). This is especially true for those who work extra hours during the week to be able to buy things that they cannot afford with their regular salaries.

If potential workers expect prices to remain stable, they will likely feel less need to work extra hours, thus they will supply less of their time to the labor market. This will shift the labor supply curve to the left (figure 13-6). However, if they expect prices to be on the rise, they will supply more of their labor hours to keep up with anticipated inflation, which would shift the labor supply curve to the right (figure 13-7A).

Therefore, if workers expect less income or compensation for their work, if they expect that they will likely consume or spend less, and/or if they expect lower prices to prevail in our economy in the near future, these expectations will usually cause the labor supply curve to shift to the left. The opposite is also true.

POPULATION

If there is a decline in population, the labor supply curve typically shifts left and the opposite is true. Obviously fewer people living in a country or a community means that fewer qualified workers will be available to take care of a firm's needs. Population shifts can occur when firms move out of a community, and workers often follow those employers to their new locations. Others will leave their region in search of more opportunities for work, if enough employers close their businesses, or leave a vicinity. There are other reasons for shifts in a population, and they will certainly determine the supply of labor.

TAXES

High taxes will likely make workers want to supply less of their time to the labor market. This is the same thing that happens with producers, as discussed before. In this respect, workers are no different. Higher taxes have the same effect as lower wages, as they reduce the reward for a person's work, shifting the labor supply curve to the left. Lower taxes will conversely, therefore, shift the labor supply curve outward, or to the right (figure 13-7A).

EMPLOYER INCENTIVES

Some people want to supply their labor, but they can't. If they have children or loved ones at home who need their care or attention, they are unavailable to work at an employer's location. Sometimes employers will offer opportunities to them such as flextime, daycare, transportation, or telecommuting in order to make a job more practical for them. **Flextime** is an arrangement with employers that allows workers to pick the times they want to work as long as they accomplish the objectives that the employer requires. By doing this, workers can get children to school and take care of personal needs that happen in the middle of the day that would otherwise draw them away from a job that required them to work specific hours each day. **Daycare facilities** are also offered to those who cannot afford to pay a babysitter or home health care service to watch their children or loved ones while they work. Thus, if there is an abundance of such programs, more workers will become available, as they feel that accepting employment is more practical. **Transportation** may even be offered to those who have no means of getting to work or if they have physical challenges that keep them from being able to drive themselves to work. **Telecommuting** is a tool used by many employers who can offer jobs to workers who want to work in their homes. If the jobs can be performed online or if the nature of the jobs are such that it is not necessary for the workers to work in a given location, once again, those jobs become more practical for those who have no transportation or have to stay at home to care for loved ones. All of these initiatives by employers will shift the labor supply curve to the right (figure 13-7A).

EQUILIBRIUM FOR LABOR

Equilibrium for labor also becomes a factor in this market, just as it does for goods and services. When wages are driven up—again, whether it is because of high minimum wage laws, or for whatever reason—it can cause a surplus of labor if wages rise above the point of equilibrium (figure 13-7B). A surplus of labor is not good for workers. In the context of goods and services, it creates warehouses full of merchandise that is difficult to sell. In the context of labor, it means that some people will not be hired. In fact, it could lead to layoffs of existing workers. Just like a surplus of goods and services requires vendors to lower their prices, sometimes workers must begin to accept lower wages in order to be hired or to keep their jobs.

In the early 1980s, such an idea was initially dismissed, especially by workers in union shops. However, labor and management of various firms found that they could begin to negotiate wage concessions and profit sharing. Many workers agreed to receive profit sharing in return for such wage concessions.

What about **minimum wage laws**? They are in effect across the country, and they have been effective toward getting a decent wage for workers over the decades. Many economists believe, however, that they can have the same effect as a price floor where surpluses then cannot self-correct as was discussed in chapter 5. This doesn't only affect those who will take a wage that is lower than the minimum wage. A few states around the country have their own minimum wage laws that are higher than that of the federal level. Other states have tried to pass such laws without success, while still others have passed them only to have the laws struck down when they were challenged in the courts. In those cases, it is argued that labor surpluses will remain intact if workers cannot legally accept wages low enough that will get the wages back to the equilibrium level.

One more thing to note here is that federal minimum wage laws only affect firms doing business on an interstate level. If you are a small firm and if the activities of your business do not cross state lines, the federal laws don't apply to you. This is the reason that some states have their own minimum wage laws, in which case no firm can legally escape paying a minimum wage to their workers.

Politicians who have opposed minimum wage laws have not necessarily been opposed to the cause of the worker, especially if those laws are causing wages to rise too quickly. They cite the demand curve for labor, arguing that higher minimum wages cause a loss of jobs as quantity demanded for labor falls with legal requirements of higher wages. Some argue that a good wage for a job is no good if you can't get a job due to the higher wage that is required. Minimum wage laws are also very ineffective during times when the economy is booming and when we are experiencing full employment. During such times, employers experience a shortage of qualified workers that they can hire, and thus they often raise wages above the minimum wage levels.

A shortage of labor exists when wages are below equilibrium (Figure 13-7B). This is good news for workers, as worker shortages are often remedied by employers offering higher wages. Worker shortages also increase the likelihood that you will be hired quickly if you are looking for a job. This is typical when the economy is reaching or is at full employment and applicants for jobs, especially minimum wage jobs, are scarce. Employers also will take measures such as providing perks to those workers such as transportation to work, added sick days, personal days, vacation time, and some benefits to entice them to apply for such jobs.

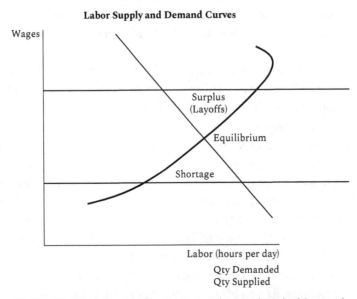

FIGURE 13-7B   Labor Supply and Demand Curve (Surplus/Shortage)

WAGE ELASTICITY OF LABOR

Just as there is elasticity of supply in goods and services, there is also that same effect in labor supply and demand.

If we are having boom times, higher wages don't have as much of an impact on demand for labor as they do during a recession. The reason for this is that during boom times, applicants for jobs have less competition for those jobs. But when a recession is in full force, the competition for those jobs becomes very fierce and the elasticity of demand becomes very high. This is the same as that of goods and services, as competition (whether it is low during good economic times or high during a recession) will indeed drive price elasticity of demand for goods and services. It will also be affected by the nature of the jobs in question. For example, a physician's **wage elasticity of demand** (the level of change in demand for labor derived from a change in wages) will be much lower than that of a person whose job skills are very low, because there is a shortage of those who are qualified to do medical work and it is a very much needed service. People or clinics will simply have to bite the bullet and pay the higher rate when physicians require higher wages. On the other hand, during recessions there are typically many applicants for jobs that require few skills. If they demand a higher wage, they will simply lose their jobs to those who do not.

As far as **wage elasticity of supply**, it differs between people of given demographics, such as current income levels, age groups, family status, and the need for job security. For example, a teenage worker may be inclined to move from job to job as the wages offered increase by only a few dollars per hour, thus supplying their labor hours to you if you offer them a slightly higher wage. But as they get older and have a family, they are less inclined to change jobs unless the prospective employer is offering some level of job security with their offer of a higher wage. The older some people get, the more reluctant they are to leave an existing employer and to burn the bridges with that employer where they may have worked for many years. There is a risk when you change jobs. When you go to a job that offers a higher wage, it is possible that you could lose that job soon after you are hired. Therefore, as people's demographics change, many will not change jobs unless the wage offered is significantly higher than what they are being paid now. Such a higher wage would be demanded by the worker to justify the risk of a job change.

THINGS THAT DRIVE HIRING COSTS AND HIRING CONDITIONS

When hiring, you have only a limited number of human resources from which to choose.

First, you can seek those who are out of work. A person experiencing **cyclical unemployment** is one who has been unemployed due to bad economic times. This type of unemployment exists when the business or economic cycle is experiencing low gross domestic product (GDP). A **business** or **economic cycle** is one that can peak at prosperity (or a boom time with full employment), or it can fall to a deep recession. Please look at figure 13-8. The blue line represents the growth and decline of GDP mentioned in chapter 2 that changed dramatically between the 1930s and the 1940s, and it still changes to this day. When it falls, there are layoffs, and workers experience cyclical unemployment because they lost their jobs when the economic cycle was not in a boom time or was not at full employment. Those experiencing cyclical unemployment are the easiest to hire because they are more anxious to get back to work. They may still have the skills you need, and they may be willing to work for a lower wage to get back to work quickly. Then there are those who are experiencing **frictional unemployment**. They could be out of work even during boom times. They are not as aggressively seeking work, and they may even have a job lined up but are still looking for something better until that new job begins. If you attempt to hire them and they are not as adamant about being hired, you may have to offer them more money to entice them to apply for your open position. Or, you may have to pay more for their labor as they may already be expecting a higher wage at a job they have lined up. Those experiencing **structural unemployment** could also be out of work even during boom times because they lack the skills that employers need. If you hire them, you may have to offer them a great deal of training, and it may take a significant amount of time before they become productive for you.

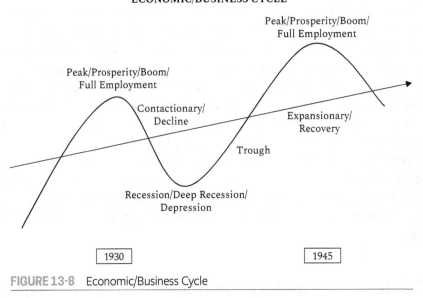

FIGURE 13-8   Economic/Business Cycle

You could also encourage those who are currently working for another firm to apply for your position openings. However, you must first make sure that you are not breaking laws by doing so. If you hire an employee from a competitor, it is illegal to do so if that employee has knowledge about your competitor's operations that you are not entitled to know. It is also difficult in that you have to truly offer a higher wage to them, because, as mentioned earlier, workers are very leery of leaving a job where they have built up a relevant degree of job security and status.

You can hire those who are currently in your firm. It is important to note, however that doing so requires you to then hire someone to replace them within your firm. It also limits the reservoir of skills from which you must choose when filling positions in your firm, whereas looking outside your firm for new workers gives you greater skill possibilities from which to choose.

You can also recruit labor from those who are currently entering the job market for the first time. High school or college graduates are great prospects in that regard, except that many may lack the experience you need. Recruitment can happen at aggressive job fairs and in cooperation with job placement programs in such schools.

There are also those who are willing to work a second job in the evenings or on weekends. Thus, you can recruit them without requiring them to leave their existing situation. This doesn't work, of course, if the times of day you need workers to work conflict with their existing work schedules.

Another thing to remember is that laws have existed in our country ever since the passage of the **Fair Labor Standards Act of 1938**, which outlaw the hiring of children (except for theatrical jobs or home-owned farms). The law also requires employers to pay time and a half wages (150 percent of the existing wage rate) to workers if they work more than forty hours in a given week, depending upon their status in the firm. Employees who are paid a salary are usually exempt from receiving overtime pay, while wage earners are nonexempt from it.

Skill level needed and supply and demand for that skill is also a factor, as mentioned earlier. Higher skills needed and higher demand for those workers drives up the price or wage that you must offer such workers.

UNIONIZATION

Seniority drives the level of wages, and it will also drive your decisions as to who will be hired in a given position in union shops. Seniority is often what rules in union shops, and the wages are already preset by a negotiated contract. In many cases union shops also require employers to first promote workers who have worked for their organizations the longest, regardless of their job performance and qualifications. Union contracts require seniority to be the driving force deciding which workers will be let go during bad economic times or rehired when economic times are good again.

In 1935, the **Wagner Act** was passed. It was also known as the **National Labor Relations Act**. It set up what is now known as the **National Labor Relations Board (NLRB)**. The act of having a union is called **collective bargaining**, because it sets up a system where each worker need not negotiate the pay or conditions of their jobs individually with an employer. Instead, the bargaining is done collectively for all of the workers in the organization who are represented by that union's negotiators. As mentioned earlier, until the law was passed, joining a union was deemed by the courts as being in violation of antitrust laws, as they felt it was an attempt by workers to monopolize the labor market. In those days, belonging to a union was not a criminal act, but any contract that a union negotiated with a firm was simply not legally enforceable. If the firms failed to live by the contract guidelines, the union members could not use the court system to force them to comply.

When the law was passed, it set down guidelines for employers to follow as workers began to organize unions. It established the process by which an election could be held by workers to determine whether they wanted a union to represent them or not. Also, the law made it clear that employers are not to interfere with the process of unions organizing. If they do, it could be considered an **unfair labor practice**. Employers are not allowed to intimidate those who are in favor of organizing a union. For example, if it is proven that an employer threatened to fire workers because they are in some way involved with organizing a union or wanting to join a union, this is considered an unfair labor practice. If an employer threatens to cut wages or threatens to make things difficult for workers if they vote in favor of starting a union, or if management does anything that would taint the outcome of a union election, the National Labor Relations Board would rule on what the penalty for the employer would be. It could lead to the employer's forfeiting the election, which would automatically put the union in the organization for a set period of time. Once a union is put in place in any organization, it is very difficult for leaders of those organizations to compel workers to vote the union out.

If a union is voted in and can begin to represent the workers, there are several arrangements that can exist. The first is called a **closed shop**. This exists if a firm will only hire a worker if that worker agrees to belong to the union once they are hired. In other words, the hiring of a worker is conditional upon the worker agreeing to join the union prior to being hired. This arrangement, however, was outlawed in large part by what are called **right-to-work laws**, which will be discussed shortly.

A **union shop** is more common, and workers are not hired upon condition that they will agree to join the union once hired. However, they usually must join the union within a specified time after being employed there. Many argue that this ultimately has the same effect as a closed shop, unless the job in question is perhaps only a summer job that will not last beyond the date where the worker would have to join the union.

In **agency shops**, workers don't have to join the union at any time but must pay union dues as if they were in the union, because it is believed that said workers benefit from the union's negotiations of higher wages. **Union dues** are what each union member must pay the union organization for their work and expenses to maintain union activity within an organization. The only difference, therefore, is that if the union goes on strike during a contract **impasse** (when a contract agreement is in a stalemate and workers refuse to work), nonunion workers would not have to go on strike along with the union workers. It is, however, very difficult for such workers to "cross a picket line" and go to work for that firm each day when a strike is taking place. As union workers engage in demonstrations and picketing outside a workplace, it is very intimidating to walk past those workers and continue to work and draw wages. If more workers continue to work during a strike, making things appear to be as business as usual, workers are less likely to be successful in motivating management to agree to their terms. Union workers who strike do not get paid until the strike is over and they return to work.

An **open shop** exists when workers who decide they don't want to join the union still benefit from the wages and working conditions negotiated by the union, but they do not have to pay union dues.

Lastly, the **maintenance of membership** arrangement is such that workers for that organization who wish to remain as nonunion workers will pay no dues and must negotiate their own wages. The first two of these union arrangements, the closed shop and union shop, are the most desired by union leaders.

Unionization attempts to engage in what is known as **exclusion**, which attempts to keep workers who are willing to work cheaper out of the work force. Unions are always willing to help workers in any organization to start a union if they feel that the workers are not being treated fairly by their employers, particularly in the areas of pay rates, hiring and firing decisions, working conditions, and the level of participation that workers may have in the making of any major decisions within an organization. Therefore, unionization within an organization specifically drives hiring and firing decisions in these areas. Firing is also addressed, as union workers fired for misconduct or incompetence can initiate a process in which union representatives will be deeply involved to represent them, making sure that no worker is fired without just cause.

The **Taft Hartley Act of 1947** was passed, according to some, to create a balance in labor laws. It set up guidelines that union organizers must also follow while trying to form or maintain a collective bargaining unit. It declared that some conduct can be considered an unfair labor practice by union representatives. For example, it considers it to be an unfair labor practice on the part of the union if there is coercion of workers to join a union.

Both the Wagner Act and the Taft Hartley Act require that both labor and management within an organization bargain in good faith. If there is a time when either labor or management is not as eager to settle a labor contract dispute, they cannot just refuse to negotiate, nor can they make demands that are unreasonable. The NLRB is often asked to decide what conduct may be deemed as failure to bargain in good faith.

LABOR UNION SUPPLY

The labor supply in the United States is one that can be broken down into two categories: unionized workers and nonunionized workers. Workers are often displaced from the unionized market when they lose their jobs during bad economic times, or when unionized shops close or move away. When this happens, they often seek work in places that pay a lower wage to increase their chances of finding work. They often find these jobs in nonunionized markets, thereby shifting the nonunion supply of labor curve to the right (figure 13-9A). In the same way, the supply for unionized workers would shift to the left (figure 13-9B).

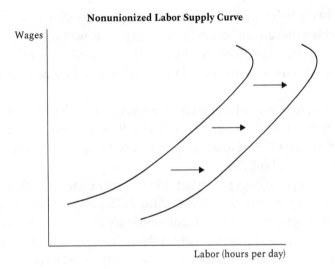

FIGURE 13-9A   Nonunionized Labor Supply Curve (Shift Right)

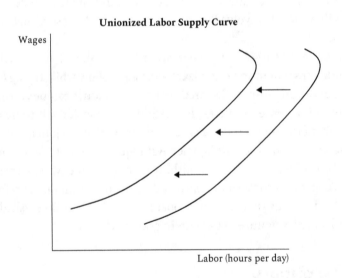

FIGURE 13-9B   Unionized Supply Curve (Shift Left)

IMPASSE

In labor/management impasses over contracts, usually both labor and management will suffer when work stoppages exist, such as a strike. When workers strike, they don't get paid. If they get an extra dollar per hour after negotiations, sometimes the wages lost from the strike take many years to regain from the wage increase, especially after factoring in the cost of income taxes. Some strikes have lasted many months, costing workers thousands of dollars in lost wages. Suppose, for example, that you lose in excess of $4,000 in lost wages from a strike. If you receive a $1 per hour wage increase from the renegotiated contract, you would have to work at least 4,000 hours to recoup that money. If you work 40 hours per week, you would have to work 100 weeks, or nearly two years, to get back the lost wages from the strike. Employers too will suffer, not only from the bad publicity that can exist if workers make their issues public but also from the business lost during those work stoppages. It is usually better for both labor and management to resolve disputes quickly.

MARGINAL FACTOR COST

The more workers you need or demand, the higher will be your **marginal factor cost**. With labor being a factor of production, the added cost you have in labor is driven by how much labor you need. Figure 13-10 shows, for example, that if you need more workers, you must offer wages that will encourage them to apply to work for you. If you offer only $1 per hour for workers, no one in this day and age will likely apply. Even at the rate of $3 or $4 per hour, the number of hours supplied are very low and certainly are not even in compliance with minimum wage laws. Workers who accept such wages would have to be very desperate for work. If you need more hours than that from workers, you must raise the wage. Suppose, in this example, that you are the employer shown in figure 13-10 and you need 300 hours of labor supplied. According to the labor market in your area shown in figure 13-10, you would need to offer a wage of $9 per hour. Your total wage cost (or total labor factor cost) would be $2,700 ($9 × 300 hours). Now suppose that your business gets better and your needs for more labor increases to 800 hours of labor supplied. You will then need to pay $10 per hour to attract workers to work that many hours, bringing your factor cost to $8,000 ($10 × 800 hours). That is $5,300 higher than what the total wage or factor cost would have been if you only needed 300 hours. Therefore, your marginal factor cost (or the change in your cost of the factor of production of labor) would be $5,300.

Scenario	Wage Rate/ Hour	×	Quantity of Labor Supplied (Workers Per Hour)	Total Wage Cost	Marginal Factor Cost (Per Labor-Hour)
A	$ –		0	$ –	
B	$ 1.00	×	0	$ –	
C	$ 2.00	×	0	$ –	$ –
D	$ 3.00	×	1	$ 3.00	$ 3.00
E	$ 4.00	×	3	$ 12.00	$ 9.00
F	$ 5.00	×	4	$ 20.00	$ 8.00
G	$ 6.00	×	10	$ 60.00	$ 40.00
H	$ 7.00	×	30	$ 210.00	$ 150.00
I	$ 8.00	×	100	$ 800.00	$ 590.00
J	$ 9.00	×	300	$ 2,700.00	$ 1,900.00
K	$ 10.00	×	800	$ 8,000.00	$ 5,300.00
L	$ 11.00	×	1000	$ 11,000.00	$ 3,000.00

FIGURE 13-10   Marginal Factor Cost

TAXES AND EFFICIENCY

As mentioned earlier, if income tax rates go higher, the incentive for people to work is diminished and the labor supply curve for all employers will be shifted to the left. It is important, therefore, to have a basic understanding of how the tax system works. Many years ago, if a person earned income above a certain level, that person's tax rate would increase, and the government would retroactively charge that higher rate to *all* of their income. The problem was that such a person could feasibly get lower net pay (income after they paid their taxes) even if they worked more hours and had earned more money. This is illustrated in figure 13-11A, where the person earned $1,000 more in wages but netted $150 less in net pay during that year after paying income taxes.

Wage	Tax Rate	Taxes	Income After Taxes
$19,000	15%	$2,850	$16,150
$20,000	20%	$4,000	$16,000

FIGURE 13-11A   Old Retroactive Tax Rate System

This is because the person was taxed at a lower rate of 15 percent until they earned income at the level of $20,000, when the tax rate increased retroactively to 20 percent (tax rates in figure 13-11A are pure estimates of state and national rates). This required the person to pay $4,000 in taxes after earning the $20,000 rather than paying $2,850 in taxes after earning $19,000. As you can see, when you subtract the taxes from the income at each level, the net income after taxes after earning the higher income of $20,000 is $150 below the level of what was netted at the $19,000 level.

In America, we now use what is called a **marginal tax rate system**. The marginal tax rate system only increases your tax rate on the money that you have earned beyond a certain point. In figure 13-11B, you can see an example of what the rates were for a single person in years past using the marginal tax rate system.

Marginal Tax Rate System

Income From	To	Marginal Tax Rate	Base Tax	Added Tax	Income Examples	Tax
0$	$2,650	0.0%	$0			$0
$2,650	$9,800	10.0%	$0	+ 0.1 × Income Exceeding 2650	$5,000	$235
$9,800	$31,500	15.0%	$715	+ 0.15 × Income Exceeding 9800	$10,000	$745
$31,500	$69,750	25.0%	$3,970	+ 0.25 × Income Exceeding 31500	$35,000	$4,845
$69,750	$151,950	28.0%	$13,533	+ 0.28 × Income Exceeding 69750	$75,000	$15,003
$151,950	$328,250	33.0%	$36,549	+ 0.33 × Income Exceeding 151950	$170,000	$42,505
$328,250	$999,999	35.0%	$94,728	+ 0.35 × Income Exceeding 328250	$350,000	$102,340

FIGURE 13-11B   Marginal Tax Rate System

With the tax structure like what you see here, you'll note that your workers will pay no tax on the first $2,650 that they earn per year. The money they earn between $2,650 and $9,800 is taxed at a rate of 10 percent. Rather than you having to figure out what the taxes are at each level and then adding them up, you can simply find the bracket in question and then add the taxes from the previous brackets to the taxes paid in this existing one. For example, suppose your workers earn $35,000 per year. This is between $31,500 and $69,750. To compute their income tax, you first find the **base tax** (which is found by adding the total taxes paid at each level previous to the one you are in now) as shown in figure 13-11B. This would be $3,970. In addition to that, you will see that at that level of income, your workers will pay 25 percent on any income above $31,500. This is found by taking their income of $35,000 and subtracting $31,500. This would be $3,500. That $3,500 would then be multiplied by 25 percent. This would come to $875. When you add that $875 to the base tax of $3,970, this would give you a tax of $4,845 as seen in figure 13-11B.

CHAPTER 13 REVIEW

QUESTIONS TO THINK ABOUT

1. What are you views about the labor laws? If you are a worker, do you feel that they are fair for the workers? If you hope to be an entrepreneur, do you feel that they are fair for managers or business owners?
2. What conduct is deemed as an unfair labor practice for workers to commit, and what laws define them?
3. What conduct is deemed as an unfair labor practice for management to commit, what laws define them?

TERMS TO KNOW

Agency shop
Bilateral monopoly
Business cycle
Closed shop
Collective bargaining
Cyclical unemployment
Derived demand
Economic cycle
Equilibrium for labor
Exclusion
Frictional unemployment
Income effect
Labor demand curve
Labor supply curve
Maintenance of membership

Marginal factor cost
Marginal tax rate system
Minimum wage laws
Monopsony
National Labor Relations Act of 1935
National Labor Relations Board
Right-to-work laws
Structural unemployment
Substitution effect
Taft Hartley Act of 1947
Unfair labor practice
Wage elasticity of labor
Wagner Act
Welfare Reform Act of 1995

CHAPTER FOURTEEN

A Closer Look at Capital

NOW THAT WE have a firm understanding of labor issues, the focus in this chapter will now shift to that of purchases of plants and capital equipment.

To get more plant or building space and capital equipment, it takes capital dollars. This chapter will show you the two roles you will play in getting capital equipment if you wisely raise and use your capital dollars.

When you buy capital equipment, in some cases there is also the need to expand plant space to accommodate the added machinery. Before you move forward, however, you will need to make sure that doing so will bring you added profits that will be a good enough return for the investment you make. This is known as the **investment decision**. To maximize profits, a firm should increase its plant size and use more capital equipment only if the profits from the marginal revenue product from that expansion of plant and added capital exceeds the investment price of buying them. These profits must exceed investment costs at a rate that is acceptable, just as it would be for any investment. If you buy a stock, for example, you must get dollar returns from that stock that exceed what you paid for it, and the return rate on those profits must be acceptable depending upon how risky this purchase will be. Higher risk requires a higher rate of profit returns from any investment. This principal is just as true for buying added plant space and added capital equipment.

For our purposes, from this point on we will call this process **capital equipment purchases (CEPs)** with the understanding that buildings and real estate are commonly included in the mix.

Remember, capital equipment must be purchased when needed in order to maximize output and marginal physical product. You don't want too much capital equipment or too little, just as you don't want to have too much labor or not enough labor.

A firm's requirements or demand for financial capital is usually derived from its need or demand for physical capital equipment. When you are buying equipment, you can do one of two things. You could become an investor in order to invest now, save up for the capital equipment over the next few months or years, and then make the capital equipment purchase later. Or, you could raise the money to buy the capital equipment now by borrowing (or issuing stock if you are a corporation), requiring you to find investors who are willing to make those funds available.

Figure 14-1 shows you what your three options are to make either of these choices happen. Your first option would be to invest directly in organizations who need funds. This is called **private placement** (illustrated in figure 14-1). You can negotiate a rate of return with them that they will pay you for the use of your money. If you invest directly with those people, you don't have to pay anyone a cut in the earnings or returns you receive when you do not use an **intermediary** (or one who negotiates these things for you) One problem with this is that it takes time for you to find a suitable firm in which you can invest, especially if you are not experienced at finding such firms. The same is true if you need someone to invest in your firm. You can decide on a return you will give them for doing so, but where do you go to find them? This is why many use the second option by going to **financial markets**, where there are always people needing money or wanting to invest money (also shown in figure 14-1). However, by doing so you run a high risk of losing that investment if people take your money you have invested in them and lose it by making bad business decisions or even by skipping town with your money. If they invest in you, you must still be very savvy to the point that you make a deal where you are not overpaying them for the use of the money they invest in you.

Whether you need money for capital equipment purchases now or if you want to invest money today to buy equipment later, it is often best to engage intermediaries in this process as long as you are willing to absorb the cost of using those intermediaries or **financial institutions,** also shown in figure 14-1. Those financial institutions that are reputable will be more experienced to work for you whether you are investing or seeking investors, but they will require a commission for doing so, which adds to your costs of raising money or reduces your net returns if you are investing money.

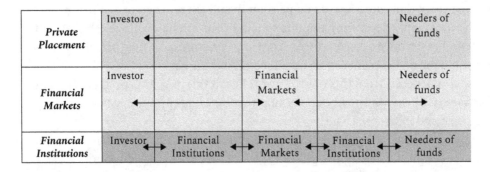

FIGURE 14-1 Private Placement, Financial Markets, Financial Institutions
Source: https://en.wikipedia.org/wiki/Dow_Jones_Industrial_Average

If you or your organization puts money aside in a bank, or into any investment, you make more funds available for those who wish to raise money and spend it. You can invest in many things, but the most typical investments involve stocks and bonds. All investment markets thrive on information, so you can better judge which of them are good or bad.

It is important to know that if you save or invest, you should require a higher return from those investments if they are riskier (as mentioned before). If you are seeking investors, they will require more money from you for the use of their money if your firm's financial status or the CEP itself is perceived by them as being riskier.

The market for buying stocks and bonds is often referred to as the **capital market**. As we discuss stocks and bonds, you need to think about this information from the perspective of being an investor saving up for a future purchase of capital equipment or as one who seeks investors for you to buy capital equipment now.

THE NATURE OF STOCKS

Please recall the process of how stocks are sold and how dividends are generated as was discussed in chapter 8. When you buy stock, they are usually broken down into two types: **common stock** and **preferred stock**. The examples given in previous chapters were based upon common stock.

Common stock is the most basic ownership you can have in a corporation. It gives you, the owner, several rights. The first is **voting rights**. You will need this, because if the firm is being managed in a way that makes profits low, the dividends and the stock value will also be low. With voting rights, you have the right to vote on certain corporate policies or you can vote for or against the admission or removal of members of your firm's **board of directors**. The board is the group of people to whom you delegate other major decisions, such as whether top management is performing well enough, and if they are not, whether to have them removed. Voting rights can either be on the basis of **one-person, one-vote** or **one-share, one-vote**. The latter is most typical because it is usually the shareholders who own the most shares of stock who have the most power in a corporation. If you own 50 percent of the stock plus one share, you will have the final say in all issues. Otherwise, if you use the one-person, one-vote arrangement, a person who owns one hundred shares could have as much power as one who owns thousands of shares. This one-share, one-vote approach creates the need for **preemptive rights** for common stock owners. Suppose you own stock in a corporation that issues more stock shares to raise more money. If they do, it could dilute that amount of clout you have with the number of shares you own. Therefore, when they issue the stock, they must first ask you if you want to buy some of the newly issued shares in order to maintain your percentage of ownership of the firm and thus maintain your current level of influence. With preemptive rights, you have the first right to buy it or refuse it.

Dividends are not always promised or paid to stockholders. If the corporation's net profit after taxes is zero or negative, you will not likely be paid dividends unless the firm has promised to pay dividends out of their reserves during bad times. However, even if the firm is profitable, many times firms choose to keep that money in the firm to make it grow rather than paying it out in cash dividends to investors. Many firms offer a **dividend reinvestment plan (DRP)**. When dividend season arrives, they can automatically take your dividends and buy more of their stock for you. Many investors, especially those saving up for their retirements, prefer DRPs, because cash dividends are taxed, and many investors would rather defer those dividends until later when they are nearing retirement and thus when they may be in a lower tax bracket. Anytime a board of directors decides that a dividend is to be paid, they **declare a dividend** and owners as of a certain date will be the recipients of those dividends.

So how does one put a price on a stock? First, as stated earlier, when you buy stock or any investment, you should require a higher rate of return for any added risk you take if the firm's status is less than completely stable. Second, you then find out what kind of dividend or net profit after taxes per share the firm is expecting. For example, suppose you own stock in a firm that is promising a dividend of $3 per share. If you feel that the risk of that stock is high enough that you should require a rate of return of perhaps 15 percent, then you have a good way of putting a value on that stock. How? If you know you need a 15 percent return of whatever price you pay for the stock, and you already know that they expect to pay you a $3 dividend, then the price times 15 percent should be equal to $3. Let's do a little algebra (don't panic—this will be simple).

In this example, let's set the value, or recommended price, for the stock equal to V. You would then be able to create the following equation:

$$V(15\%) = \$3$$

How do we solve for V? Of course, we divide both sides of the equation by 15 percent. In other words,

$$V = \text{The Expected Dividend (D)}/\text{The Required Rate of Return (R)}$$

In other words,

$$V = D/R$$

In our example, the value of the stock would be $3/15 percent, which would be $20.

This is why **profit warnings** are often issued at times when bad news about companies or the economy drives profits down. People who based their purchase price on a given expected dividend will then find themselves having paid too much for the stock if those profits and ultimately those dividends are lower than expected. The opposite is true. If the actual profits and thus the actual dividend is higher than expected, the stock price will go up. The key here is that you want to have profits, and ultimately dividends, rise faster than the rise in the required rate of return. Higher dividends do not bring up stock prices if the firm is simultaneously taking bigger risks, perhaps to obtain those higher profits and dividends. In the example below, you see that the stock price in scenario A has a lower dividend than the stock in scenario B, but the price for stock A is higher because it is much less risky and therefore does not require such a high return for its investors.

$$A: \$1.50/10\% = \$15$$

$$B: \$2.00/20\% = \$10$$

If you buy preferred stock, your rights are different. For one thing, you get preferred treatment in many respects; this is why it is called preferred stock. For example, if a company goes bankrupt, it will liquidate the firm by selling off its assets (buildings, equipment, land, or whatever has any value). With that money, they pay the auctioneer, back taxes, and those to whom they owe debts. If there is money left over, they will pay the preferred shareholders back for their investments. At liquidation, common stockholders are paid last, and only if there is enough money left after all of the others are paid in the order given here.

Another thing to consider here is that preferred shareholders (stockholders) are more likely to be paid a dividend. In fact, the preferred stock is named after the dividend. For example, $5 preferred stock means it pays $5 per year in a dividend. It may also be expressed as a percent. For example, if you pay $50 for a share of preferred stock and it pays a $5 dividend per year, it would be giving you a 10 percent return, thus it will also be called 10 percent preferred stock. If a firm is unable to pay the preferred dividends to their preferred shareholders, they better have a good reason for it, because the preferred shareholders expect the dividend that is stated. Maybe the firm has had a bad year or perhaps they have a cash crunch. Either way, they will have trouble selling preferred stock in the future if they have a reputation for not paying the dividend when it is due. This is why preferred stock is often called **quasi debt**, because just like a bank, a payment is expected. However, you can't actually straight out call it debt, because no one is going to foreclose on a corporation if they don't pay the dividend. Accountants will also tell you that dividends are never a liability (or an actual debt) until they have been declared. **Cumulative preferred stock** is a kind of stock that you can buy in the event that the corporation fails to pay a dividend. Rather than just miss the expected dividend and let it go by the wayside, missed dividends are paid up later (or paid in arrears). In other words, the dividends owed to you, as a preferred shareholder, when they are missed, accumulate or are cumulative until they are paid to you.

Because preferred shareholders' dividends do not go up or down based directly upon current profits, preferred stockholders typically will have no voting rights.

Another type of preferred stock exists where you as a shareholder can participate in the dividends paid to common shareholders as well as the one promised to you by your own preferred stock, even if you don't own common stock in the firm. Hence, they are called **participating preferred stock.**

Stocks are considered to be the owners' equity in a corporation; the stock market is often called the **equity market**.

BONDS

If you *buy* a bond, you become a lender of money to someone. If you *issue* a bond, it is the same as *selling* a bond, and when you do, you become a *borrower*. Think of buying a **certificate of deposit (CD)** at a bank. Buying a certificate of deposit is an arrangement where you lend money to a bank for a set amount of time. The bank sells it to you because they are borrowing it from you. By tying up your money for a minimum amount of time, banks will pay you a higher interest rate than they would for a regular savings or checking account. Even so, CDs are not good investments if you need a large return to buy capital equipment.

Let's use an example to see how a bond could work. Suppose on January 1, 2020, you buy a $10,000 bond from a company. Eventually that borrower from whom you bought it must pay that back to you. The $10,000 is called the **face value** (or **par value**). It is the amount of the loan. Suppose the borrower promises to pay you a yield (or an interest rate) each year on that $10,000 of 10 percent. This is called the **coupon rate**. It is the rate of return you would receive on the bond, and in most cases it is fixed. Suppose also that you and the borrower agree that the $10,000 is to be paid back to you in full by January 1, 2025. This is called the **maturity date**. The face value, the interest rate (or annual yield), and the maturity date that you agreed upon cannot be changed (unless you have a special bond with special arrangements). A bond, therefore, is a contract.

At the end of each year, you would receive an interest check for $1,000 ($10,000 × 10 percent). That's all. Nothing would be paid to you toward the balance of the $10,000 debt owed to you until the maturity date. At that point, the entire $10,000 would be paid to you in addition to the last payment of interest of $1,000. In other words, you should receive a check for a total of $11,000 at the time of maturity.

Bonds are an IOU, and they can also be bought and sold in a market called the **bond market**. People buy them as their prices go down in hopes that after they do so, their values will rise again, at which point they can make a profit. How can bond values change? Let's talk about that.

Bond values *fall* when the interest rates for them rise *above* the coupon rate. Why? Let's return to the bond you just bought. Suppose interest rates in the overall bond market rise above the coupon rate of 10 percent, to perhaps 15 percent. One reason they could rise would be if the economy starts to boom. When that happens, the Federal Reserve and/or many lending institutions would wish to raise their interest rates to reduce the growth of the economy so it doesn't get to the point of creating shortages. Rates can also rise if the financial status of the borrowing company or organization you loan to becomes shaky and their ability to pay you back may not be as certain. That would increase the risk of you being paid back, and higher-risk investments require a higher rate of return. If the rate does go above the coupon rate, you, the lender, are not happy, because you need to be getting a higher rate. Everyone else who buys a bond like yours at that time will be getting paid much more (15 percent), but you can't raise the coupon rate of your bond. Your bond is a contract. You are stuck with the lousy rate of 10 percent return in this example. Therefore, if you wanted to sell the bond, there would be very few takers. Thus, the value of the bond would decline. Remember, when people are reluctant to buy something or when its demand is very low, so too will be its price. Later, we will show mathematically why the value of any investment will go down when its required rate of return goes up.

Bond values *rise* when the interest rates for them fall *below* the coupon rate. Why? Let's return once more to the bond you just bought. Suppose now that interest rates fall below the coupon rate of 10 percent. One reason they could fall would be because the economy may start to experience a decline in GDP. Remember, that would be the sign of a recession. When that happens, the Federal Reserve and/or many lending institutions would wish to lower their rates to encourage people to borrow money for car and home purchases in order to stimulate the economy. The rates can also fall if the financial status of the borrowing company or organization becomes more secure, and their ability to pay you back is more certain and less risky. This would reduce the risk of the borrower being unable to back the loan, and lower-risk investments usually accept a lower rate of return. If the rate does go below the coupon rate, you, the lender, will be very happy, because you will be getting a higher rate on that type of bond than anyone else. Therefore, if you wanted to sell the bond, there would be very many takers.

Remember, when people are wanting to buy, or are demanding more of, something, its price will rise.

The bond market facilitates bond sales, and by doing so, more of such funds become available for new ventures, purchases of capital equipment, and for other borrowers.

If you loan money to someone, there are three things you need to charge the parties to whom you loan the money. The first is called the **risk-free rate**. This is the rate of return you want if you don't expect that there will be any risk for that investment or inflation in the near future. However, risk and inflation are almost always in existence. Historically, there are very few times when there was no inflation or when there were investments with no risk.

Let's talk about inflation first. If inflation begins to rise, and thus if the costs of things are expected to rise each year, perhaps by 3 percent, we would then have to add that inflation rate to our return in addition to the risk-free rate we seek. Why? Suppose you put $1,000 into a savings account for one year that pays you 3 percent per year. Assume that inflation is also expected to be 3 percent during that same year. At the end of one year, you would have $1,030 in your savings account ($1,000 × 3% added back to your original $1,000). But because of inflation, that $1,030 would not be able to buy any more at that time than your $1,000 could have purchased a year earlier when you put it into the savings account. In other words, you broke even on this investment. You have to make a higher return than that of the inflation rate (or the expected inflation rate) when you charge a borrower interest. This is called the **inflation premium**.

What about the risk of you not getting paid back by the person to whom you loan? This is called the **risk of default** or **default risk**. If their financial condition is questionable, you need to add an additional rate of return to reward you, the lender, for your risk. That added return is called the **risk premium**.

Suppose, for example, that you would like to have a rate of return after all is said and done of 5 percent. In other words, let's assume that is the risk-free rate you seek. Also suppose that the inflation rate is in fact expected to be 3 percent in the foreseeable future, or at least for the time in which this loan is in play (between now and the time that the bond matures). Finally, let's assume that, because the borrower's financial condition is somewhat risky, you would seek an additional 4 percent return from the borrower as a risk premium. The required rate of return you would charge them would then be calculated as follows:

$$Require\ Rate\ Return = Risk\ Free\ Rate + Inflation\ Premium + Risk\ Premium$$

Therefore, you would have to ask the borrower to pay you the required rate of return of 12 percent which is calculated as follows:

$$Require\ Rate\ Return = 5\% + 3\% + 4\% = 12\%$$

THE SUPPLY OF BOND DOLLARS FOR YOU

If you are raising money by borrowing, and if your firm's financial status becomes more sound and solid, the risk to investors of you losing the funds loaned to your firm declines. Suppose, then, that you were being charged an interest rate of 18 percent when your firm was not very stable. When your risk declines, one of two things will happen. More investors will be willing to lend you more money at that same rate because that would be a bargain for them (for reasons mentioned earlier). Thus, the quantity of dollars in bonds available or supplied to you will shift to the right as shown in figure 14-2 where your Money Supply Curve S1 becomes the Money Supply Curve S2. Thus, more funds are available to you at the same rate. The other possibility is that the same number of investors would be willing to loan you the same amount of money but at lower rates. Another way to look at these bonds, if you are trying to borrow, is that if you offer investors a higher rate of interest, especially if that rate is higher than what they would expect, they will supply more dollars to you for loans.

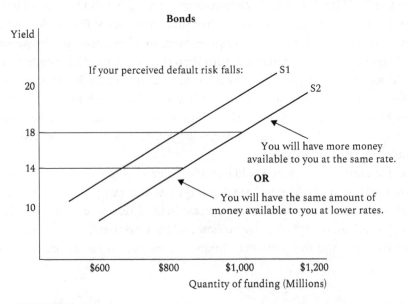

FIGURE 14-2   Bonds

DIVERSIFICATION

Many investors prefer to invest in many ventures rather than putting all their eggs into one basket. Therefore, many prefer to invest in both stocks and bonds, and with many different companies.

Years ago, if you bought stock, you had to buy a minimum number of shares from one corporation. You could not just buy a few shares at a time from a given firm. Suppose a corporation required a minimum purchase of their stocks to be 10,000 shares and their stock price was $10 for each share. In those cases, people with savings accounts worth $100,000 used up all of their savings or investment dollars to buy stocks from only one firm. This is very risky, because if you own stocks in only one or two firms, and if one or both of those firms in which you invested experienced a huge decline in their stock value or went bankrupt, you would lose much or all of your investments and most if not all of your life savings. That's why many didn't invest much in stocks decades ago unless they were exceptionally wealthy and could afford to take such risks. Today, this is not the case. The vast majority of households now own stocks and bonds, either directly or indirectly.

You can buy stocks directly by using the method just mentioned, by owning stock in only a few companies. Today, however, there are investments such as **mutual funds** that you can buy. These are a mixture of stocks and bonds in thousands of different companies. This way, if only one, two, or a few of those thousands of firms were to go bankrupt or if the value of their stocks declines dramatically, you will hardly know it, as the investments in the other firms will make up for such losses. The fund is managed by a money manager, and many small investors put their money in these funds in the hope that the manager is skilled at getting the most return out of their money. There are fees paid to the manager for doing so, with the hopes that your return on the funds exceeds the manager's fees. This allows you as an investor to spread out your risk among many of these firms or ventures in order to minimize risk. In other words, you can diversify your investments to eliminate some (but not all) risk. Risk that can be removed by **diversification** (investing in many different firms of many types) is called **diversifiable risk** or **(nonsystematic risk)**. Figure 14-3 shows how diversification can reduce risk by investing in stocks and bonds in these funds that comprise many different companies, and are of different sizes, in different industries, and even in different countries.

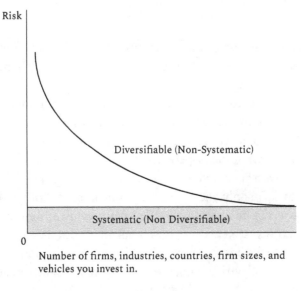

FIGURE 14-3 Diversifiable and Systematic Risk

Notice in figure 14-3 that as you buy investments that are more and more diversified, risk declines but it does not go to zero. Why? Because there is always a risk that all firms will take losses if our economic system finds itself in a bad economy, such as a recession. At that point, all firms will likely have lower returns, and, in some cases, some may go bankrupt. The risk that the economic system could falter and thus cause the stock or bond markets to decline or even collapse (as happened in the crash of 1929) is always in existence. Therefore, the risk you cannot remove by diversification is called **systematic risk** or **nondiversifiable risk.** Diversifiable risk, discussed earlier, is also called nonsystematic risk because it is implying that by diversification, you are not removing systematic risk or the risk of an economic system's decline.

> Economics Myth #5: The Dow Jones Industrial Average was created by the government during the Roosevelt Administration and the number represents the number of shares that have increased in value in a given day.

There are many misunderstandings as to what the **Dow Jones Industrial Average (DJIA)** represents. It is the most common thing that the average person sees or hears about in the news on a given day regarding stock performance. Most people have heard of it and watch it daily, but very few people know what it actually represents.

Dow Jones & Company is a news corporation company and a leading provider of global business news and information services. For a fee, many news providers publish their work on a minute-by-minute basis on their websites or on their news broadcasts. It was established by two journalists and financial reporters, **Charles Dow** (1851–1902) and **Edward Jones** (1856–1920).

In November 1883, they started Dow Jones & Company, which published and distributed a two-page report regarding the financial news that was prevalent on any given day. It was distributed every afternoon, hence the name it was given was the **Customers' Afternoon Letter.** It gave information regarding the overall market as well as a few stocks of particular interest. It was also the first publication to have the Dow Jones stock average, which reported the stock prices and performance of mostly railroads (New World Encyclopedia 2017). The Customers' Afternoon Letter is still in publication today, but its name has since been changed to what we now know as the **Wall Street Journal.** The industrial average did not exist until May 26, 1896, and it became what we now know as the Dow Jones Industrial Average (DJIA). **General Electric Corporation** is the only company whose stock has been tracked in recent years that was among the original stocks in the DJIA.

Observe figure 14-4, which shows the different firms that are now or have once been among the thirty stocks tracked by the DJIA. You can see that it was set up to represent stock prices of all major industries. When it was first created over a century ago, without computers, they could not quickly get an average of all stocks. The average would have been wrong by the time all the stock prices would have been compiled. That's why they were forced to take a sample that represented the entire spectrum of stocks.

The first average was at 62.76. This represented the dollar average of the index. To calculate the average, you need to add up the prices of all of the stocks in the index and then divide the total by the **Dow divisor,** or the number of stocks you are tracking. The divisor is the denominator. Originally, they divided the price totals by twelve. By doing this, there was soon a problem. Some stocks are given what is called a **stock split**, where firms cut the price of a stock in half. When stock prices are cut in half, it is not because of bad performance, but it is done by firms when they feel the stock is becoming too pricey. After doing so, they would then double the number of shares owned by each stockholder, thus their wealth would be unchanged. For example, if you own one thousand shares of stock of a firm for which you paid $50 each, your stock's total value would be $50,000. If the firm splits the stock price in half, you would immediately have two thousand shares of stock worth $25 each, and your stock value would remain at $50,000 ($25 × 2,000 shares). The splits would often frighten those who followed the Dow Jones Industrial Average, as they would think that a drop in the average was due to a drop in the value of the stocks in the market. The divisor or denominator, therefore, has been adjusted over many decades due to things such as stock splits by lowering it in order to put the average back to where it would have been had there been no stock splits. They will also change the denominator to adjust for the times that stocks are removed from the sample and replaced by another stock because the prices of those stocks are usually different. Changing the stocks tracked is often done when it is believed that the new stock placed into the index is a better representative of its industry than the one it replaced. As a result of adjusting the Dow divisor, the average really is not a dollar average any more.

Since the index is no longer a dollar average, the percent changes each day are more relevant than the numeric size of the index. As of this writing, the DJIA is above 25,000 and, once again you can see the firms of which the index is comprised in figure 14-4. In 1981, if

Company	Where Traded	Symbol	Industry	Year Added
3M	NYSE	MMM	Conglomerate	09/08/1976
American Express	NYSE	AXP	Consumer finance	30/08/1982
Apple	NASDAQ	AAPL	Consumer electronics	19/03/2015
Boeing	NYSE	BA	Aerospace and defense	12/03/1987
Caterpillar	NYSE	CAT	Construction and mining equipment	06/05/1991
Chevron	NYSE	CVX	Oil & gas	19/02/2008
Cisco Systems	NASDAQ	CSCO	Computer networking	08/06/2009
Coca-Cola	NYSE	KO	Beverages	12/03/1987
DowDuPont	NYSE	DWDP	Chemical industry	01/09/2017
ExxonMobil	NYSE	XOM	Oil & gas	01/10/1928
General Electric	NYSE	GE	Conglomerate	1896-26-05
Goldman Sachs	NYSE	GS	Banking, Financial services	09/20/2013
The Home Depot	NYSE	HD	Home improvement retailer	01/11/1999
IBM	NYSE	IBM	Computers and technology	29/06/1979
Intel	NASDAQ	INTC	Semiconductors	01/11/1999
Johnson & Johnson	NYSE	JNJ	Pharmaceuticals	17/03/1997
JPMorgan Chase	NYSE	JPM	Banking	06/05/1991
McDonald's	NYSE	MCD	Fast food	30/10/1985
Merck	NYSE	MRK	Pharmaceuticals	29/06/1979
Microsoft	NASDAQ	MSFT	Software	01/11/1999
Nike	NYSE	NKE	Apparel	20/09/2013
Pfizer	NYSE	PFE	Pharmaceuticals	08/04/2004
Procter & Gamble	NYSE	PG	Consumer goods	26/05/1932
Travelers	NYSE	TRV	Insurance	08/06/2009
UnitedHealth Group	NYSE	UNH	Managed health care	24/09/2012
United Technologies	NYSE	UTX	Conglomerate	14/03/1939
Verizon	NYSE	VZ	Telecommunication	08/04/2004
Visa	NYSE	V	Consumer banking	20/09/2013
Walmart	NYSE	WMT	Retail	17/03/1997
Walt Disney	NYSE	DIS	Broadcasting and entertainment	06/05/1991

FIGURE 14-4 Companies Tracked in the DJIA

Source: https://en.wikipedia.org/wiki/Dow_Jones_Industrial_Average.

the DJIA had changed by 100 points, that would have been more than an 11 percent change, because that average was only 875. This would have been big news. Today, however, a 100-point change would not be nearly as significant because the percent change would be so small (less than 1 percent).

Other indexes include the **Standard & Poor's 500,** which basically uses the same methodology of watching stocks that the DJIA does except that it uses a bigger sample size of 500 stocks. Statisticians will tell you that a sample size of thirty is adequate to use for such an average but that a bigger sample size gives a more accurate picture of what the actual stock average is, and it is less likely to change much when only a few stock prices change.

For many years, the **over-the-counter trade (OTC)** of stocks was the means by which smaller firms could sell their stocks if they could not afford to purchase a seat on one of the bigger, face-to-face, formal stock exchanges such as the **New York Stock Exchange**, which is very expensive. Representatives of those small firms would have to literally go to a brokerage house and do business "over the counter." When telephones began to be used to complete stock purchases, the need to go to a firm's office to make a transaction was no longer needed, but it was still called the over-the-counter trade. In 1971, a group was formed to computerize this process; stock prices could be quoted without people having to speak to one another or play phone tag. This computerized process was created by the **National Association of Securities Dealers' Automated Quotes (Nasdaq).** It was what we now know as the **Nasdaq Stock Market.** At the time that it began trading on February 8, 1971, it was considered to be the world's first electronic stock market. It started out to be only a quotation system and did not provide a way to perform electronic trades, but over the years the computer then began to facilitate sales as well. Some still call it the OTC (over-the-counter trade) even though the idea of using the front counter in an office is long gone.

Please remember that you can apply all of this information either as an investor, so you can buy capital equipment later, or while seeking investors to make it possible to buy capital equipment now.

Let us now focus on the idea of investing money now to buy capital equipment later. It is more likely that you would do so in order to replace machinery that has a relatively finite life span. If you have a machine that usually lasts five years and then needs to be replaced, either because of wearing out or by becoming obsolete, you can begin to invest now to replace it rather than having to cough up a lot of money in five years. Roof replacements are often done this way as well.

While you're at it, putting business aside for a moment, you can even use this concept to prepare for your retirement fund or for a college fund for your children or grandchildren.

THE TIME VALUE OF MONEY (FUTURE VALUE)

If you want to put money aside today to save up for a future purpose, there is a concept that you need to understand called the **time value of money**. The concept assumes that when you make an investment, either in a savings account, a bond, or in stocks, you will take your returns and buy more of those investments, thus your returns themselves will also be getting returns. In banks, they call it **compounded interest**. In stocks, they call it **dividend reinvestment plans (DRPs).**

For simplicity, we will use an example of you putting $1,000 into an investment that gets an average return of 10 percent annually. At the end of one year, your investment would be worth $1,100. Why? Because your 10 percent return of $1,000 is equal to $100 (10% × $1,000). When you add that $100 to the original $1,000 investment, it has now grown to $1,100 by the end of the first year. In other words, the **future value** of that investment under these circumstances would be $1,100. If you keep all of that money in that investment for a second year, it will grow to $1,210. Why? Because if you assume that the $1,100 will still be getting the average rate of return of 10 percent, that 10 percent of $1,100 would be $110. If you add $110 to the original $1,100 investment, it would give you $1,210. Therefore, the future value of a $1,000 investment, getting a 10 percent return compounded annually for two years, would be $1,210. Let's go one more year. Once again, if you keep all of the $1,210 in that investment for a third year in a row, it will grow to $1,331. Why? Because if the $1,210 will still be getting the average rate of return of 10 percent, that 10 percent of $1,210 would be $121. If you add that $121 to the original $1,210 investment, it would give you $1,331. Therefore, the future value of a $1,000 investment, getting a 10 percent return compounded annually for three years, would be $1,331.

There is a much easier way to determine the level to which your investment will grow. Would you agree that we just performed the following calculation?

$$\$1,000 + (\$1,000 \times 10\%) + (\$1,100 \times 10\%) + (\$1,210 \times 10\%) = \$1,331$$

Mathematical principles tell us that if I want to know what $1,000 times 10 percent added to $1,000 is equal to, I can simply add 10 percent to one (with one always being a constant) and then multiply that times $1,000. I can do this for any return rate. If the return is 10 percent, I can take 110% (1 + 10%) times $1,000 and doing so would give me the same result as (10% × $1,000) + $1,000. Doing it this way saves a step. In other words,

$$\$1,000 \times 110\% = \$1,100$$

$$\$1,100 \times 110\% = \$1,210$$

$$\$1,210 \times 110\% = \$1,331$$

There is an even faster way to do this. Math principals tell us that if I were to do this math by multiplying $1,000 times 110 percent three times, I will get the same results:

$$\$1,000 \times 110\% \times 110\% \times 110\% = \$1,331$$

Let's go faster. You can then save time by using the same formula, but by instead using an exponent of 3, which represents the three years that the money was growing. In other words,

$$\$1,000 \times (110\%)^3 = \$1,331 \text{ or } \$1,000 \times (1.10)^3 = \$1,331$$

Therefore, we can now extract a formula from this exercise that will always tell us the future value of any investment. It can always be found as follows:

$$\text{Future Value of an Investment (FV)} = \text{Investment (I)} \times$$
$$(1 + \text{Return Rate (r)})^{\text{Number of Years Invested (y)}}$$

or

$$FV = I \times (1 + r)^y$$

We can then draw from this formula another formula. This formula would be the means to calculate the amount to which *any* investment will grow over a period of time. We call it the **future value interest factor,** and in this example it would be $(1.10)^3$ or 1.331. It is expressed as follows:

$$(1 + r)^y$$

Let's play around with it for a moment, shall we?

If my return is 12 percent and the investment is for 10 years, it would be expressed as follows:

$$(1 + 12\%)^{10} = 3.106 \text{ (Rounded)}$$

Therefore, if you invest your $1,000 under these circumstances, the future value of your investment in 10 years would be $3,106. Not bad. If you invest $6,500 today in such an investment, 10 years from now it would be worth $20,189 (3.106 × $6,500).

Rather than having to do the math like that each time, a spreadsheet can be constructed to do the math for you. That very thing has already been done for you in figure 14-5. Please notice that the intersection of the return rate of 12 percent with 10 years (or periods) is already created for you. Such a chart is helpful only if your returns are not expected to be values such as 5.6 percent or 8.2 percent or any number that is between those listed in the top row of figure 14-5.

Suppose now that you have an investment where you plan to put money aside each year in order to buy your new machinery 10 years from now to replace existing equipment that will be worn out or obsolete by then. Also assume that you want to save $1,000 per year, and at the end of each year you will then put that $1,000 into an investment that promises to bring you an average of 12 percent per year. Putting the same amount of money into an investment annually is called an **ordinary annuity.** Once again, referring to figure 14-5, the future value interest factors (FVIF) will help you to calculate what the entire investment will be worth at the end of 10 years after having put the $1,000 per year into it.

$$P = \frac{D_1}{R_R}$$

Periods	1%	2%	3%	4%	5%	6%	7%	8%	9%	10%	11%	12%	13%	14%	15%
1	1.010	1.020	1.030	1.040	1.050	1.060	1.070	1.080	1.090	1.100	1.110	1.120	1.130	1.140	1.150
2	1.020	1.040	1.061	1.082	1.103	1.124	1.145	1.166	1.188	1.210	1.232	1.254	1.277	1.300	1.323
3	1.030	1.061	1.093	1.125	1.158	1.191	1.225	1.260	1.295	1.331	1.368	1.405	1.443	1.482	1.521
4	1.041	1.082	1.126	1.170	1.216	1.262	1.311	1.360	1.412	1.464	1.518	1.574	1.630	1.689	1.749
5	1.051	1.104	1.159	1.217	1.276	1.338	1.403	1.469	1.539	1.611	1.685	1.762	1.842	1.925	2.011
6	1.062	1.126	1.194	1.265	1.340	1.419	1.501	1.587	1.677	1.772	1.870	1.974	2.082	2.195	2.313
7	1.072	1.149	1.230	1.316	1.407	1.504	1.606	1.714	1.828	1.949	2.076	2.211	2.353	2.502	2.660
8	1.083	1.172	1.267	1.369	1.477	1.594	1.718	1.851	1.993	2.144	2.305	2.476	2.658	2.853	3.059
9	1.094	1.195	1.305	1.423	1.551	1.689	1.838	1.999	2.172	2.358	2.558	2.773	3.004	3.252	3.518
10	1.105	1.219	1.344	1.480	1.629	1.791	1.967	2.159	2.367	2.594	2.839	3.106	3.395	3.707	4.046
11	1.116	1.243	1.384	1.539	1.710	1.898	2.105	2.332	2.580	2.853	3.152	3.479	3.836	4.226	4.652
12	1.127	1.268	1.426	1.601	1.796	2.012	2.252	2.518	2.813	3.138	3.498	3.896	4.335	4.818	5.350
13	1.138	1.294	1.469	1.665	1.886	2.133	2.410	2.720	3.066	3.452	3.883	4.363	4.898	5.492	6.153
14	1.149	1.319	1.513	1.732	1.980	2.261	2.579	2.937	3.342	3.797	4.310	4.887	5.535	6.261	7.076
15	1.161	1.346	1.558	1.801	2.079	2.397	2.759	3.172	3.642	4.177	4.785	5.474	6.254	7.138	8.137

FIGURE 14-5 Table FVIF

Present value
Future value

Invested At The End of Year	Annual Investment		Future Value Interest Factor		Future Value	Number Of Year(s) It Will Be Able To Grow
Year 10	$ 1,000	×	1.000	=	$ 1,000.00	0
Year 9	$ 1,000	×	1.120	=	$ 1,120.00	1
Year 8	$ 1,000	×	1.254	=	$ 1,254.00	2
Year 7	$ 1,000	×	1.405	=	$ 1,405.00	3
Year 6	$ 1,000	×	1.574	=	$ 1,574.00	4
Year 5	$ 1,000	×	1.762	=	$ 1,762.00	5
Year 4	$ 1,000	×	1.974	=	$ 1,974.00	6
Year 3	$ 1,000	×	2.211	=	$ 2,211.00	7
Year 2	$ 1,000	×	2.476	=	$ 2,476.00	8
Year 1	$ 1,000	×	2.773	=	$ 2,773.00	9
		Totals	17.549		$ 17,549.00	

FIGURE 14-6   Future Value of an Annuity (The Long Way)

Figure 14-6 will show you what the future values will be. Please notice that the $1,000 you put in at the end of year 10 will have no time to grow, therefore its future value at that time will be no different than $1,000 (or $1,000 × 1.000). Also notice that the money you invest at the end of year one will only have the remaining nine years of the investment to grow, because of your having waited for a year to invest it. This is why we use the FVIF of nine years for that investment. After adding up the future values, you will see that the investment will be worth $17,549 (rounded) at the end of 10 years. Not bad at all, especially considering that you only invested $10,000 in this venture. You are close to doubling your money!

Is there an easier way to do this? Absolutely. If you add up all of the future value interest factors, you will see that their sum comes to 17.549. If you multiply that times $1,000, you will get the same answer, only much faster.

Once again, rather than having to do the math like that each time, a spreadsheet can be constructed to do the math for you. That very thing has already been done for you in figure 14-7. As before, such a chart is helpful only if your returns are not between the numbers given. These sums of the future value interest factors at each scenario are called the **future value interest factors of an annuity**. Please notice again that the intersection of the return rate of 12 percent with 10 years (or periods) is already created for you. You will see that it is 17.549 (rounded) as we said it would be if you added up the future value interest factors.

Once you have the chart, there are all kinds of scenarios you can apply. For example, if you intend to replace a machine in 15 years and thus plan to put $5,000 aside at the end of each year for the next 15 years, and if the investment you have in mind is promising an average rate of return of 14 percent per year, your future value interest factor of an annuity would be 43.842. Multiplying that times $5,000 will tell you that the future value of that investment will be $219,210. Once again, that isn't bad, seeing as how you would have only put $75,000 ($5,000 × 15 years) into the investment!

Another instance in which you cannot use the chart in figure 14-7 would be if you do not plan to put equal amounts of money aside each year. Such a set of cash flows is called a **mixed**

Periods	1%	2%	3%	4%	5%	6%	7%	8%	9%	10%	11%	12%	13%	14%
1	1.000	1.000	1.000	1.000	1.000	1.000	1.000	1.000	1.000	1.000	1.000	1.000	1.000	1.000
2	2.010	2.020	2.030	2.040	2.050	2.060	2.070	2.080	2.090	2.100	2.110	2.120	2.130	2.140
3	3.030	3.060	3.091	3.122	3.153	3.184	3.215	3.246	3.278	3.310	3.342	3.374	3.407	3.440
4	4.060	4.122	4.184	4.246	4.310	4.375	4.440	4.506	4.573	4.641	4.710	4.779	4.850	4.921
5	5.101	5.204	5.309	5.416	5.526	5.637	5.751	5.867	5.985	6.105	6.228	6.353	6.480	6.610
6	6.152	6.308	6.468	6.633	6.802	6.975	7.153	7.336	7.523	7.716	7.913	8.115	8.323	8.536
7	7.214	7.434	7.662	7.898	8.142	8.394	8.654	8.923	9.200	9.487	9.783	10.089	10.405	10.730
8	8.286	8.583	8.892	9.214	9.549	9.897	10.260	10.637	11.028	11.436	11.859	12.300	12.757	13.233
9	9.369	9.755	10.159	10.583	11.027	11.491	11.978	12.488	13.021	13.579	14.164	14.776	15.416	16.085
10	10.462	10.950	11.464	12.006	12.578	13.181	13.816	14.487	15.193	15.937	16.722	17.549	18.420	19.337
11	11.567	12.169	12.808	13.486	14.207	14.972	15.784	16.645	17.560	18.531	19.561	20.655	21.814	23.045
12	12.683	13.412	14.192	15.026	15.917	16.870	17.888	18.977	20.141	21.384	22.713	24.133	25.650	27.271
13	13.809	14.680	15.618	16.627	17.713	18.882	20.141	21.495	22.953	24.523	26.212	28.029	29.985	32.089
14	14.947	15.974	17.086	18.292	19.599	21.015	22.550	24.215	26.019	27.975	30.095	32.393	34.883	37.581
15	16.097	17.293	18.599	20.024	21.579	23.276	25.129	27.152	29.361	31.772	34.405	37.280	40.417	43.842

FIGURE 14-7 Table FVIFA

stream of cash flows, and you would need to do the calculation the long way as seen in figure 14-6 (unless you perform this calculation with a financial calculator).

Now we come to the point of this discussion that is very important when making capital equipment decisions. We will discuss different ways to answer very important questions that will arise through this process.

HOW MUCH IS NEEDED TO SET ASIDE EACH YEAR TO FUND A FUTURE CAPITAL EQUIPMENT PURCHASE?

In the scenario just mentioned, I know that $5,000 invested each year will give me $219,210. That's great if that's how much I need. But how can one figure out what to put aside each year if we need to raise a given amount by a certain date in the future?

It's simple. Once again, all you need is some simple algebra. Suppose you need $50,000 in five years to replace a machine that is likely to be obsolete at that time. Let's set the amount of money that we need to set aside each year equal to S. We know that whatever is set aside multiplied times the future value interest factor of an annuity is equal to what you will have in the future. Also assume that you have an investment available that will give you a return averaging 9 percent per year. Using figure 14-7, we see that the future value interest factor of an annuity under those circumstances (at the intersection of 9 percent and five periods) would be 5.985. We can use the following equation:

$$S \times FVIFA = \$Capital\ Needed\ (for\ the\ Capital\ Equipment\ Purchase)$$

Thus, in our example, after replacing the variables in the equation with the numbers that we know, it would read as follows:

$$S \times 5.985 = \$50,000$$

To solve for the variable S, you can divide both sides of the equation by 5.985. Now the equation reads as follows:

$$S = \$50,000/5.985 = \$8,354.22$$

Therefore, to find that amount you need to set aside each year, the formula would be as follows:

$$S = \$Capital\ Needed/FVIFA$$

Let's try another one. Suppose you feel you need $1,000,000 to replace a roof on your factory 35 years from now, because that is when the warranty will run out. Also assume that you can get an average annual return of 11 percent per year on an investment. Figure 14-8 will show you that the future value interest factor of an annuity at the intersection of the 11 percent return rate column and the 35 periods row would be 341.590. Therefore, the formula would be as follows:

$$S = \$1,000,000/341.590 = \$2,927.49$$

Therefore, if you put $2,927.49 into that investment each year, you will have $1,000,000 waiting for you in that account in 30 years.

That's a very good deal! You could also use this on a personal level. If you want to retire with $1 million dollars in your possession in 35 years, find an investment that will promise to give you an average rate of return each year of 11 percent. If you put $2,927.49 into it, you will be a millionaire in 35 years! The same could be true if you are setting money aside each year to pay for college for your children or grandchildren. If you can estimate what it will cost to educate them in 18 years, you can use this same method to learn how much you should invest each year to make it happen.

TIME VALUE OF MONEY (PRESENT VALUE)

Now we need to look at the other side of the time value of money. It is called **present value**. In order to understand present value, we must first review the concept of future value. Let's return to our original example with the $1,000 investment that grew to $1,331 in three years with an average annual rate of return of 10 percent. Suppose you were promised by an investment firm that if you bought a specific investment from them, your investment will grow to $1,331 by the end of three years from now. Also suppose that you could get an average rate of return per year of 10 percent on an investment with the same level of risk. You know from our example that you would need to invest $1,000 in that investment and no more than that, because doing so would give you $1,331 in three years. If the firm promising you that you would receive $1,331 in three years (if you invest with them) requires you to pay more than $1,000 for that investment, your answer would be no. The investment is simply not worth more than that. The present value of that investment is therefore $1,000.

But what if you didn't know that by having just done the calculation earlier? What if you needed to figure it out?

Periods	1%	2%	3%	4%	5%	6%	7%	8%	9%	10%	11%	12%	13%	14%
1	1.000	1.000	1.000	1.000	1.000	1.000	1.000	1.000	1.000	1.000	1.000	1.000	1.000	1.000
2	2.010	2.020	2.030	2.040	2.050	2.060	2.070	2.080	2.090	2.100	2.110	2.120	2.130	2.140
3	3.030	3.060	3.091	3.122	3.153	3.184	3.215	3.246	3.278	3.310	3.342	3.374	3.407	3.440
4	4.060	4.122	4.184	4.246	4.310	4.375	4.440	4.506	4.573	4.641	4.710	4.779	4.850	4.921
5	5.101	5.204	5.309	5.416	5.526	5.637	5.751	5.867	5.985	6.105	6.228	6.353	6.480	6.610
6	6.152	6.308	6.468	6.633	6.802	6.975	7.153	7.336	7.523	7.716	7.913	8.115	8.323	8.536
7	7.214	7.434	7.662	7.898	8.142	8.394	8.654	8.923	9.200	9.487	9.783	10.089	10.405	10.730
8	8.286	8.583	8.892	9.214	9.549	9.897	10.260	10.637	11.028	11.436	11.859	12.300	12.757	13.233
9	9.369	9.755	10.159	10.583	11.027	11.491	11.978	12.488	13.021	13.579	14.164	14.776	15.416	16.085
10	10.462	10.950	11.464	12.006	12.578	13.181	13.816	14.487	15.193	15.937	16.722	17.549	18.420	19.337
11	11.567	12.169	12.808	13.486	14.207	14.972	15.784	16.645	17.560	18.531	19.561	20.655	21.814	23.045
12	12.683	13.412	14.192	15.026	15.917	16.870	17.888	18.977	20.141	21.384	22.713	24.133	25.650	27.271
13	13.809	14.680	15.618	16.627	17.713	18.882	20.141	21.495	22.953	24.523	26.212	28.029	29.985	32.089
14	14.947	15.974	17.086	18.292	19.599	21.015	22.550	24.215	26.019	27.975	30.095	32.393	34.883	37.581
15	16.097	17.293	18.599	20.024	21.579	23.276	25.129	27.152	29.361	31.772	34.405	37.280	40.417	43.842
16	17.258	18.639	20.157	21.825	23.657	25.673	27.888	30.324	33.003	35.950	39.190	42.753	46.672	50.980
17	18.430	20.012	21.762	23.698	25.840	28.213	30.840	33.750	36.974	40.545	44.501	48.884	53.739	59.118
18	19.615	21.412	23.414	25.645	28.132	30.906	33.999	37.450	41.301	45.599	50.396	55.750	61.725	68.394
19	20.811	22.841	25.117	27.671	30.539	33.760	37.379	41.446	46.018	51.159	56.939	63.440	70.749	78.969
20	22.019	24.297	26.870	29.778	33.066	36.786	40.995	45.762	51.160	57.275	64.203	72.052	80.947	91.025
21	23.239	25.783	28.676	31.969	35.719	39.993	44.865	50.423	56.765	64.002	72.265	81.699	92.470	104.768
22	24.472	27.299	30.537	34.248	38.505	43.392	49.006	55.457	62.873	71.403	81.214	92.503	105.491	120.436
23	25.716	28.845	32.453	36.618	41.430	46.996	53.436	60.893	69.532	79.543	91.148	104.603	120.205	138.297
24	26.973	30.422	34.426	39.083	44.502	50.816	58.177	66.765	76.790	88.497	102.174	118.155	136.831	158.659
25	28.243	32.030	36.459	41.646	47.727	54.865	63.249	73.106	84.701	98.347	114.413	133.334	155.620	181.871
26	29.526	33.671	38.553	44.312	51.113	59.156	68.676	79.954	93.324	109.182	127.999	150.334	176.850	208.333
27	30.821	35.344	40.710	47.084	54.669	63.706	74.484	87.351	102.723	121.100	143.079	169.374	200.841	238.499
28	32.129	37.051	42.931	49.968	58.403	68.528	80.698	95.339	112.968	134.210	159.817	190.699	227.950	272.889
29	33.450	38.792	45.219	52.966	62.323	73.640	87.347	103.966	124.135	148.631	178.397	214.583	258.583	312.094
30	34.785	40.568	47.575	56.085	66.439	79.058	94.461	113.283	136.308	164.494	199.021	241.333	293.199	356.787
31	36.133	42.379	50.003	59.328	70.761	84.802	102.073	123.346	149.575	181.943	221.913	271.293	332.315	407.737
32	37.494	44.227	52.503	62.701	75.299	90.890	110.218	134.214	164.037	201.138	247.324	304.848	376.516	465.820
33	38.869	46.112	55.078	66.210	80.064	97.343	118.933	145.951	179.800	222.252	275.529	342.429	426.463	532.035
34	40.258	48.034	57.730	69.858	85.067	104.184	128.259	158.627	196.982	245.477	306.837	384.521	482.903	607.520
35	41.660	49.994	60.462	73.652	90.320	111.435	138.237	172.317	215.711	271.024	341.590	431.663	546.681	693.573

FIGURE 14-8   Table FVIFA (Up to 35 Years)

The answer is simple. Once again, we use some simple algebra. We would set the amount we need to invest today equal to I (which stands for "investment"). We know that the future interest factor for three years at 10 percent is 1.331. Thus, we would have this equation:

$$I \times FVIF = \text{Promised Amount}$$

Thus, in our example, after exchanging the variables we know, it would read as follows:

$$I \times 1.331 = \$1,331$$

To solve for the variable I, you can divide both sides of the equation by 1.331. Now the equation reads as follows:

$$I = \$1,331/1.331 = \$1,000$$

Therefore, to find the amount you need to invest today to get a promised amount in the future, the formula would be as follows:

$$I = \text{Promised Amount}/FVIF$$

If we are talking about present value, then why are we using the future interest factor? Very good question. The answer is that we can now rewrite the equation and make a brand-new formula. This time, however, the formula will be for **the present value interest factor**. Would you agree that the following holds true?

$$\$1,331/1.331 \text{ is the same as } \$1,331 \times (1/1.331)$$

You should agree, because the answer is the same. Thus, you could say the following:

$$\$1,331 \times (1/1.331) = \$1,000$$

Therefore, the formula to find the present value interest factor is as follows:

$$PVIF = 1/FVIF \text{ or } 1/(1 + r)^y$$

The present value interest factor would then be $1/(1 + 10\%)^3$ in this example, which would be 0.751. Thus, if you multiply the expected or promised value of the investment of $1,331 times 0.751, which (rounded) would give you $1,000, that would give you the amount that you need to invest today to get $1,331 three years from now.

Thus, in our example, if someone promised to give you $1,331 three years from today if you pay them an investment of $1,000 today, you would have to decide if that is a good investment or not. If you know, based upon the risk of the investment (after researching its risk), that you should require an annual return of at least 10 percent, then (as stated earlier) you would be able to invest that $1,000 with no regrets. Why? Because the present value of $1,331 you would receive three years from now at a required annual return of 10 percent would be $1,000. However, what if someone gave you the same investment opportunity, with the exception that they required you to invest $1,100 today instead? As we stated earlier, your answer would be a flat no! Why would you pay $1,100 today to get $1,331 in three years if you know that doing so would not be giving you your **required rate of return** of 10 percent? You could simply tell that person that you would rather put $1,000 into an investment getting 10 percent, which gives you the same outcome. The present value of this investment, with these circumstances, is $1,000, and you should pay no more for it. Therefore, you should never pay more for an investment than the present value of its expected or promised cash flow(s).

Is there an easier way to find the present value interest factor? Yes. There is also a chart one can make with a spreadsheet, just like the one used to find the future value interest factors. The only difference is that each of the present value interest factors would be inverted future value interest factors (figure 14-9). Please note that at the intersection of 10 percent and three years in figure 14-9 is the present value interest factor of 0.751.

Let's try another example. If you expect or are promised a cash flow return from an investment six years from now of $2,500, and after researching its risk you find that such an investment should give you at least an 8 percent return, you would first find the present value interest factor (PVIF) of 0.630, because that is where the 8 percent interest rate column and the six-period row intersect. If you multiply 0.630 times $2,500, the present value of that investment would only be $1,575. If the person offering you this investment demanded any more from you in order to buy it, you would politely turn them down because that investment, under those circumstances, would be worth no more than $1,575.

It's very important to understand at this point why this is relevant. Please remember that when you buy capital equipment, you are making an investment. The investment is expected to give you returns of added profits or cost savings. If you make an investment in capital equipment, you have to find out what cash flows the equipment will give you in the way of added profits or savings. Let's try an example. Suppose you are considering buying capital equipment. Also assume that the machine life is expected to be five years and that it is expected to save you $3,000 per year in operating costs (see figure 14-10). If the cost of buying the machine requires you to pay investors or lenders an average of 7 percent per year on the money you raise to buy it, then your required return will be at least 6 percent. There is another way to determine your required rate of return. Suppose you discover that you could pay for the capital equipment with what money you now have. If that money is now invested in stocks or bonds and getting an 8 percent return, then that would be your required rate of return. Let's go with the 6 percent in this example. So, how would you find out the present value of these cash flows? According to figure 14-9, the PVIF for 6 percent for the $3,000 you expect to receive by the end of year one would be 0.943. The PVIF for 6 percent for the $3,000 you expect to receive by the end of year two would be 0.890. The PVIF for 6 percent for the $3,000 you expect to receive by the end

	1%	2%	3%	4%	5%	6%	7%	8%	9%	10%	11%	12%	13%	14%	15%
1	0.990	0.980	0.971	0.962	0.952	0.943	0.935	0.926	0.917	0.909	0.901	0.893	0.885	0.877	0.870
2	0.980	0.961	0.943	0.925	0.907	0.890	0.873	0.857	0.842	0.826	0.812	0.797	0.783	0.769	0.756
3	0.971	0.942	0.915	0.889	0.864	0.840	0.816	0.794	0.772	0.751	0.731	0.712	0.693	0.675	0.658
4	0.961	0.924	0.888	0.855	0.823	0.792	0.763	0.735	0.708	0.683	0.659	0.636	0.613	0.592	0.572
5	0.951	0.906	0.863	0.822	0.784	0.747	0.713	0.681	0.650	0.621	0.593	0.567	0.543	0.519	0.497
6	0.942	0.888	0.837	0.790	0.746	0.705	0.666	0.630	0.596	0.564	0.535	0.507	0.480	0.456	0.432
7	0.933	0.871	0.813	0.760	0.711	0.665	0.623	0.583	0.547	0.513	0.482	0.452	0.425	0.400	0.376
8	0.923	0.853	0.789	0.731	0.677	0.627	0.582	0.540	0.502	0.467	0.434	0.404	0.376	0.351	0.327
9	0.914	0.837	0.766	0.703	0.645	0.592	0.544	0.500	0.460	0.424	0.391	0.361	0.333	0.308	0.284
10	0.905	0.820	0.744	0.676	0.614	0.558	0.508	0.463	0.422	0.386	0.352	0.322	0.295	0.270	0.247
11	0.896	0.804	0.722	0.650	0.585	0.527	0.475	0.429	0.388	0.350	0.317	0.287	0.261	0.237	0.215
12	0.887	0.788	0.701	0.625	0.557	0.497	0.444	0.397	0.356	0.319	0.286	0.257	0.231	0.208	0.187
13	0.879	0.773	0.681	0.601	0.530	0.469	0.415	0.368	0.326	0.290	0.258	0.229	0.204	0.182	0.163
14	0.870	0.758	0.661	0.577	0.505	0.442	0.388	0.340	0.299	0.263	0.232	0.205	0.181	0.160	0.141
15	0.861	0.743	0.642	0.555	0.481	0.417	0.362	0.315	0.275	0.239	0.209	0.183	0.160	0.140	0.123
16	0.853	0.728	0.623	0.534	0.458	0.394	0.339	0.292	0.252	0.218	0.188	0.163	0.141	0.123	0.107
17	0.844	0.714	0.605	0.513	0.436	0.371	0.317	0.270	0.231	0.198	0.170	0.146	0.125	0.108	0.093
18	0.836	0.700	0.587	0.494	0.416	0.350	0.296	0.250	0.212	0.180	0.153	0.130	0.111	0.095	0.081
19	0.828	0.686	0.570	0.475	0.396	0.331	0.277	0.232	0.194	0.164	0.138	0.116	0.098	0.083	0.070
20	0.820	0.673	0.554	0.456	0.377	0.312	0.258	0.215	0.178	0.149	0.124	0.104	0.087	0.073	0.061

FIGURE 14-9   Table PVIF

of year three would be 0.840. The $3,000 you expect to receive by the end of year four would have a PVIF of 0.792, and finally the 3,000 you expect to receive by the end of year five would have a PVIF of 0.747. Figure 14-10 shows a summary of these assumptions and how the present value of these cash flows would be found.

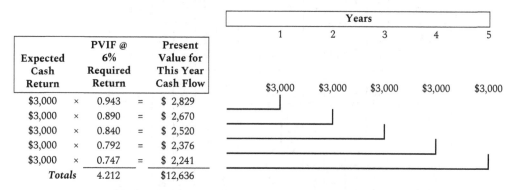

Expected Cash Return		PVIF @ 6% Required Return		Present Value for This Year Cash Flow
$3,000	×	0.943	=	$ 2,829
$3,000	×	0.890	=	$ 2,670
$3,000	×	0.840	=	$ 2,520
$3,000	×	0.792	=	$ 2,376
$3,000	×	0.747	=	$ 2,241
Totals		4.212		$12,636

FIGURE 14-10   Finding Present Value of an Annuity (The Long Way)

Once you multiply those PVIFs times the promised savings or returns of each year, you will see the present value of each of those annual returns. If you add up those present values, the total comes to $12,636. Should you buy this capital equipment? Only if the cost of it is less than or equal to $12,636. If the price is $12,000 and the value is $12,636, you are getting a bargain. The answer would be yes! You would want to buy the capital equipment! Anytime you can buy something for less than its value, you would do it, wouldn't you? That would be very economical. On the other hand, if the cost of this investment was $13,000, you shouldn't do it. No one would pay $13,000 for something that is worth only $12,630. That would be like paying someone $12 for a $10 bill. Ironically, many people say yes to doing such things every day without knowing it.

There is still a faster way to do the math in this analysis. Please note that this example is also using the same annual cash flow. Remember, cash flows that are expected to be the same each year are called an **ordinary annuity**. Just like that of finding future value interest factors of annuities, you can add up the present value interest factors for each year and multiply that total times the $3,000 annuity. Once again, this has been done for you as you can see in figure 14-11.

Just like before, if you add up the present value interest factors in this problem, their total would be 4.212. In figure 14-11 you can see that for a required rate of 6 percent for five periods, the total of the PVIFs would be 4.212 (with rounding). Each of these are called the **present value interest factor of an annuity (PVIFA)**.

Let's try a new example. Suppose you are promised returns of $6,500 in cash savings and/or added profits from the purchase of some capital equipment (or machinery) for your factory for the next 15 years. If the needed rate of return is 9 percent, you would find the present value interest factor of an annuity (PVIFA) at the intersection of the 9 percent column and the 15-year row, which would be 8.061. Multiplying 8.061 times $6,500 would give you a present value of

	1%	2%	3%	4%	5%	6%	7%	8%	9%	10%	11%	12%	13%	14%	15%
1	0.990	0.980	0.971	0.962	0.952	0.943	0.935	0.926	0.917	0.909	0.901	0.893	0.885	0.877	0.870
2	1.970	1.942	1.913	1.886	1.859	1.833	1.808	1.783	1.759	1.736	1.713	1.690	1.668	1.647	1.626
3	2.941	2.884	2.829	2.775	2.723	2.673	2.624	2.577	2.531	2.487	2.444	2.402	2.361	2.322	2.283
4	3.902	3.808	3.717	3.630	3.546	3.465	3.387	3.312	3.240	3.170	3.102	3.037	2.974	2.914	2.855
5	4.853	4.713	4.580	4.452	4.329	4.212	4.100	3.993	3.890	3.791	3.696	3.605	3.517	3.433	3.352
6	5.795	5.601	5.417	5.242	5.076	4.917	4.767	4.623	4.486	4.355	4.231	4.111	3.998	3.889	3.784
7	6.728	6.472	6.230	6.002	5.786	5.582	5.389	5.206	5.033	4.868	4.712	4.564	4.423	4.288	4.160
8	7.652	7.325	7.020	6.733	6.463	6.210	5.971	5.747	5.535	5.335	5.146	4.968	4.799	4.639	4.487
9	8.566	8.162	7.786	7.435	7.108	6.802	6.515	6.247	5.995	5.759	5.537	5.328	5.132	4.946	4.772
10	9.471	8.983	8.530	8.111	7.722	7.360	7.024	6.710	6.418	6.145	5.889	5.650	5.426	5.216	5.019
11	10.368	9.787	9.253	8.760	8.306	7.887	7.499	7.139	6.805	6.495	6.207	5.938	5.687	5.453	5.234
12	11.255	10.575	9.954	9.385	8.863	8.384	7.943	7.536	7.161	6.814	6.492	6.194	5.918	5.660	5.421
13	12.134	11.348	10.635	9.986	9.394	8.853	8.358	7.904	7.487	7.103	6.750	6.424	6.122	5.842	5.583
14	13.004	12.106	11.296	10.563	9.899	9.295	8.745	8.244	7.786	7.367	6.982	6.628	6.302	6.002	5.724
15	13.865	12.849	11.938	11.118	10.380	9.712	9.108	8.559	8.061	7.606	7.191	6.811	6.462	6.142	5.847

FIGURE 14-11   Table PVIFA

$52,396.50 for that machinery. If the price of the machine is $60,000, you would be advised *not* to buy the machinery because the present value of its added profits is only worth $52,396.50. If the price was $50,000, you would be wise to buy the machinery. If you pay $50,000 for something worth $52,396.50, you would have a true bargain of $2,396 (found by $52,396.50 – $50,000).

The bargain, such as this one of $2,396, is called **the net present value**. It is found by subtracting the cost of the capital equipment from the present value of its forecasted or promised cash savings and/or profits. Another way to answer the question, then, as to whether the purchase of capital equipment is advisable is by following the rule that you would be well to buy a piece of capital equipment as long as the **net present value** of its expected cash savings is greater than or equal to zero.

What about promised savings that are not expected to be equal each year? Such savings would be referred to as a mixed stream of cash flows, as mentioned before. In those circumstances, you must then return to the slow way of getting their present values as was shown in figure 14-10. You would need to get the present value of each cash flow and once again add those present values together to find the present value of all of the cash flows from the savings they are promising to generate.

If required rates of return rise due to added risks of the purchase or your firm or both, or if the cost of capital equipment goes up in price, the present value, and therefore the net present value, of a venture will go down. Thus, there will be less demand for capital for such projects or ventures. To prove this, please note that as you move from the 1 percent column to the 15 percent column in the PVIF chart in figure 14-9, the present value interest factors, and thus present values, would decline.

An organization must never undertake a venture in which the present value of such a venture is less than the initial cost or investment.

CHOOSING BETWEEN MULTIPLE CAPITAL EQUIPMENT PURCHASES (CEPS)

Sometimes your organization may be limited in what purchases of capital equipment it can undertake, either because you are limited in funds or because more than one supplier is proposing to make the equipment available. If you only need one machine but several proposals are given, you will need to pick the best of them because they are then mutually exclusive.

We will now give an example, and for simplicity, let's assume for our purposes that there are only three CEP's from which to choose. The example of these capital equipment purchases is in figure 14-12.

		CEP 1	CEP 2	CEP 3
	Cost/Investment	$50,000	$70,000	$60,000
Cash Savings/ Added Profits	Year 1	$18,000	$20,000	$30,000
	Year 2	$18,000	$20,000	$25,000
	Year 3	$18,000	$20,000	$20,000
	Year 4	$18,000	$20,000	$15,000
	Year 5	$18,000	$20,000	$10,000
	Totals	$90,000	$1,00,000	$1,00,000
	Averages	$18,000	$20,000	$20,000

FIGURE 14-12 CEP 1, 2, and 3

Such purchases could give returns for much longer than five years, and they often are not for the same length of time. Vendors' machines may promise savings at different intervals for different reasons as one machine may be expected to last longer than others. Again, for simplicity, we have kept them to five years and with the cash flows shown.

Theoretically, the best way to decide which one of them is best is to find the one with the highest net present value (as discussed earlier). For these cases, let's assume that the required rate of return on all three of them is equal to 8 percent. Using this concept, the net present value of each case is shown in figure 14-13.

Please notice that Capital Equipment Projects 1 and 2 are annuities. Finding their present values is easy. If you refer, once again, to the chart in figure 14-11, you will see that with a five-year return at 8 percent, the present value interest factor of an annuity is 3.993. If you multiply that times the annuity amounts in CEP 1 (which is an $18,000 annuity) and CEP 2 (which is a $20,000 annuity), you will see the present values of their cash savings/added profits are equal to $71,874 and $79,860 respectively.

		CEP 1	CEP 2	CEP 3				
	Cost/ Investment	$50,000	$70,000	$60,000				
						PVIF@8%,5 Years		
Cash Savings/ Added Profits	Year 1	$18,000	$20,000	$30,000	×	0.926	=	$27,780
	Year 2	$18,000	$20,000	$25,000	×	0.857	=	$21,425
	Year 3	$18,000	$20,000	$20,000	×	0.794	=	$15,880
	Year 4	$18,000	$20,000	$15,000	×	0.735	=	$11,025
	Year 5	$18,000	$20,000	$10,000	×	0.681	=	$6,810
	Totals	$90,000	$1,00,000	$1,00,000				
	Averages	$18,000	$20,000	$20,000				

PVIFA @8%,5 Years	3.993	3.993			
Annuity Cash Flow	× $18,000	× $20,000			
Annuity Present Values	$71,874	$79,860	Total of Mixed Stream Present Values		$82,920
Cost/Investment	– $50,000	– $70,000	Cost/Investment		$60,000
Net Present Value	$21,874	$9,860	Net Present Value		$22,920

FIGURE 14-13   CEP 1, 2, and 3 Present Values @ 8 Percent

At first it appears that CEP 2 is superior to CEP 1 until you see that the cost of CEP 2 is much higher, thus its net present value is lower. When you subtract the $50,000 cost of CEP 1 from its cash flows' present value of $71,874, its NPV would be $21,874 When you subtract the $70,000 cost of CEP 2 from its cash flows' present value of $79,860, its NPV would be $9,860.

Now let's look at CEP 3. It is a mixed stream of cash savings/added profits; thus, you must find their present values individually using the chart from figure 14-9. The chart in figure 14-9 is only used for mixed streams of cash savings/added profits, while the chart in figure 14-11 is only used for annuities. After multiplying each present value interest factor times the respective cash savings, you will see that the sum of their present values is $82,920. When you subtract the $60,000 cost or investment of CEP 3 from its cash flows, you will see that its net present value is now only $22,920.

If you have to pick only one of them, the one with the highest net present value is the winner; thus, CEP 3 is the one to choose, assuming that the forecast of savings and added profits are correct.

There are vendors who tend to overstep their claims of savings; thus, it is often a good idea to track the accuracy of forecasts of the past in order to make better judgements of forecasts in the future.

Suppose CEP 2 is using a vendor in which similar, past forecasts have been recorded. A forecast for returns expected one year from now is usually going to be more accurate than one you will make for savings five years from now. This is because so many more things can happen in five years than can happen in only one year, because over time, many more unforeseeable things can occur. Therefore, let's also assume that the accuracy of the claims of forecasts for purchases similar to that of CEP 2 has historically been as you see in figure 14-14.

Year	Cash Probability
Year 1	96%
Year 2	90%
Year 3	87%
Year 4	73%
Year 5	68%

FIGURE 14-14   Cash Probabilities

These become the probability that the forecasts given will be accurate for the one that was analyzed in CEP 2. Therefore, the forecasts must be adjusted downward. Once you have fine-tuned the forecast, the risk of the purchase will also be reduced. Recall that the required return on investments includes a risk premium, but it is feasible to remove that risk premium in that the return of the risk has been removed. Suppose the risk premium for CEP 2 was 3 percent. If you remove it from the required rate of return of 8 percent, it now becomes 5 percent. In order to fine-tune the analysis of CEP 2, there are two steps. First, find the more accurate forecasts by multiplying each cash flow of $20,000 times their respective cash probability. Second, you must take those new forecasts times the present value interest factor for the lower required rate of return. Figure 14-15 shows that after finding the downwardly adjusted cash flows and multiplying them times the lower PVIFs at 5 percent, the present value of the cash savings from CEP 2 is now $72,316. Please notice that after having adjusted those $20,000 cash flows downward by applying their different cash probabilities, CEP 2 is now a mixed stream of cash flows rather than an annuity and would require the use of the table found in figure 14-9. After subtracting the cost of the purchase of $70,000, the net present value is now only $2,316. It is still not superior to the other purchases; thus, it should not be undertaken. The only way we would make all of these purchases is if they were not mutually exclusive, because they all have a positive net present value. No project should be undertaken if they have a negative net present value.

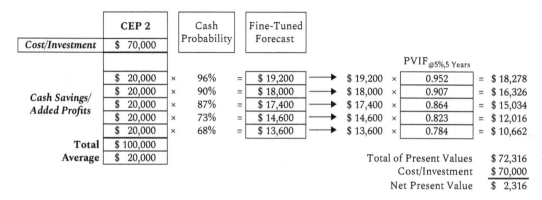

FIGURE 14-15 CEP 2 with Present Value after Cash Probability Adjustment

THE INTERNAL RATE OF RETURN (IRR) OF A CAPITAL EQUIPMENT PURCHASE

The purchase of capital equipment in any one of the scenarios of CEP 1, 2, or 3 would also involve what is called the **internal rate of return (IRR)**. To help you understand the concept of the IRR, you need to review some of the concepts discussed regarding bonds. If you buy a bond for $10,000 and if you are told that your return will be 10 percent, you know that it will give you a return per year of $1,000. However, that return is not so easy to know when you are working backward to find out what rate of return is being generated by your investment to receive the cash savings from capital equipment, especially if the cash savings per year are a mixed stream. Just as you must know the rate of return on a bond you have purchased, you must also know that rate of return on a capital equipment purchase. This book is not going to discuss the procedure for finding it mathematically, but it can be found in a spreadsheet by what is called the IRR function. If you set the cost of the capital equipment to a negative (since it is paid out as seen in figure 14-16A in cell C2) and then include the rest of the range of cash savings, you can allow the spreadsheet to find it for you. You can see the results in figure 14-16B. The IRR in CEP 1, for example, is found by the function =I RR(C2:C7). You can see that the IRRs are 23 percent, 13 percent, and 25 percent for CEP 1, 2, and 3, in that order.

		CEP 1	CEP 2	CEP 3
	Cost/Investment	$(50,000)	$(70,000)	$(60,000)
	Year 1	$18,000	$20,000	$30,000
	Year 2	$18,000	$20,000	$25,000
Cash Savings/ Added Profits	Year 3	$18,000	$20,000	$20,000
	Year 4	$18,000	$20,000	$15,000
	Year 5	$18,000	$20,000	$10,000
	Totals	$90,000	$100,000	$100,000
	Averages	$18,000	$20,000	$20,000
		= IRR(C2:C7)		25%

FIGURE 14-16A   CEP 1, 2, and 3 IRRs Showing IRR Function

		CEP 1	CEP 2	CEP 3
	Cost/Investment	$(50,000)	$(70,000)	$(60,000)
	Year 1	$18,000	$20,000	$30,000
	Year 2	$18,000	$20,000	$25,000
Cash Savings/ Added Profits	Year 3	$18,000	$20,000	$20,000
	Year 4	$18,000	$20,000	$15,000
	Year 5	$18,000	$20,000	$10,000
	Totals	$90,000	$1,00,000	$1,00,000
	Averages	$18,000	$20,000	$20,000
	IRR	23%	13%	25%

FIGURE 14-16B   CEP 1, 2, and 3 IRRs

Even though, theoretically, it is best to choose a purchase with the highest net present value, in practice the IRR is more commonly used to make this decision.

Based upon what has been said, you can see that if you have a required rate of return that is equal to your actual rate of return (or IRR), your net present value will always be zero.

Now let's take a look at some applications to the use of the IRR.

First, if your IRR is lower than the rate you will pay toward raising the funds for a purchase or if it is lower than your required rate of return, it would not be a good purchase. For example, if CEP 1 was going to cost you a rate of 25 percent to borrow or raise the money through a stock issue, a bond issue, or a bank loan, it would be very unwise to proceed because you are losing money to the tune of about 2 percent (25 percent – 23 percent). Second, you can use the IRR to analyze multiple purchases where the cost for raising the money for them may vary. Sometimes people will loan you money or buy your stock where the rate for return you pay them could fluctuate.

WHEN MULTIPLE CAPITAL EQUIPMENT PURCHASES CAN BE MADE

Sometimes you may have a list of purchases as well as a list of different costs of capital as you raise more money. As you raise more money, your cost of raising funds will also rise. Why? For one thing, if you borrow more and more money, there is always a higher probability of your defaulting on loans. The more debt that some people acquire, the more difficulty they will often have repaying those debts. This leads investors to believe that your firm is riskier, and as they perceive your firm to be a high-risk firm, they will want a higher rate of interest from you. Second, if more stocks are issued, and if your firm was to go bankrupt, each of the shareholders will get less or perhaps no money disbursed to them when the firm liquidates (as discussed earlier); thus, they will also perceive your firm as being a riskier investment, and they will also seek a higher rate of return from the stocks you issue to them.

Figure 14-17 shows a possible group of capital equipment purchases in addition to the ones already mentioned as well as the costs of raising the dollars to make those purchases as the amount of the money raised continues to go up. You can clearly see that the IRR of these purchases are ranked from highest to lowest, along with their expected IRRs and their costs. Please note that it would be okay to purchase all the machinery with exception to CEP 2. Why? Because by the time you have the money raised to make that purchase, part of its cost will be 15 percent as shown in figure 14-17, and that is above the expected IRR of 13 percent that it promises. This could thus cause you to lose money on a large portion of CEP 2. You would lose 2 percent in return (15 percent – 13 percent).

WHEN THE COST OF CAPITAL VARIES

Before you can decide what purchases to make at various changes in the cost of capital, you first want to graph them by finding at least two points for each of them and making sure that the graph intersects both axes. Let's return to the three original purchases.

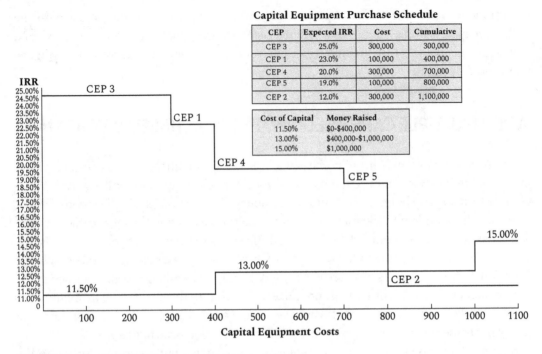

Capital Equipment Purchase Schedule

CEP	Expected IRR	Cost	Cumulative
CEP 3	25.0%	300,000	300,000
CEP 1	23.0%	100,000	400,000
CEP 4	20.0%	300,000	700,000
CEP 5	19.0%	100,000	800,000
CEP 2	12.0%	300,000	1,100,000

Cost of Capital	Money Raised
11.50%	$0-$400,000
13.00%	$400,000-$1,000,000
15.00%	$1,000,000

FIGURE 14-17 Capital Equipment Purchase Schedule

If you assume, for a moment, that there is no required rate of return for a purchase, then its present value of its cash flows/savings will be the same as their face value. Why? Because if I am not required to have any return, then the value of the money I will receive a year from now or more will be the same as what it is today. Looking at it from another perspective, if you needed $1,000 one year from today and there are no returns on investments, then I would have to put $1,000 aside today to have $1,000 a year from now; hence the present value and the investment would be equal. Therefore, we can make the purchases' net present values cross the Y axis if we set their required rates of return equal to zero. When you do, for CEP 1 you will have a net present value of $40,000 (the total $90,000 in cash savings minus the $50,000 investment). Figure 14-18A shows the other information about this purchase and the other two purchases, based upon what we already know with the required rate of return of 8 percent.

If the required rate of return of an investment is also the same as its actual internal rate of return (IRR), as explained earlier, its net present values would be zero. All of these figures are shown in the grid in the upper left of figure 14-18A, and we can now graph the data of all three purchases.

The graphing of these three purchases, their corresponding required rates of return at various levels, and their net present values at those levels shows us that at all times, CEP 3 always has the highest net present value, and thus it is always superior. Let's suppose for argument's sake, however, that the IRR for CEP 3 was only 20 percent. Figure 14-18B shows that the lines for CEP 1 and CEP 3 would now cross. When this happens, the superior of these two

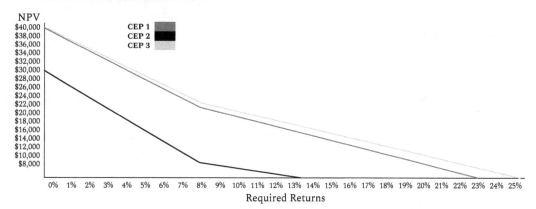

Required Return	Net Present Value		
	CEP 1	CEP 2	CEP 3
0.00%	$40,000	$30,000	$40,000
8.00%	$21,874	$9,860	$22,920
13.00%		$0	
23.00%	$0		
25.00%			$0

FIGURE 14-18A Net Present Value and Required Returns Charts (No Intersection)

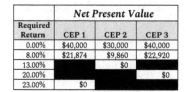

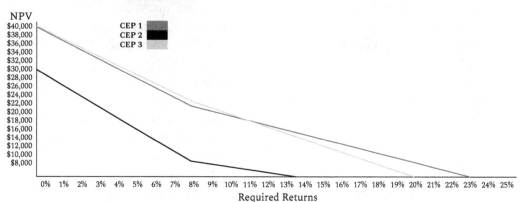

Required Return	Net Present Value		
	CEP 1	CEP 2	CEP 3
0.00%	$40,000	$30,000	$40,000
8.00%	$21,874	$9,860	$22,920
13.00%		$0	
20.00%			$0
23.00%	$0		

FIGURE 14-18B Net Present Value and Required Returns Charts (With Intersection)

purchases would always be the one with the higher net present value. The lines appear to cross at the point of a required return of just under 11 percent. That being said, if the required return goes below that point, CEP 3 would be superior with the highest net present value. However, if the required return goes above that point, CEP 1 would have the higher net present value, and it would then get the nod.

CHAPTER 14 REVIEW

QUESTIONS TO THINK ABOUT

1. Map out some of the strategies you would use to get the best possible results as you purchase capital equipment. Why did you use these strategies?
2. How can such strategies help you if you are using them to purchase things for your own personal future, such as a college education for you children or for retirement?

TERMS TO KNOW

Bond market
Bonds
Borrower
Capital equipment purchase (CEP)
Capital market
Certificate of deposit (CD)
Charles Dow (1851–1902)
Common stock
Coupon rate
Customers' Afternoon Letter
Diversifiable risk
Dividend reinvestment plan (DRP)
Dow Divisor
Dow Jones & Company
Dow Jones Industrial Average (DJIA)
Edward Jones (1856–1920)
Equity market
Face value (or par value)
Future value
Future value interest factor
Future value interest factor of an annuity
Inflation premium
Internal rate of return (IRR)
Investment decision

Lender
Maturity date
Mutual funds
National Association of Securities
    Dealers' Automated Quotes (NASDAQ)
Net present value
Nondiversifiable risk
Nonsystematic risk
One person, one vote
One share, one vote
Ordinary annuity
Over-the-counter trade (OTC)
Preemptive rights
Preferred stock
Present value
Present value interest factor
Present value interest factor of an annuity
Risk premium
Risk-free rate
Standard & Poor's 500
Systematic risk
Time value of money
Wall Street Journal

CHAPTER FIFTEEN

A Closer Look at Land

IN THIS CHAPTER we discuss the resource of land and how its use is determined.

The supply and demand of land differs from all other goods and services in that the supply of land is fixed. This would make the supply curve for land vertical, as no price changes can increase its supply. Therefore, demand for land may often exceed the supply, depending upon where you are and what uses of it are needed.

There are some exceptions. Not long before his death in the late 1960s, Walt Disney bought swamp land in Florida to create what we now know as Disney World. He drained those swamps and, in a sense, created land. This idea, however, has been applied by others, but has not historically changed the worldwide supply of land to a level of any significance.

RENT

Rent, as most of us know it, is what we pay landlords for the use of any shelter, offices, or factories. However, it's not the concept used in economic theory. Economists use the term differently in different contexts. Centuries ago in Europe, much of the farmland on which crops were grown was made available by landlords, and in addition to the space, the landlords often provided the workers to plant and harvest the crops. In our case, we will use the term *rent* as anything paid for any use of land.

Earlier in this textbook we discussed the writings of Adam Smith, who believed that the economy could manage itself with the market mechanism. We also stated that the market mechanism was a process by which society naturally allocates its resources by only paying a price for what it wants, and that society also refrains from paying a price for what it does not want. Therefore, we put more resources toward producing what society likes and for which it pays a good price, and we stop wasting resources in the production of things that society does not want to pay for. When we discussed the law of supply earlier in this textbook, we also talked about the price signal, which is the essential element of the market mechanism. Why? Because it is the prices people are willing to pay producers that tell them that consumers are either wanting more or less of something. If they want more of something, they will offer to pay a higher price for it, while their dislike of a product or service will become obvious when they no longer want to pay a high price for it or when they stop buying it altogether

The question is, what kind of rent for the use of land would be required in order to have a specific amount of land available? The answer is zero! Why? Because the supply of land never changes, whether one is paying $100,000 per day for its use or paying nothing.

When prices rise above the amount that most producers are willing to accept to supply more of a product or service, it can generate economic profit, which is also discussed earlier in this book. When it comes to land, rising rents will always exceed the amount that is required to make it available, because the land would always be available to us even if nothing was paid for it. Land was here before we were born, and it will be here long after we die. Therefore, any rent that is paid for land usage will always be greater than what is needed to make it available.

Some would then say that all money paid for rent is considered a surplus payment. That surplus payment is called **economic rent**. This concept, however, assumes that the land is pure and unimproved. By that is meant that no buildings, roadways, cultivation, irrigation, fencing, or anything that would increase its value has been added. Such land improvements require resource costs to be paid by the land owner and won't be made unless a sufficient compensation or price is offered to that land owner. In most cases, a very small fraction of the rental payment represents pure economic rent as defined here.

Pure rent as defined by economists is not the same thing as what you pay for homes or apartments, because rental payments made to landlords typically include compensation for the use of the capital (the building structure) and labor (building maintenance and management), and for the use of utilities (water, electric, and gas).

Remember, rents help us to allocate a scarce factor among other competing uses. The most valuable use of the land is what will determine what the market price or rent will be. People making less valuable use of a scarce factor will not be able to pay the higher rent and will therefore not acquire it. The market mechanism determines how scarce resources will be allocated: whoever is the highest bidder gets it. For example, if you own a plot of land in the middle of nowhere, the land value would be very small; thus there would likely be very few bidders. But if the land were at a busy intersection with high traffic, there would likely be many retailers who would bid on it and likely pay a higher price or rent for it. Retailers usually prefer and need to locate in areas where there is a lot of traffic to entice buyers to drop in and buy their products. The price would be higher because the bids are higher. This leads us to an important question. If gasoline stations are built on the higher-priced land, is it fair to say that it is the landlords who drive up the prices of gasoline by charging their higher rates? Actually, the price of gasoline is usually already high before the bidding on the land used to locate a gasoline station even begins.

Back in the nineteenth century, landlords were blamed for the high price of corn that was grown and harvested on their land. Those high corn prices were causing some to live in poverty. Many believed that it was necessary for the government to impose limits on how much rent could be charged by landlords to the corn farmers, thinking that lower rents would bring down corn prices, and thus more people would have corn that was less expensive and there would therefore be less poverty. Classical economists, including David Ricardo, one of the great classical economists (who often embrace the teachings of Adam Smith and say that government needs to remain out of the economy and all its problems in order to allow those problems to self-correct), contended that corn prices were not high because of high rent paid to harvest it, but rent costs were so high because the price of corn was so high and that corn growers were the highest bidders for the land's usage. They believed, therefore, that no government action was needed to make corn prices low.

Many who argued that landlords were the villains were indirectly contending that the increasing rent for land caused a leftward shift of the supply curve for corn because of the increased factor costs associated with producing corn. Remember, higher factor costs make supply curves shift to the left. This decline in production of corn, they believed, caused shortages that drove prices up. They also believed, of course, that the higher rent made it necessary for corn farmers to raise their prices for their corn to cover the higher rent costs.

On the other hand, Ricardo's argument is based upon marginal cost (discussed earlier), which is the increase in total costs associated with a one-unit increase in production. He felt that things such as diminishing returns were driving up labor costs, and that such increases in labor costs were driving up corn prices. Recall that producers are willing to produce and sell goods in competitive markets as long as price is equal to or exceeds marginal cost. Since the marginal cost defines the lowest price a firm will accept for a given quantity of output, it is this rise in marginal costs driving up corn prices, according to Ricardo and classical economists, not the rent charged by the landlords. He and many other economists also believed that the cost of rent was not determining the price of corn. Instead, they felt that it was the other way around. They felt that the high price of corn was determining the high cost of rent. Just as long as the price of corn was high for reasons mentioned earlier, and as long as the corn farmers were the highest bidders for the use of the land, that higher rents would continue.

These are some principals to remember as you consider the purchase or renting of land for any business operation. The cost or rent you pay will be based upon your ability and willingness to pay it. Therefore, you are likely more willing to pay a higher price for the use of land under the following circumstances:

1. If the land possesses many valuable, natural resources that can be used and/or sold
2. If its location is in a place that will bring in more business for you if you are a retailer.
3. If it is in close proximity to other needed resources, or if it has easy access to roads that will get you to the suppliers of those needed resources. Circumstances such as these are more likely going to justify the cost of land if it brings you profits in excess of its costs.

CHAPTER 15 REVIEW

QUESTIONS TO THINK ABOUT

1. Do you agree with the thinking of the classical economists regarding the need to regulate the price of land? Why or why not?
2. Why do some parcels of land cost so much to buy or to rent?
3. How does rent in this chapter differ from your previous understanding of the term *rent*?

TERMS TO KNOW

Economic rent

Pure rent

CHAPTER SIXTEEN

Bringing it All Together

WHEN WE TRY to make decisions as to what combination of land, labor, and capital equipment will be used to maximize output and minimize costs, and thus maximize the use of our resources, we have given much information to help one to make such a decision. In this chapter, we will use examples to help apply this information.

COST EFFICIENCY

When determining if you should use more machinery or not when there is a wage increase, when you want to expand production, or if you have an opportunity to purchase capital equipment at a good price, you may want to consider the concept of **cost efficiency**. This is the amount of output associated with an additional dollar spent on input. It is found by dividing the marginal physical product of an input by its cost. This is because the most cost-effective factor of production is the one that produces the most output per dollar.

Please recall that, typically, as production increases, marginal physical product will rise briefly, but then it will go down due to diminishing returns, thus sending down the marginal revenue product (MRP). It is also the dollar value of a worker's contribution to output.

Let's use an example. Suppose you are harvesting corn and that you sell the corn by the bushel. Also assume that you know that if you hire one more picker, that worker will generate an additional four bushels of corn per hour. In other words, you expect that the next worker will have a marginal physical product of four. If that grower sells the corn at $3.50 per bushel, your marginal revenue product would be $3.50 times four bushels, or $14.

Remember, the MRP sets an upper limit to the wage rate an employer will pay, and it also puts a limit on the number of workers hired. Therefore, the employer cannot pay more than $14 per hour for such labor in this example.

Assuming that the hourly wage for corn pickers is $8 per hour, the cost efficiency would be calculated as follows:

Cost Efficiency = Marginal Physical Product Per Hour/Hourly Wage

Thus, the following formula:

Cost Efficiency = Marginal Physical Product of 4/$8
Hourly Wage = 4/$8 =0.5 Bushels

Therefore, the producer is getting 0.5 or half of a bushel of corn per $1 dollar spent in labor cost.

Now, let's suppose that the employer is considering the possibility of buying a machine that will give a marginal physical product of 10 bushels of corn per hour. Also assume that the total of all costs needed to run the machine for that same hour is $11. Using the same formula, the cost efficiency would be calculated as follows:

Cost Efficiency = Marginal Physical Product of 10/$11 Cost of
Running the Capital Equipment = 10/$11 = 0.91 Bushels

This is nearly double the output per dollar spent.

Therefore, in this application, it may be best to buy the capital equipment rather than hire the added worker.

BEST PROCESS

Now it's time to bring land, labor, and capital equipment together to make decisions as to what combinations are best for production.

While the cost efficiency method is useful, employers don't typically choose between individual inputs as much as they choose between complete production processes that are either labor intensive or capital intensive. They are more likely to gather information on costs of land, labor, and capital, and then engage in output using various combinations of them.

Figure 16-1 is a good example of how such an analysis may happen. Notice that labor costs per hour and all costs associated with the operating of capital (equipment) can be changed in order to get the costs of operations down. Also notice that the cost of land doesn't change as a result of changing the combinations of the hours of use of labor and capital equipment inputs.

Process A has utilized 325 labor hours (at a cost of $10.00 per hour), thus costing a total of $3,250. Process A also uses 13 capital hours (at a cost of $15 per hour), thus costing a total of $195. When those costs are added to the cost of land, the total cost of Process A is $4,145. The output would be 10 thousand units; thus, process A will cost $0.4145 per unit of output.

Best Process

Process A	Resource	Hours Utilized	Hourly Rate		Units of Output	
	Labor	325	$10.00	$3,250.00	10,000	
	Land	N/A	$700	$700.00		
	Capital	13	$15.00	$195.00		
			Total	$4,145.00	$0.4145	*Average Total Cost*
Process B						
	Labor	250	$10.00	$2,500.00	10,000	
	Land	N/A	$700	$700.00		
	Capital	25	$15.00	$375.00		
			Total	$3,575.00	$0.3575	*Average Total Cost*
Process C						
	Labor	200	$10.00	$2,000.00	10,000	
	Land	N/A	$700	$700.00		
	Capital	35	$15.00	$525.00		
			Total	$3,225.00	$0.3225	*Average Total Cost*
Process D						
	Labor	150	$10.00	$1,500.00	10,000	
	Land	N/A	$700	$700.00	BEST	
	Capital	40	$15.00	$600.00		
			Total	$2,800.00	$0.2800	*Average Total Cost*
Process E						
	Labor	140	$10.00	$1,400.00	10,000	
	Land	N/A	$700	$700.00		
	Capital	50	$15.00	$750.00		
			Total	$2,850.00	$0.2850	*Average Total Cost*

FIGURE 16-1   Best Process

If you reduce the number of labor hours used in Process A from 325 hours down to 250 hours as suggested for Process B, you must remember that it is not likely going to keep the output level at 10 thousand units without increasing the number of hours that capital equipment is used. The only other way to get by with fewer labor hours is by making workers more efficient. Assuming that efficiency with labor is already at its highest, the hours used for capital equipment operation is raised from 13 in Process A to 25 in Process B. Also, assuming that the costs per hour of each input remain constant, we see that the output of 10 thousand units with this combination remains the same, and yet costs are lowered to $3,575 or $0.3575 per unit of output.

When finding the right combination, you can substitute capital equipment hours in place of labor hours to see if total costs, and ultimately average total costs, decline. If they do, this is an indication that you have made the right choice, once again assuming that the output remains the same and that there is no decline in the quality of the product. Notice, for example, when Process B is put into place to see if it is better than Process A, it shows that Process B is indeed less costly, and that Process A should be abandoned. But that's not the end of the story. Even though Process B is better, it's important to continue this process of reducing labor hours and adding hours to the operation of capital equipment to see if costs continue to decline. Please note that this process can also be the reverse! It is just as important to see if costs are reduced when labor hours are increased while machine hours are reduced.

Once Process C is shown to reduce total costs after an additional decrease in labor hours and an increase in the hours utilizing capital equipment, and thus reduces average total costs, Process B should be abandoned. When Process D is shown to reduce total costs using the same analysis we have been doing all along, and thus average total costs decline, Process C should then be abandoned.

So, how many times should we continue to change the combination of hours for capital equipment and labor? Until the cost no longer declines. Notice in figure 16-1 that the combination of labor and capital equipment is changed again in Process E, but in a way that causes average total costs to rise again. Therefore, it would be determined in this example that Process D is the best or superior process at the given time.

This analysis is something that needs to be performed regularly and most certainly when output levels are changed.

CHAPTER 16 REVIEW

QUESTIONS TO THINK ABOUT
1. Would you prefer to use the cost efficiency method or the best process method to decide the right combination of labor and capital equipment? Why?
2. How many times do you need to try a new combination when you are using the best process method? Why?

TERMS TO KNOW
Cost efficiency

Epilogue

BY NOW YOU should have a genuine understanding of how organizations can utilize methods that will help them to maximize the use of all resources. A very small percentage of people in this country know what you now know, and yet nearly everyone has an opinion about it. Among those you talk with, you will be one of the few who will have an educated view point. It is my hope that you use it well and for the betterment of your organizations, careers, and families, and for society.

References

Gitman, Lawrence J., and Chad J. Zutter. 2011. *Principles of Managerial Finance*. Prentice Hall.

Gregory, Paul R. 2005. *Essentials of Economics*. Pearson Publishing.

McConnell, Campbell R. 1984. *Economics*. McGraw Hill Book Co.

Schiller, Bradley R. 2016. *The Macro Economy Today*. McGraw-Hill Irwin.

Index

CPSIA information can be obtained
at www.ICGtesting.com
Printed in the USA
LVHW020733200722
723885LV00004B/21